350

DreamHOMESource

VACATION& SECOND HOMES

350 DreamHOMESource
VACATION&
SECOND HOMES
hanley▲wood

Published by Hanley Wood
One Thomas Circle, NW, Suite 600
Washington, DC 20005

Distribution Center
PBD
Hanley Wood Consumer Group
3280 Summit Ridge Parkway
Duluth, Georgia 30096

Vice President, Home Plans, Andrew Schultz
Director, Marketing, Mark Wilkin
Associate Publisher, Development, Jennifer Pearce
Editor, Simon Hyoun
Assistant Editor, Kimberly Johnson
Publications Manager, Brian Haefs
Production Manager, Theresa Emerson
Senior Plan Merchandiser, Nicole Phipps
Plan Merchandiser, Hillary Huff
Graphic Artist, Joong Min
Product Manager, Susan Jasmin
Marketing Manager, Brett Bryant

Most Hanley Wood titles are available at quantity discounts with bulk purchases for educational, business,
or sales promotional use. For information, please contact Andrew Schultz at aschultz@hanleywood.com.

VC Graphics, Inc.
Creative Director, Veronica Vannoy
Graphic Designer, Jennifer Gerstein
Graphic Designer, Denise Reiffenstein
Graphic Designer, Jeanne-Erin Worster

Photo Credits
Front Cover, Main: Design HPK2500413 on page 21; photo by Chris A. Little of Atlanta, courtesy of Chatham Home Planning, Inc. Front Cover, Inset: Design HWEPL13691 on eplans.com; photo courtesy of Tom Harper. Back Cover, Left: Design HPK2500012 on page 10; photo courtesy of Donald A. Gardner Architects, Inc. Back Cover, Top: Design HPK2500064 on page 66; photo by Arthur Manns Harden Architect. Page 4, Top: Sam Gray. Page 4, Bottom: Southern Pine Council. Page 5, Top: Mark Samu. Page 14, Left: Sam Gray. Page 14, Top: Mark Samu. Page 15: Mark Samu. Page 72, Left: Mark Samu. Page 72, Bottom: Design HWEPL07112 on eplans.com; photo by Donald A. Gardner Architects, Inc. Page 73, Top and Right: Design HPK2500078 on page 82 and design HPK2500079 on page 83; photos by Donald A. Gardner Architects, Inc. Page 142: Peter Loppacher. Page 143, Top: Design HPK2500211 on page 198; photo by Donald A. Gardner, Inc. Page 143, Bottom: Tony Giammarino. Page 242, Top: Design HPK2500293 on page 269; photo by Laurence Taylor. Page 242, Bottom: Design HPK2500294 on page 270; photo courtesy of the Sater Design Collection, Inc. Page 243, Top: Design HPK2500268 on page 246; photo by John Sciarrino, courtesy of Giovanni Photography. Page 243, Bottom: Design HPK2500297 on page 273; photo by Laurence Taylor Photography. Page 328, Bottom: Jessie Walker. Page 328, Top: Karen Bussolini. Page 328-329: Mark Lohman. Page 329, Top: Karen Bussolini. Page 329, Bottom: Ernest Braun.

10 9 8 7 6 5 4 3 2 1

Printed in the United States of America

Library of Congress Control Number: 2006935044

ISBN-13: 978-1-931131-71-1
ISBN-10: 1-931131-71-6

350
DreamHOMESource
VACATION&
SECOND HOMES

CONTENTS

Far and Away

Many dream of a house on the shore or a cottage in the woods, and the house plans in this book can make that dream a reality! However, to get started you should know what to look for in the perfect vacation home. As you flip through the pages of *Vacation & Second Homes*, there are a few details to consider that will help you narrow options and find the home that's just right.

ORGANIC MATERIALS and finishes for the floors and walls connect this rustic home with its environment.

WHAT IS A VACATION HOME?

A vacation home can be that weekend getaway just outside the city, where you can retreat to an environment of peace and quiet, leaving work and stress behind. It can be that special place on the shore that your family treks to each year via road trip or quick flight. Often, it's a cozy, laid-back place where families bond and reacquaint themselves with nature, forgetting that suitcases and Blackberries even exist. Whatever your vacation home will be to you and your family, the following questions should help you decide if you want to build the weekend getaway, the special place, or something totally unique and all your own.

WHERE ARE YOU BUILDING?

There can be significant differences between a home designed for the coast and one designed for a mountaintop. Coastal homes are designed to welcome ocean breezes, with open airy spaces for casual gatherings. Special features, such as outdoor showers and mudrooms, equip the home to withstand wear and tear, heading off the sand before the kids and track it into the family room. Lots of windows welcome the sunshine, but special coastal windows also block UV rays and keep the home safe from storms.

Mountain homes have a more rustic feel. Large stone fireplaces are the centerpieces to great rooms, and even master bedrooms, ready to warm the family as everyone sips hot cocoa. Steep roof pitches let snow run off the eaves, and storage space houses all the ski equipment on and off season.

INVITING OUTDOOR SPACES, like this boardwalk that ends with twin pergolas, are what make vacation homes special.

SIMPLICITY IS WHAT DELIGHTS in the no-fuss comfort of this sunroom.

WHAT KIND OF LOT DO YOU HAVE?

The lot you have largely determines the best type of house to build. Seaside homes on sand-filled lots benefit from pier and island foundations. You may refer to a house with a pier foundation as being "on stilts," elevating the main level a story above ground. The bottom level is open and often used as garage and storage space. An island foundation is similar, except that it is enclosed with walls that break away in the event of a storm surge or flooding, again keeping the main stories above water.

As you can image, most lots found amid the mountains are hillside lots, which—unless you choose to spend the time and money to reground the lot—can mean a walkout basement foundation. This style of basement is below ground level at the front of the home, but is open at ground level in the back, where the lot slopes toward the lake or valley. Walkout basements can turn the rear of the home into the feature side, revealing a second or

third level where the front only shows one or two. The direct access to the backyard is particularly beneficial to a waterfront lot, where one can enter the home directly from the landscape. It also makes for convenient storage for such equipment as skis and snow mobiles.

HOW DO YOU ORDER?

This part is easy! Simply turn to page 376 for details on the ordering process and what you'll receive with your purchase. A materials list, customization, home automation, and other options are also explained in this section, followed by the list of prices on page 382. Please note that the plans are organized by page number, not plan number. Any time you have a question or simply would like a second opinion about a plan, please feel free to contact our representatives at 1-800-521-6797. And, for even more vacation home choices, go to www.eplans.com.

Fun in the Sun

This plan was made for warm weather and salty, sea breezes

The bold exterior and colorful interior reveal the island influence of this Key West home. Designed for a balmy climate, the plan boasts expansive porches and decks accessible from every area of the plan. The back of the home provides French doors and full-height windows that bring in surrounding views, as well as stairs to the rear property.

Beyond the front entry, a sun-dappled foyer leads via a stately midlevel staircase to a splendid great room, which features a fireplace—for those breezy autumn nights—surrounded by beautiful built-in cabinetry. Highlighted by a wall of windows along the rear porch, this two-story living space opens to the formal dining room and a well-appointed kitchen. Whole-family dining, as well as causal meals and larger affairs, occur in the combined space.

At the opposite end of the main level, spacious secondary bedrooms open privately to porches and decks. The two rooms share a full bath, which doubles as a guest bath.

The second level has been reserved for the homeowners. Just beyond the interior overlook, the master suite is surrounded by views from three

1 VIVID WALLS AND ACCENTS were drawn from the lush colors of the home's coastal surroundings.

2 THE SPACIOUS MASTER SUITE allows for a king-sized bed with room to spare. Tray ceilings add elegance to the space.

Photo by Doug Thompson Photography

3 A WALK-UP ENTRY and paired columns are prominent features of the home's facade.

FIRST FLOOR

SECOND FLOOR

BASEMENT

④ NESTLED BETWEEN THE KITCHEN and the covered porch, the dining room is suitable for everyday meals as well as formal dinners. A simple modification converted the nearby deck into an accessible sunroom.

directions, including a private porch at the rear of the plan. The master bath is well-lit by front-facing windows and includes a whirlpool tub and steam shower. The walk-in closet is appropriately spacious.

Lastly, consider the island basement. With walls designed to break away during floods, this foundation option is ideal for coastal dwellers. Others may choose to finish the space fully, as a storage area, recreation room, or home theater.

⑤ PLENTY OF CABINETS AND COUNTER SPACE make storage and food preparation easy. In this photo, the homeowners have moved the cooktop peninsula toward the wall, to create easier flow into the great room.

6 DIRECT ACCESS FROM BED-ROOMS to the decks pampers guests and family alike.

7 BONUS SPACE in the island basement can be finished into a large common area such as this media room.

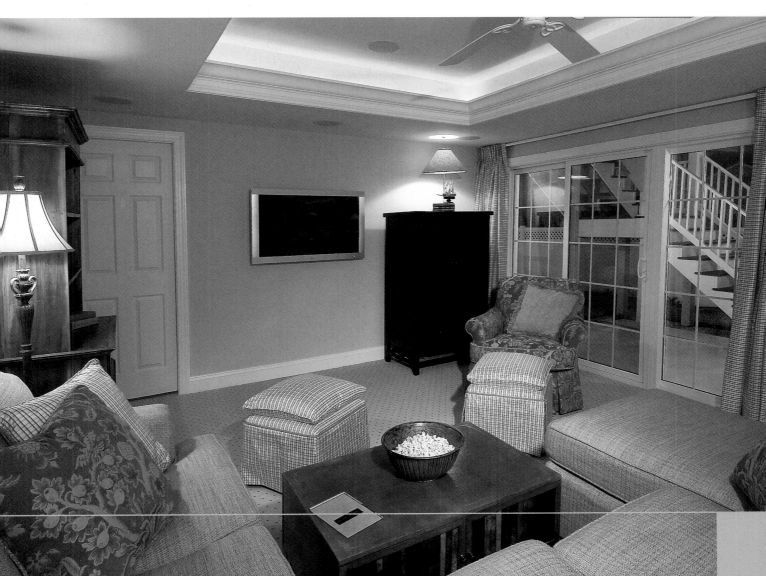

Mountain High Life

A resort-style estate specializes in outdoor spaces

1 **THIS CONVERSATION AREA** takes advantage of the great room's rearward orientation. Note the arched windows, which match the front entry.

A pleasing blend of gables and dormers embellishes the courtyard-style facade of this grand home. Decorative stickwork in the front-facing gable, stone accents, and transomed windows are Craftsman details—but the home does not commit to any single architectural precedent. An arched entryway is matched by carriage-style garage doors, creating a well-unified exterior.

Inside, decorative ceiling treatments and long sightlines define areas without compromising the open-living philosophy guiding the design. For instance, dramatically framed views of the rear landscape beckon visitors from the prominent foyer and through the tremendous great room. The centerpiece of the home, the great room features a full-height stone fireplace, cathedral ceiling crossed by exposed wood beams, and a wide wall of windows. As shown here, this is an ideal design for waterfront or mountainside property.

The foyer also introduces the spacious island kitchen, at left. The nearby dining room is situated at the back of the plan for flexibility of use: as an everyday gathering spot, extended entertaining area, or formal dining space. At the other end of the foyer are two of the home's bedrooms, which share a large bath with separate vanities and toilets.

The master suite receives special privilege at the back of the home, beyond the study. Attended by a luxurious bath, wardrobe, and private porch, and featuring 180-degree views, the master bedroom is a true haven for vacationing homeowners. Additional suites reside upstairs and are just as

2 **A MASSIVE STONE HEARTH** is the focal point of the great room. Exposed beams and columns and hardwood floors add rustic elegance.

3 IN THE MASTER BATH, a garden tub and abundant storage make life easier.

MAIN LEVEL

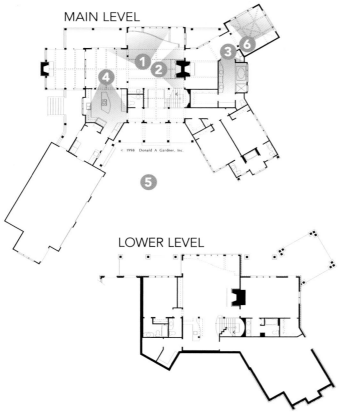

© 1998 Donald A Gardner, Inc.

LOWER LEVEL

special. The media room between them includes a fireplace and wet bar.

The screened porch at the left of the plan deserves notable mention. Perfect by itself as family space or employed as an extension of the dining area for very large gatherings, the room is bound to be a favorite in the home. Seasonal use of the space is enhanced by a handsome stone fireplace.

4 DISTRESSED CABINETRY is an appropriate choice for this home. The layout ensures abundant storage and workspace.

5 FULL-HEIGHT WINDOWS and transoms brighten the home's forward spaces. The wings of the wide floor plan angle toward the front of the home to frame a courtyard entry.

6 PICTURE WINDOWS provide panoramic views from the master bedroom, where exposed wood brings interest to the pitched ceiling.

By the Sea

A MUTED PALETTE of creams and tans reinforces the laid-back atmosphere of the coast.

Imagine a view of the sun setting over the ocean from the porch of your very own beach house. If you choose one of the plans in this coastal designs section, you could have a home for enjoying that wonderful view and more. A coastal design has open, airy spaces that let in plenty of sunshine in a style that suits the sand or the tropical community down the road; it has the low maintenance of a seasonal vacation spot or the comforts and luxuries of everyday living.

There are several styles of homes that fit beautifully in a coastal location, but it's good to know your future intentions before deciding on one. A tidewater home's simplicity and size make it perfect for week-long, annual vacations with the family. For year-round entertaining, Plantation homes have room for everyone, plus lots of decks and porches for outdoor festivities.

A POOLSIDE BAR is a must-have for summer celebrations.

The foundation of a coastal home is an important consideration when choosing an appropriate plan for your lot. A pier, or piling, foundation is what many commonly refer to as stilts and is best for beachfront sites. The elevation protects living spaces from sand and moisture while providing space beneath the home for parking and outdoor storage. For a more enclosed look, island basements have the same structure as pier foundations but with breakaway walls that absorb the impact of severe conditions, such as flooding, by separating from the home and leaving the main structure standing on columns.

A house—whether vacation, second, or year-round—is little more than a roof and four walls without the special touches that make it a

home. Many of the plans in this section have abundant outdoor living spaces for entertaining or simply enjoying the ocean air. Cupolas top some designs for a relaxing retreat with a bird's-eye view. Spacious great rooms and guest bedrooms allow you to share your new home with friends and family. And, if you see a plan that's almost perfect, our modification services will help turn your ideal vision into a reality.

So, no matter the style or purpose of your future coastal home, this section provides a wide selection that will surely lead you to that porch with the sunset view.

LOOK TO TAKE ADVANTAGE of seaside views from wide windows and patios.

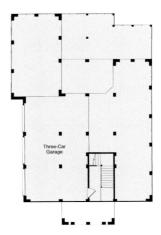

Master Bedroom 16'10"x 17'8"

Wood Deck 30'10"x 16'

Master Bath

Porch 17'7"x 12'

Breakfast 12'8"x 13'4"

Walk-In Closet

Family 17'6"x 20'6"

Kitchen 12'8"x 16'

Utility

1/2 Ba.

Study 12'6'x 13'

Foyer

Dining 12'4"x 14'4"

Porch 18'x 8'

FIRST FLOOR

Balcony 17'10"x 10'

Playroom 13'10"x 15'

Bath

Bedroom 12'2"x 11'4"

Bedroom 13'2"x 11'4"

Library/Office 11'8"x 12'

Three-Car Garage

SECOND FLOOR

(#) HPK2500013

Plan: HPK2500013

Style: Tidewater

First Floor: 2,331 sq. ft.

Second Floor: 988 sq. ft.

Total: 3,319 sq. ft.

Bedrooms: 3

Bathrooms: 2 ½

Width: 48' - 0"

Depth: 66' - 0"

Foundation: Pier (same as Piling)

eplans.com

HISTORY-RICH DETAILS LOVINGLY RETHINK TRADITION throughout this waterfront plan to form a new notion of home and create comfort. The strength of the design lies in its simplicity, with an open interior and plenty of breezy outdoor spaces. Walls of energy-efficient glass filter sunlight to the heart of the home and allow generous views of the landscape. A gallery provides guest amenities, such as a powder room. A servery area with its own walk-in pantry links a well-equipped kitchen to the formal dining room. French doors lead from the master suite and morning area to an extensive outdoor space that includes a covered porch. Upstairs, a wraparound loft leads to an open library.

REAR EXTERIOR

A RAISED PORCH WELCOMES GUESTS AND HOMEOWNERS to relax in this four-bedroom design. French doors let in fresh breezes and allow entry to the dining room and guest bedroom on the first floor. The master bedroom sits to the right of the plan and enjoys deck and rear-porch access as well as a private front porch. The kitchen also features a private porch and adjoins a sunlit breakfast nook. A fireplace with built-ins adorns the living room. Two family bedrooms, two baths, and an exercise room fill the second floor.

HOME PLAN # HPK2500014

Plan: HPK2500014

Style: Tidewater

First Floor: 2,213 sq. ft.

Second Floor: 1,010 sq. ft.

Total: 3,223 sq. ft.

Bedrooms: 4

Bathrooms: 4

Width: 61' - 4"

Depth: 67' - 0"

Foundation: Pier (same as Piling)

eplans.com

FIRST FLOOR

- Deck 27'x 12'
- Porch 30'x 8'
- Breakfast 11'3"x 16'6"
- Master Bedroom 16'4"x 16'6"
- Living Room 24'x 17'4"
- Util.
- WIC
- WIC
- Kitchen 11'3"x 19'
- Bath
- Ma. Bath
- Porch 11'8"x 6'
- Dining Room 13'3"x 13'10"
- Guest Bedroom 12'6"x 12'
- Porch 11'8"x 6'
- Porch 26'x 7'

SECOND FLOOR

- Bath
- Balcony
- Exercise Room 12'6"x 12'5"
- WIC
- Bedroom 13'6"x 12'6"
- Open to Below
- Bedroom 12'6"x 12'6"
- WIC
- WIC

COASTAL DESIGNS

FIRST FLOOR

Wood Deck 36'7" x 10'
Master Bath
Master Bedroom 15'8" x 16'3"
Covered Porch 20' x 13'
Breakfast 12'8" x 13'2"
WIC
Living 20' x 18'
Kitchen 12'6" x 13'2"
Bath
Bedroom 12'8" x 13'
Study 13' x 13'
Foyer
Dining 12'10" x 13'
Utility
Porch 51' x 8'

SECOND FLOOR

Multimedia Room 16' x 19'
WIC
Bath
Open To Below
WIC
Balcony
Bedroom 13' x 13'
Open to Below
Bedroom 13' x 13'
WIC

THIS LUXURIOUS WATERFRONT DESIGN SINGS OF SOUTHERN ISLAND INFLUENCES. A front covered porch opens to a foyer, flanked by a study and dining room. The living room, warmed by a fireplace and safe from off-season ocean breezes, overlooks the rear covered porch. The island kitchen extends into a breakfast room. Beyond the covered porch, the wood deck is also accessed privately from the master suite. This suite includes a private whirlpool bath and huge walk-in closet. A guest suite is located on the first floor, while two additional bedrooms and a multimedia room are located on the second level.

HPK2500015

HOME PLAN

Style: Tidewater

First Floor: 2,390 sq. ft.

Second Floor: 1,200 sq. ft.

Total: 3,590 sq. ft.

Bedrooms: 4

Bathrooms: 3

Width: 61' - 0"

Depth: 64' - 4"

Foundation: Pier (same as Piling)

eplans.com

REAR EXTERIOR

THIS PIER-FOUNDATION HOME HAS AN ABUNDANCE OF AMENITIES TO OFFER, not the least being the loft lookout. Inside, the living room is complete with a corner gas fireplace. The spacious kitchen features a cooktop island, an adjacent breakfast nook, and easy access to the dining room. From this room, a set of French doors leads out to a small deck—perfect for dining alfresco. Upstairs, the sleeping zone consists of two family bedrooms sharing a full hall bath, and a deluxe master suite. Amenities in this suite include two closets and a private bath.

HPK2500016

HOME PLAN

Style: Cracker

First Floor: 731 sq. ft.

Second Floor: 935 sq. ft.

Third Floor: 138 sq. ft.

Total: 1,804 sq. ft.

Bedrooms: 3

Bathrooms: 3

Width: 35' - 0"

Depth: 38' - 0"

Foundation: Pier (same as Piling)

eplans.com

COASTAL DESIGNS

FIRST FLOOR

Deck

Dining 9'x 13'8"

Living 14'x 19'

Screen Porch

SECOND FLOOR

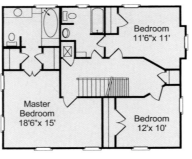

Bedroom 11'6"x 11'

Master Bedroom 18'6"x 15'

Bedroom 12'x 10'

THIRD FLOOR

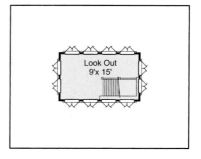

Look Out 9'x 15'

Dining 11'x 11'

Living 16'6" x 21'

Bedroom 13'x 11'

Bedroom 13'x 11'

Porch

Deck

FIRST FLOOR

Master Bedroom 16'6"x 19'

Bedroom 13'x 13'

Balcony

SECOND FLOOR

HOME PLAN

HPK2500017

Style: Tidewater

First Floor: 1,056 sq. ft.

Second Floor: 807 sq. ft.

Total: 1,863 sq. ft.

Bedrooms: 4

Bathrooms: 3

Width: 33' - 0"

Depth: 54' - 0"

Foundation: Crawlspace, Pier (same as Piling)

Photo Courtesy of Chatham Home Planning, Inc. Chris A. Little of Atlanta (Photographer). This home, as shown in photographs, may differ from the actual blueprints. For more detailed information, please check the floor plans carefully.

HOME PLAN

HPK2500018

Style: Tidewater

First Floor: 1,122 sq. ft.

Second Floor: 528 sq. ft.

Total: 1,650 sq. ft.

Bedrooms: 4

Bathrooms: 2

Width: 34' - 0"

Depth: 52' - 5"

Foundation: Pier (same as Piling)

Porch 12'x 9'5"

Kitchen 8'8"x 18'

Dining 11'6"x 18'

Bedroom 13'x 10'11"

Living 16'6"x 14'5"

Bedroom 13'x 10'9"

Porch 20'6"x 5'

Deck 34'x 10'

FIRST FLOOR

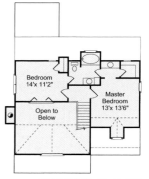

Bedroom 14'x 11'2"

Open to Below

Master Bedroom 13'x 13'6"

SECOND FLOOR

Photos by Chris A. Little of Atlanta. This home, as shown in photographs, may differ from the actual blueprints. For more detailed information, please check the floor plans carefully.

HOME PLAN

(#) HPK2500413

Style: Tidewater

First Floor: 1,552 sq. ft.

Second Floor: 653 sq. ft.

Total: 2,205 sq. ft.

Bedrooms: 3

Bathrooms: 2

Width: 60' - 0"

Depth: 50' - 0"

Foundation: Pier (same as Piling)

eplans.com

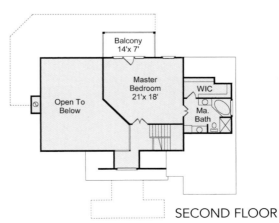

REAR EXTERIOR

A SPLIT STAIRCASE ADDS FLAIR TO THIS EUROPEAN-STYLE COASTAL HOME, where a fireplace brings warmth on chilly evenings. The foyer opens to the expansive living/dining area and island kitchen. A multitude of windows fills the interior with sunlight and ocean breezes. The wraparound rear deck finds access near the kitchen. The utility room is conveniently tucked between the kitchen and the two first-floor bedrooms. The second-floor master suite offers a private deck and a luxurious bath with a garden tub, shower, and walk-in closet.

COASTAL DESIGNS

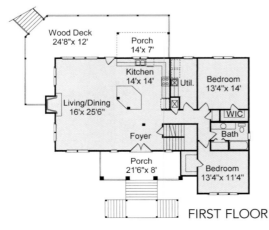

Wood Deck 24'8"x 12'
Porch 14'x 7'
Kitchen 14'x 14'
Util.
Bedroom 13'4"x 14'
Living/Dining 16'x 25'6"
WIC
Foyer
Bath
Porch 21'6"x 8'
Bedroom 13'4"x 11'4"

FIRST FLOOR

Balcony 14'x 7'
Open To Below
Master Bedroom 21'x 18'
WIC
Ma. Bath

SECOND FLOOR

THIS ELEGANT CHARLESTON TOWNHOUSE IS ENHANCED BY SOUTHERN GRACE and three levels of charming livability. Covered porches offer outdoor living space at every level. The first floor offers a living room with fireplace, an island kitchen serving a bayed nook, and a formal dining room. A first-floor guest bedroom is located at the front of the plan, along with a laundry and powder room. The second level offers a sumptuous master suite boasting a private balcony, a master bath, and an enormous walk-in closet. Two other bedrooms sharing a Jack-and-Jill bath are also on this level. The basement level includes a three-car garage.

HOME PLAN #

HPK2500019

Style: Plantation

First Floor: 1,901 sq. ft.

Second Floor: 1,874 sq. ft.

Total: 3,775 sq. ft.

Bedrooms: 4

Bathrooms: 3 ½

Width: 50' - 0"

Depth: 70' - 0"

Foundation: Pier (same as Piling)

eplans.com

FIRST FLOOR

SECOND FLOOR

FIRST FLOOR

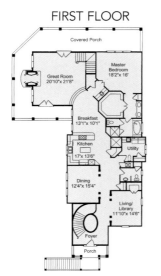

Covered Porch

Great Room
20'10"x 21'8"

Master Bedroom
18'2"x 16'

Breakfast
13'1"x 10'1"

Kitchen
17'x 13'6"

Utility

Dining
12'4"x 15'4"

Living/ Library
11'10"x 14'6"

Foyer

Porch

SECOND FLOOR

Bedroom
17'10"x 11'1"

Media Room
8'7"x 21'

Bedroom
17'4"x 11'1"

Bedroom
13'2"x 11'4"

Future Gameroom
27'x 12'10"

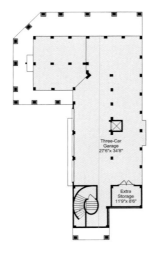

Three-Car Garage
27'6"x 34'8"

Extra Storage
11'9"x 8'6"

HOME PLAN

HPK2500020

Style: Plantation

First Floor: 2,578 sq. ft.

Second Floor: 1,277 sq. ft.

Total: 3,855 sq. ft.

Bonus Space: 347 sq. ft.

Bedrooms: 4

Bathrooms: 3 ½

Width: 53' - 6"

Depth: 97' - 0"

Foundation: Pier (same as Piling)

eplans.com

THIS CHARMING CHARLESTON DESIGN IS FULL OF SURPRISES! Perfect for a narrow lot, the raised foundation is ideal for a waterfront location. An entry porch introduces a winding staircase. To the right is a living room/library that functions as a formal entertaining space. A large hearth and two sets of French doors to the covered porch enhance the great room. The master suite is positioned for privacy and includes great amenities that work to relax the homeowners. Upstairs, three family bedrooms, two full baths, an open media room, and a future game room create a fantastic casual family space.

COASTAL DESIGNS

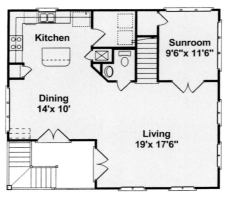

FIRST FLOOR

Kitchen

Dining
14'x 10'

Sunroom
9'6"x 11'6"

Living
19'x 17'6"

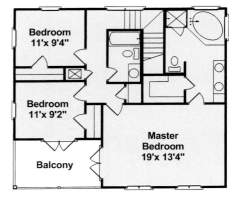

SECOND FLOOR

Bedroom
11'x 9'4"

Bedroom
11'x 9'2"

Balcony

Master
Bedroom
19'x 13'4"

(#) **HPK2500021**

Style: Tidewater

First Floor: 907 sq. ft.

Second Floor: 872 sq. ft.

Total: 1,779 sq. ft.

Bedrooms: 3

Bathrooms: 2 ½

Width: 34' - 0"

Depth: 30' - 0"

Foundation: Pier (same as Piling)

eplans.com

THIS TWO-STORY SEASIDE HOME HAS A DISTINCTIVE ELEVATION. A covered front porch leads to two sets of French doors—one to the spacious living room and one to the dining area. An L-shaped kitchen features a work island, a nearby utility room, and plenty of counter and cabinet space. A sun room finishes off this floor with class. Upstairs, the sleeping zone consists of two family bedrooms—one with access to a balcony—a full bath and a master suite. Here, the homeowner will surely be pleased with a walk-in closet, a corner tub, and a separate shower, as well as balcony access.

HOME PLAN

HPK2500022

Style: Tidewater

First Floor: 1,252 sq. ft.

Second Floor: 920 sq. ft.

Total: 2,172 sq. ft.

Bedrooms: 3

Bathrooms: 2

Width: 37' - 0"

Depth: 46' - 0"

Foundation: Crawlspace, Pier (same as Piling), Slab

FIRST FLOOR

SECOND FLOOR

HOME PLAN

HPK2500023

Style: Craftsman

First Floor: 912 sq. ft.

Second Floor: 831 sq. ft.

Total: 1,743 sq. ft.

Bedrooms: 3

Bathrooms: 3

Width: 34' - 0"

Depth: 32' - 0"

Foundation: Pier (same as Piling)

FIRST FLOOR

SECOND FLOOR

COASTAL DESIGNS

FOR FAMILIES THAT ENJOY LOTS OF SUN AND OCEAN BREEZES, this dazzling Sun Country home is made for you. Rear and front covered porches and a rear screened porch extend the living space outdoors. A sunroom, perfect for your favorite plants, opens to the dining area and grand room. The kitchen and a half-bath are also located on the main floor. Two bedrooms, each with a private bath, are found upstairs. The plan comes with an optional one-car garage with room for storage.

HOME PLAN

HPK2500024

Style: Italianate

First Floor: 754 sq. ft.

Second Floor: 662 sq. ft.

Total: 1,416 sq. ft.

Bonus Space: 96 sq. ft.

Bedrooms: 2

Bathrooms: 2 ½

Width: 38' - 0"

Depth: 44' - 0"

Foundation: Crawlspace

eplans.com

FIRST FLOOR

SECOND FLOOR

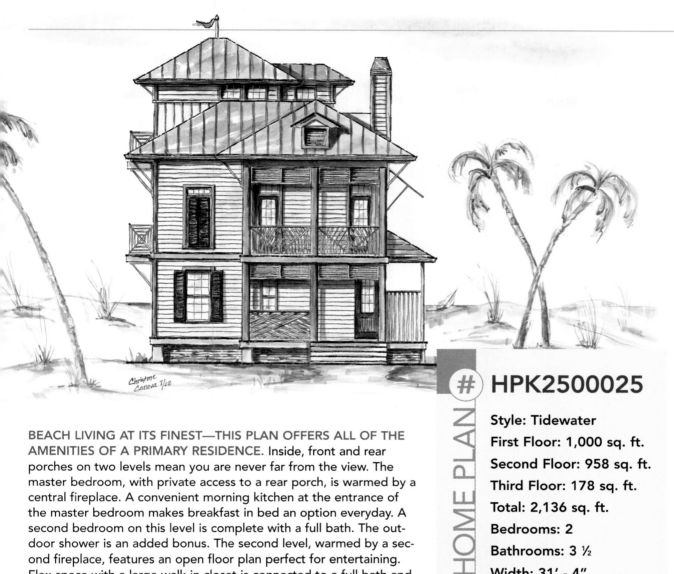

BEACH LIVING AT ITS FINEST—THIS PLAN OFFERS ALL OF THE AMENITIES OF A PRIMARY RESIDENCE. Inside, front and rear porches on two levels mean you are never far from the view. The master bedroom, with private access to a rear porch, is warmed by a central fireplace. A convenient morning kitchen at the entrance of the master bedroom makes breakfast in bed an option everyday. A second bedroom on this level is complete with a full bath. The outdoor shower is an added bonus. The second level, warmed by a second fireplace, features an open floor plan perfect for entertaining. Flex space with a large walk-in closet is connected to a full bath and could be used as a guest suite. The third level will surely be a family favorite. A cupola beach view, sleeping loft, morning kitchen, and private balcony make this area a relaxing retreat.

HOME PLAN

(#) HPK2500025

Style: Tidewater
First Floor: 1,000 sq. ft.
Second Floor: 958 sq. ft.
Third Floor: 178 sq. ft.
Total: 2,136 sq. ft.
Bedrooms: 2
Bathrooms: 3 ½
Width: 31' - 4"
Depth: 52' - 0"
Foundation: Crawlspace

eplans.com

FIRST FLOOR

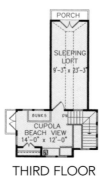

SECOND FLOOR

THIRD FLOOR

COASTAL DESIGNS

HOME PLAN

HPK2500026

Style: Cottage
Main Level: 1,342 sq. ft.
Second Level: 511 sq. ft.
Lower Level: 33 sq. ft.
Total: 1,886 sq. ft.
Bedrooms: 3
Bathrooms: 2 ½
Width: 44' - 0"
Depth: 40' - 0"
Foundation: Island Basement

LOWER LEVEL   MAIN LEVEL   SECOND LEVEL

HOME PLAN

HPK2500027

Style: New American
First Floor: 1,342 sq. ft.
Second Floor: 511 sq. ft.
Total: 1,853 sq. ft.
Bedrooms: 3
Bathrooms: 2 ½
Width: 44' - 0"
Depth: 44' - 0"
Foundation: Island Basement

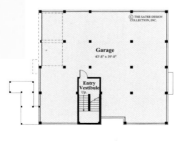

FIRST FLOOR   SECOND FLOOR

REAR EXTERIOR

© The Sater Design Collection, Inc.

HOME PLAN

HPK2500028

Style: Cottage

First Floor: 1,342 sq. ft.

Second Floor: 511 sq. ft.

Total: 1,853 sq. ft.

Bedrooms: 3

Bathrooms: 2

Width: 44' - 0"

Depth: 40' - 0"

Foundation: Pier (same as Piling)

eplans.com

AMENITIES ABOUND IN THIS DELIGHTFUL TWO-STORY HOME. The foyer opens directly into the fantastic grand room, which offers a warming fireplace and two sets of double doors to the rear deck. The dining room also accesses this deck and a second deck shared with Bedroom 2. A convenient kitchen and another bedroom also reside on this level. Upstairs, the master bedroom reigns supreme. Entered through double doors, it pampers with a luxurious bath, walk-in closet, morning kitchen, and private observation deck.

SECOND FLOOR

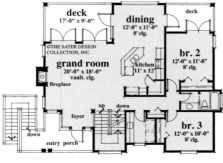

FIRST FLOOR

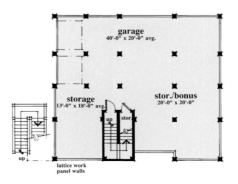

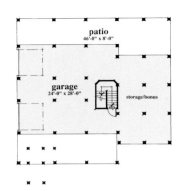

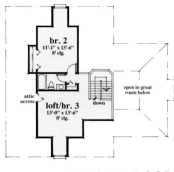

patio
46'-0" x 8'-0"

garage
24'-0" x 28'-0"

storage/bonus

up

screened
verandah
30'-8" x 8'-0"

sundeck
15'-0" x 11'-0"

© THE SATER DESIGN COLLECTION, INC.

down

master
bath

kitchen

dining
10'-0" x 11'-0"
vault clg.

laundry

great
room
15'-0" x 26'-7"
vault clg.

master
suite
17'-3" x 11'-0"
8' clg.

pwdr.

up

foyer

fireplace

down

down

down

entry porch

FIRST FLOOR

br. 2
11'-1" x 13'-6"
8' clg.

attic
access

loft/br. 3
13'-0" x 13'-6"
8' clg.

down

open to great
room below

SECOND FLOOR

AN ABUNDANCE OF PORCHES AND A DECK ENCOUR-
AGE YEAR-ROUND INDOOR/OUTDOOR RELATIONSHIPS in
this classic two-story home. The spacious great room, with its
cozy fireplace, and the adjacent dining room both offer access
to the screened porch/deck area through French doors. The
private master suite accesses both front and rear porches and
leads into a relaxing private bath, complete with dual vanities
and a walk-in closet. An additional family bedroom and a
loft/bedroom are also available.

REAR EXTERIOR

 # HPK2500029

Style: Cottage

First Floor: 1,302 sq. ft.

Second Floor: 602 sq. ft.

Total: 1,904 sq. ft.

Bedrooms: 3

Bathrooms: 2 ½

Width: 48' - 0"

Depth: 45' - 0"

Foundation: Pier (same
as Piling)

eplans.com

Oscar Thompson. This home, as shown in photographs, may differ from the actual blueprints.
For more detailed information, please check the floor plans carefully.

FRONT EXTERIOR

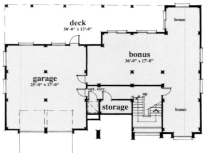

FIRST FLOOR

SECOND FLOOR

HOME PLAN

HPK2500030

Style: Cottage

First Floor: 2,066 sq. ft.

Second Floor: 809 sq. ft.

Total: 2,875 sq. ft.

Bonus Space: 1,260 sq. ft.

Bedrooms: 3

Bathrooms: 3 ½

Width: 64' - 0"

Depth: 45' - 0"

Foundation: Pier (same as Piling)

eplans.com

IF ENTERTAINING IS YOUR PASSION, THEN THIS IS THE DESIGN FOR YOU. With a large, open floor plan and an array of amenities, every gathering will be a success. The foyer embraces living areas accented by a glass fireplace and a wet bar. The grand room and dining room each access a screened veranda for outside enjoyment. The gourmet kitchen delights with its openness to the rest of the house. A morning nook here also adds a nice touch. Two bedrooms and a study radiate from the first-floor living areas. Upstairs is a masterful master suite. It contains a huge walk-in closet, a whirlpool tub, and a private sundeck with a spa.

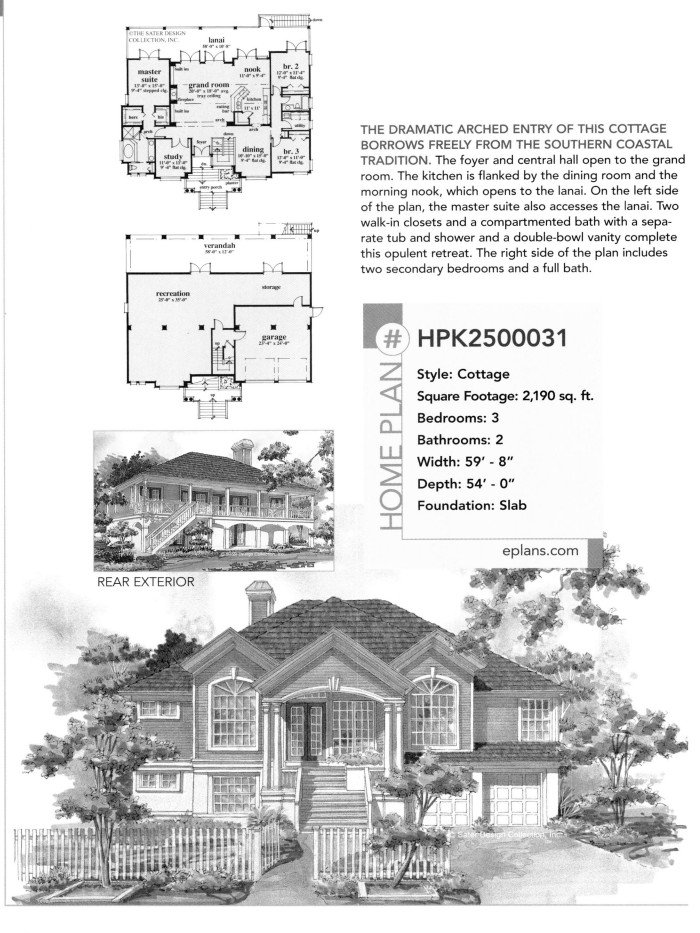

REAR EXTERIOR

THE DRAMATIC ARCHED ENTRY OF THIS COTTAGE BORROWS FREELY FROM THE SOUTHERN COASTAL TRADITION. The foyer and central hall open to the grand room. The kitchen is flanked by the dining room and the morning nook, which opens to the lanai. On the left side of the plan, the master suite also accesses the lanai. Two walk-in closets and a compartmented bath with a separate tub and shower and a double-bowl vanity complete this opulent retreat. The right side of the plan includes two secondary bedrooms and a full bath.

HPK2500031

Style: Cottage
Square Footage: 2,190 sq. ft.
Bedrooms: 3
Bathrooms: 2
Width: 59' - 8"
Depth: 54' - 0"
Foundation: Slab

HOME PLAN

eplans.com

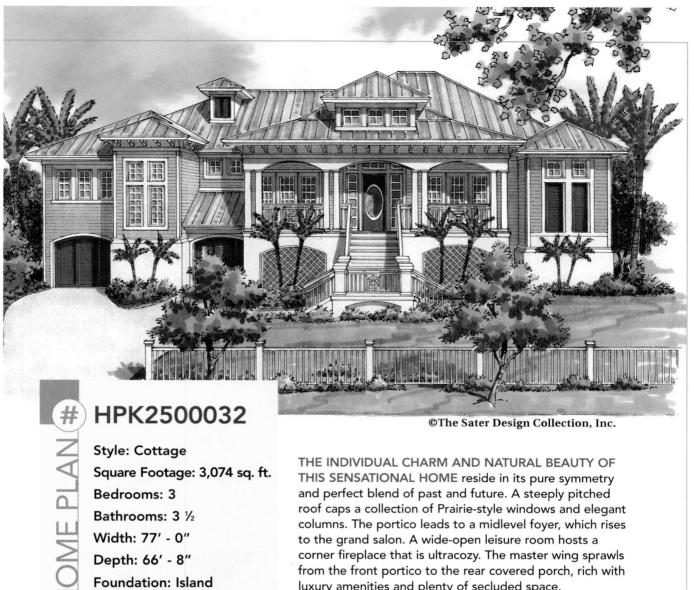

©The Sater Design Collection, Inc.

HPK2500032

Style: Cottage

Square Footage: 3,074 sq. ft.

Bedrooms: 3

Bathrooms: 3 ½

Width: 77' - 0"

Depth: 66' - 8"

Foundation: Island Basement

eplans.com

THE INDIVIDUAL CHARM AND NATURAL BEAUTY OF THIS SENSATIONAL HOME reside in its pure symmetry and perfect blend of past and future. A steeply pitched roof caps a collection of Prairie-style windows and elegant columns. The portico leads to a midlevel foyer, which rises to the grand salon. A wide-open leisure room hosts a corner fireplace that is ultracozy. The master wing sprawls from the front portico to the rear covered porch, rich with luxury amenities and plenty of secluded space.

COASTAL DESIGNS

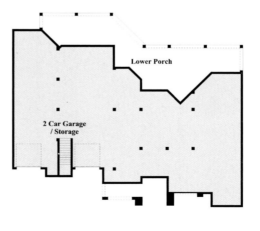

COTTAGE ACCOMMODATIONS ARE PROVIDED WITH THIS SEASIDE VACATION DREAM HOME. Once inside, the foyer steps lead up to the formal living areas on the main floor. To the left, a study is enhanced by a vaulted ceiling and double doors that open to a front balcony. Vaulted ceilings create a lofty feel throughout the home, especially in the central great room. The island kitchen is open to an adjacent breakfast nook. Guest quarters reside on the right side of the plan—one boasts a private bath. The master suite is secluded on the left for privacy and features two walk-in closets and a pampering whirlpool master bath. Downstairs, storage space abounds alongside the two-car garage.

HOME PLAN # HPK2500033

Style: Italianate
Square Footage: 2,385 sq. ft.
Bedrooms: 3
Bathrooms: 3
Width: 60' - 0"
Depth: 52' - 0"
Foundation: Island Basement

eplans.com

© The Sater Design Collection, Inc.

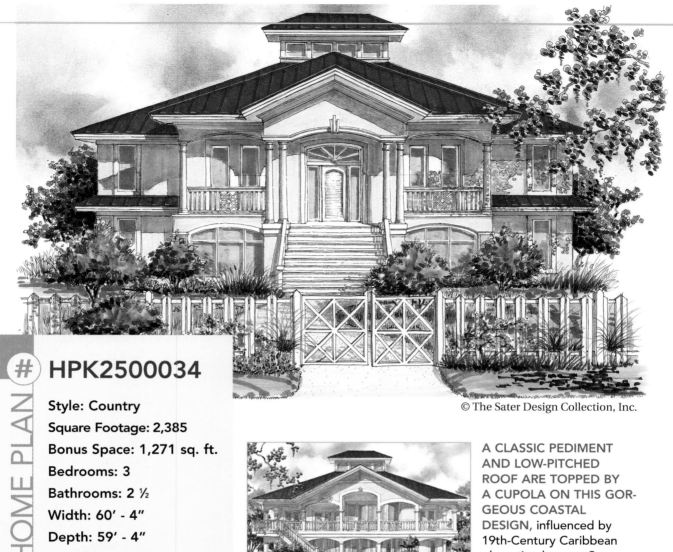

© The Sater Design Collection, Inc.

REAR EXTERIOR

A CLASSIC PEDIMENT AND LOW-PITCHED ROOF ARE TOPPED BY A CUPOLA ON THIS GORGEOUS COASTAL DESIGN, influenced by 19th-Century Caribbean plantation houses. Savory style blended with a contemporary seaside spirit invites entertaining as well as year-round living—plus room to grow. The beauty and warmth of natural light splash the spacious living area with a sense of the outdoors and a touch of joie de vivre. The great room features a wall of built-ins designed for even the most technology-savvy entertainment buff. Dazzling views through walls of glass are enlivened by the presence of a breezy porch. The master suite features a luxurious bath, a dressing area, and two walk-in closets. Glass doors open to the porch and provide generous views of the seascape; a nearby study offers an indoor retreat.

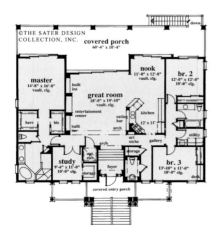

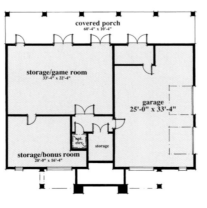

COASTAL DESIGNS

FIRST FLOOR

SECOND FLOOR

LATTICE WALLS, PICKETS, AND HORIZONTAL SIDING COMPLEMENT A RELAXED KEY WEST DESIGN that's perfect for waterfront properties. The grand room with a fireplace, the dining room, and Bedroom 2 open through French doors to the veranda. The master suite occupies the entire second floor and features access to a private balcony through double doors. This pampering suite also includes a spacious walk-in closet and a full bath with a whirlpool tub. Enclosed storage/bonus space and a garage are available on the lower level.

REAR EXTERIOR

HPK2500035

HOME PLAN

Style: Cottage

First Floor: 1,586 sq. ft.

Second Floor: 601 sq. ft.

Total: 2,187 sq. ft.

Bedrooms: 3

Bathrooms: 2

Width: 50' - 0"

Depth: 44' - 0"

Foundation: Pier (same as Piling)

eplans.com

© Sater Design Collection, Inc.

(#) HPK2500036

Style: Plantation

First Floor: 1,855 sq. ft.

Second Floor: 901 sq. ft.

Total: 2,756 sq. ft.

Bedrooms: 3

Bathrooms: 3 ½

Width: 66' - 0"

Depth: 50' - 0"

Foundation: Island Basement

eplans.com

THIS SOUTHERN TIDEWATER COTTAGE IS THE PERFECT VACATION HIDEAWAY. An octagonal great room with a multifaceted vaulted ceiling illuminates the interior. The island kitchen is brightened by a bumped-out window and a pass-through to the lanai. Two walk-in closets and a whirlpool bath await to indulge the homeowner in the master suite. A set of double doors opens to the vaulted master lanai for quiet comfort. The U-shaped staircase leads to a loft, which overlooks the great room and the foyer. Two additional family bedrooms offer private baths. A computer center and a morning kitchen complete the upper level.

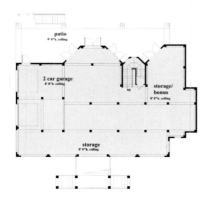

FIRST FLOOR

SECOND FLOOR

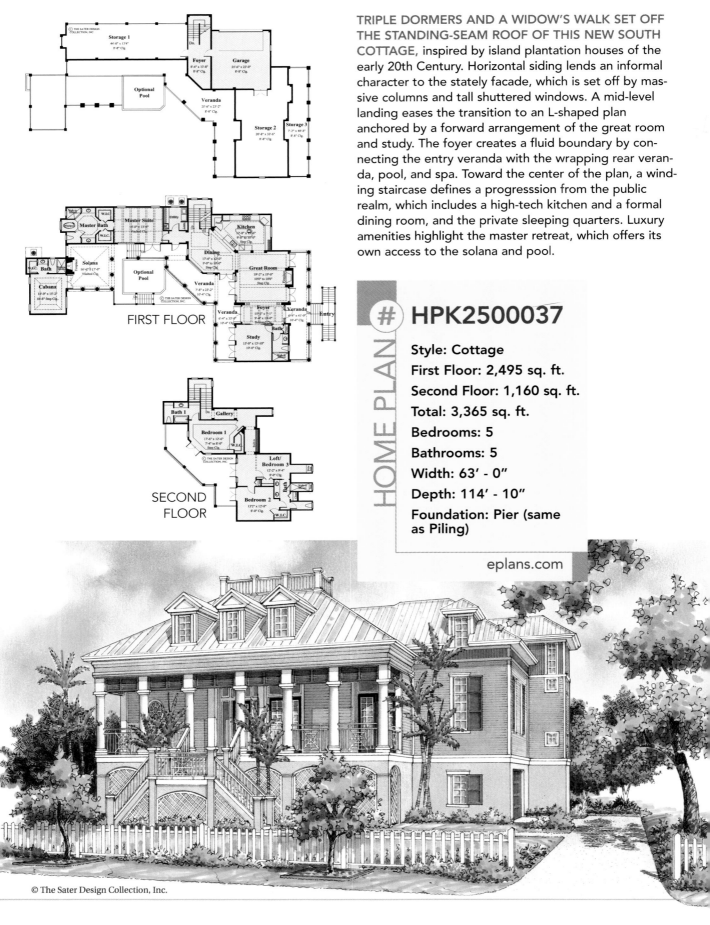

FIRST FLOOR

SECOND FLOOR

TRIPLE DORMERS AND A WIDOW'S WALK SET OFF THE STANDING-SEAM ROOF OF THIS NEW SOUTH COTTAGE, inspired by island plantation houses of the early 20th Century. Horizontal siding lends an informal character to the stately facade, which is set off by massive columns and tall shuttered windows. A mid-level landing eases the transition to an L-shaped plan anchored by a forward arrangement of the great room and study. The foyer creates a fluid boundary by connecting the entry veranda with the wrapping rear veranda, pool, and spa. Toward the center of the plan, a winding staircase defines a progresssion from the public realm, which includes a high-tech kitchen and a formal dining room, and the private sleeping quarters. Luxury amenities highlight the master retreat, which offers its own access to the solana and pool.

HOME PLAN

HPK2500037

Style: Cottage
First Floor: 2,495 sq. ft.
Second Floor: 1,160 sq. ft.
Total: 3,365 sq. ft.
Bedrooms: 5
Bathrooms: 5
Width: 63' - 0"
Depth: 114' - 10"
Foundation: Pier (same as Piling)

eplans.com

© The Sater Design Collection, Inc.

© The Sater Design Collection, Inc.

OUTDOOR SPACES, SUCH AS THE INVITING WRAPAROUND PORCH AND THE REAR VERANDA, are the living areas of this cottage. French doors, a fireplace, and built-in cabinets adorn the great room. A private hall leads to the first-floor master suite. The upper level boasts a catwalk that overlooks the great room and the foyer. A secluded master wing enjoys a bumped-out window, a stunning tray ceiling, and two walk-in closets. The island kitchen conveniently accesses the nook, dining area, and the wet bar.

HOME PLAN #

HPK2500038

Style: Plantation

Main Level: 2,146 sq. ft.

Second Level: 952 sq. ft.

Lower Level: 187 sq. ft.

Total: 3,285 sq. ft.

Bedrooms: 3

Bathrooms: 3 ½

Width: 52' - 0"

Depth: 65' - 4"

Foundation: Island Basement

eplans.com

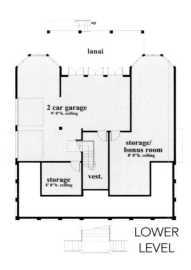

LOWER LEVEL

MAIN LEVEL

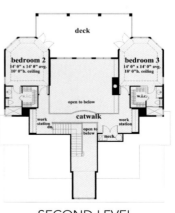

SECOND LEVEL

COASTAL DESIGNS

FIRST FLOOR

SECOND FLOOR

HPK2500039

Style: Mediterranean

First Floor: 1,383 sq. ft.

Second Floor: 595 sq. ft.

Total: 1,978 sq. ft.

Bonus Space: 617 sq. ft.

Bedrooms: 3

Bathrooms: 2

Width: 48' - 0"

Depth: 42' - 0"

Foundation: Island Basement

eplans.com

THE MIXTURE OF GRAND DETAILS WITH A COMFORTABLE LAYOUT MAKES THIS HOME A PERFECT COMBINATION OF ELEGANCE AND EASY LIVING. Those who prefer a spacious master suite set apart from the rest of the home will love this arrangement. The top story is devoted to a master suite with double doors leading to a private porch and a loft that overlooks the vaulted great room below. On the first floor, each of the two family bedrooms has an adjoining porch. The built-ins and fireplace in the great room give a feeling of casual sophistication.

© The Sater Design Collection, Inc.

GREAT INDOOR/OUTDOOR LIVING IS ACCOMPLISHED IN THIS HOME THROUGH GLASS DOORS THAT OFFER EASY ACCESS TO REAR PORCHES, providing perfect areas to entertain. The gourmet kitchen boasts an interior vista that includes the great room's fireplace. The formal dining room features a wall of glass, which furthers the spacious feeling of the interior and allows outdoor views that are simply dazzling. Two family bedrooms, a crow's nest, and a loft reside on the second level. A storage or expandable living space is available in the basement.

HOME PLAN

HPK2500040

Style: Italianate

First Floor: 1,537 sq. ft.

Second Floor: 812 sq. ft.

Total: 2,349 sq. ft.

Bonus Space: 800 sq. ft.

Bedrooms: 3

Bathrooms: 2 ½

Width: 45' - 4"

Depth: 50' - 0"

Foundation: Island Basement

eplans.com

FIRST FLOOR

SECOND FLOOR

COASTAL DESIGNS

LOWER LEVEL

lanai

2 1/2 car garage
20' 0" x 29' 0" avg.
10' 0"h. Ceiling

Optional
Utility

mech.

foyer
up

entry porch

MAIN LEVEL

© THE SATER DESIGN
COLLECTION, INC.

Veranda
39'-0" x 9'-6"
10'-6" Clg.

Window
Seat

Built-in
Cabinetry

Dining
10'-0" x 13'-0"
10'-0" Clg.

Great Room
18'-0" x 20'-0"
10'-0" Clg.

Fireplace

Built-in
Cabinetry

Window
Seat

Kitchen
15'-0" x 13'-0"
10'-0" Clg.

Dn.   Up.

P.B.

SECOND LEVEL

deck

bedrm 3
10' 0" x 13' 0"
9' 4" clg.

master
suite
13' 0" x 13' 0"
10' 4"h. clg.

w.i.c.

w.i.c.

linen

dn.

bedroom 2
12' 8" x 11' 0"
9' 4"h. clg.

A STATELY TOWER ADDS A SENSE OF GRANDEUR TO CONTEMPORARY HIGH-PITCHED ROOFLINES on this dreamy Mediterranean-style villa. Surrounded by outdoor views, the living space extends to a veranda through three sets of French doors. Decorative columns announce the dining area, which boasts a 10-foot ceiling and views of its own. Tall arch-top windows bathe a winding staircase with sunlight or moonlight. The upper-level sleeping quarters include a master retreat that offers a bedroom with views and access to the observation deck. Secondary bedrooms share a full bath and linen storage. Bedroom 3 features a walk-in closet and French doors to the deck.

HPK2500041

Style: Italianate

Main Level: 874 sq. ft.

Second Level: 880 sq. ft.

Lower Level: 242 sq. ft.

Total: 1,754 sq. ft.

Bedrooms: 3

Bathrooms: 2 ½

Width: 34' - 0"

Depth: 43' - 0"

Foundation: Island Basement

HOME PLAN

eplans.com

© Sater Design Collection, Inc.

HOME PLAN

HPK2500042

Style: Cottage

First Floor: 1,305 sq. ft.

Second Floor: 1,215 sq. ft.

Total: 2,520 sq. ft.

Bonus Space: 935 sq. ft.

Bedrooms: 3

Bathrooms: 2 ½

Width: 30' - 6"

Depth: 72' - 2"

Foundation: Slab

eplans.com

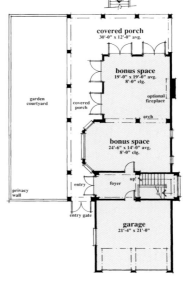

REAR EXTERIOR

FIRST FLOOR

covered porch
30'-0" x 12'-0" avg.

great room
19'-0" x 19'-0"
10'-0" clg.

built ins

fireplace

built ins

eating bar

kitchen

dining
11'-4" x 14'-0"
10'-0" clg.

gallery

study
10'-4" x 11'-4"
10'-0" clg.

util.

SECOND FLOOR

observation deck
30'-0" x 12'-0" avg.

master
19'-0" x 13'-8"
10'-0" tray clg.

sundeck

his

hers

br. 2
9'-6" x 12'-8"
9'-0" clg.

gallery

guest
10'-4" x 15'-8"
9'-0" clg.

equip.

covered porch
30'-0" x 12'-0" avg.

bonus space
19'-0" x 19'-0" avg.
8'-0" clg.

optional fireplace

bonus space
24'-6" x 14'-0" avg.
8'-0" clg.

garden courtyard

covered porch

privacy wall

entry

foyer

entry gate

garage
21'-4" x 21'-0"

THIS ELEGANT OLD CHARLESTON ROW DESIGN BLENDS HIGH VOGUE WITH A RESTFUL CHARACTER that says shoes are optional. A flexible interior enjoys modern space that welcomes sunlight. Wraparound porticos on two levels offer views to the living areas, and a "sit-and-watch-the-stars" observation deck opens from the master suite. Four sets of French doors bring the outside into the great room. The second-floor master suite features a spacious bath and three sets of doors that open to the observation deck. A guest bedroom on this level leads to a gallery hall with its own access to the deck. Bonus space awaits development on the lower level, which—true to its Old Charleston roots—opens gloriously to a garden courtyard.

COASTAL DESIGNS

FIRST FLOOR

SECOND FLOOR

Photo by Doug Thompson Photography. This home, as shown in photographs, may differ from the actual blueprints. For more detailed information, please check the floor plans carefully.

HOME PLAN

HPK2500001

Style: Cottage

First Floor: 1,383 sq. ft.

Second Floor: 595 sq. ft.

Total: 1,978 sq. ft.

Bonus Space: 617 sq. ft.

Bedrooms: 3

Bathrooms: 2

Width: 48' - 0"

Depth: 42' - 0"

Foundation: Island Basement

eplans.com

THIS FABULOUS KEY WEST HOME BLENDS INTERIOR SPACE WITH THE GREAT OUTDOORS. Designed for a balmy climate, the home boasts expansive porches and decks—with outside access from every area of the home. A sun-dappled foyer leads via a stately mid-level staircase to a splendid great room, which features a warming fireplace tucked in beside beautiful built-in cabinetry. Highlighted by a wall of glass that opens to the rear porch, this two-story living space opens to the formal dining room and a well-appointed kitchen. Spacious secondary bedrooms on the main level open to outside spaces and share a full bath. Upstairs, a 10-foot tray ceiling highlights a private master suite, which provides French doors to an upper-level porch.

THE VARIETY IN THE ROOFLINES OF THIS STRIKING WATERFRONT HOME WILL CERTAINLY MAKE IT THE ENVY OF THE NEIGHBORHOOD. The two-story great room, with its fireplace and built-ins, is a short flight down from the foyer. The three sets of French doors give access to the veranda. The huge, well-equipped kitchen will easily serve the gourmet who loves to entertain. The stepped ceiling and bay window in the dining room will add style to every meal. The master suite completes the first level. Two bedrooms and two full baths, along with an expansive loft, constitute the second level. One guest suite has an attached sundeck.

HOME PLAN

(#) HPK2500043

Style: Cottage

First Floor: 2,096 sq. ft.

Second Floor: 892 sq. ft.

Total: 2,988 sq. ft.

Bedrooms: 3

Bathrooms: 3 ½

Width: 58' - 0"

Depth: 54' - 0"

Foundation: Island Basement

eplans.com

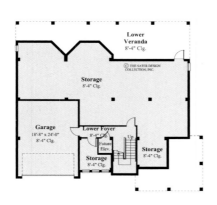

FIRST FLOOR

SECOND FLOOR

COASTAL DESIGNS

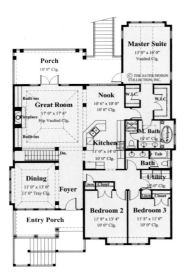

Master Suite
13' 0" x 16' 0"
Vaulted Clg.

Porch
10' 0" Clg.

© THE SATER DESIGN
COLLECTION, INC.

Nook
10' 6" x 9' 0"
10' 0" Clg.

W.I.C.

W.I.C.

Built-ins

Great Room
17' 0" x 17' 6"
Hip Vaulted Clg.

Fireplace

M. Bath
10' 6" Clg.

Built-ins

Kitchen
11' 0" x 14' 0"
10' 0" Clg.

Dn.

Tub

Bath

Dining
11' 0" x 13' 0"
11' 0" Tray Clg.

Foyer

Utility
10' 0" Clg.

Linen Closet

Bedroom 2
11' 8" x 13' 4"
10' 0" Clg.

Bedroom 3
11' 8" x 11' 0"
10' 0" Clg.

Linen Closet

Entry Porch

THE GRAND BALUSTRADE AND RECESSED ENTRY are just the beginning of this truly spectacular home. A hip vaulted ceiling highlights the great room—a perfect place to entertain, made cozy by a massive fireplace and built-in cabinetry. An angled snack counter provides an uninterrupted interior vista of the living area from the gourmet kitchen. To the rear of the plan, French doors open to a spacious lanai—a beautiful spot for enjoying the harmonious sounds of the sea. On the lower level, separate bonus spaces easily convert to hobby rooms or can be used for additional storage. An additional storage area promises room for unused toys and furnishings.

REAR EXTERIOR

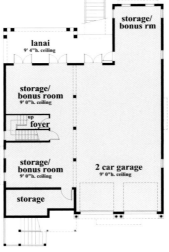

storage/
bonus rm

lanai
9' 4" h. ceiling

storage/
bonus room
9' 0" h. ceiling

up
foyer

storage/
bonus room
9' 0" h. ceiling

2 car garage
9' 0" h. ceiling

storage

HOME PLAN

HPK2500044

Style: Italianate

Square Footage: 2,137

Bedrooms: 3

Bathrooms: 2

Width: 44' - 0"

Depth: 61' - 0"

Foundation: Island Basement

eplans.com

©The Sater Design Collection, Inc.

©The Sater Design Collection, Inc.

HPK2500045

Style: Mediterranean

First Floor: 1,510 sq. ft.

Second Floor: 864 sq. ft.

Total: 2,374 sq. ft.

Bedrooms: 3

Bathrooms: 3 ½

Width: 44' - 0"

Depth: 49' - 0"

Foundation: Unfinished Basement

eplans.com

THE STAIRCASE LEADING TO A COLUMNED FRONT PORCH LENDS A TOUCH OF GRANDEUR to this coastal residence. The great room is inviting, with a fireplace and twin sets of double doors opening to a wraparound porch that's also accessed by the master suite. This spacious suite features luxurious extras like His and Hers sinks, a separate garden tub and shower, and a huge walk-in closet. The kitchen provides plenty of counter space and overlooks the formal dining room. Upstairs, two additional bedrooms open up to a second-floor porch and have their own private baths and walk-in closets.

FIRST FLOOR

SECOND FLOOR

COASTAL DESIGNS

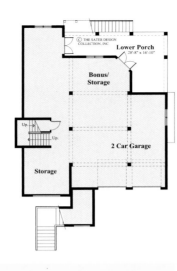

FIRST FLOOR

SECOND FLOOR

HOME PLAN # HPK2500046

Style: Cottage

First Floor: 1,542 sq. ft.

Second Floor: 971 sq. ft.

Total: 2,513 sq. ft.

Bedrooms: 3

Bathrooms: 3

Width: 46' - 0"

Depth: 51' - 0"

Foundation: Island Basement

eplans.com

ARCHES, COLUMNS, AND FRENCH DOORS PAY HOMAGE TO A CAP-TIVATING KEY WEST STYLE that's light, airy, and fully au courant. French doors lead to a study or parlor, which features a wall of built-in shelves and a view of the front property through an arch-topped window. Built-ins frame the fireplace in the great room too, providing an anchor for a wall of glass that brings in a sense of the outdoors. The main level includes a secluded secondary bedroom that's thoughtfully placed near a full bath, coat closet, and linen storage. Upstairs, a balcony hall allows interior vistas of the living area below and connects a secondary bedroom and bath with the master suite. French doors open from both bedrooms to a wrapping deck. The master bath provides a bumped-out garden tub and a walk-in closet designed for two.

© Sater Design Collection

ASYMMETRICAL ROOFLINES SET OFF A GRAND TURRET AND A TWO-STORY BAY that allow glorious views from the front of this home. Arch-top clerestory windows bring natural light into the great room, which shares a corner fireplace and a wet bar with the dining room. Two guest suites are located on this floor. A winding staircase leads to a luxurious master suite that shares a fireplace with the bath and includes a morning kitchen, French doors to the balcony, and a double walk-in closet. Down the hall, a study and a balcony overlooking the great room complete the plan.

REAR EXTERIOR

HOME PLAN

 # HPK2500047

Style: Cottage

First Floor: 1,684 sq. ft.

Second Floor: 1,195 sq. ft.

Total: 2,879 sq. ft.

Bonus Space: 674 sq. ft.

Bedrooms: 3

Bathrooms: 3

Width: 45' - 0"

Depth: 52' - 0"

Foundation: Pier (same as Piling)

eplans.com

COASTAL DESIGNS

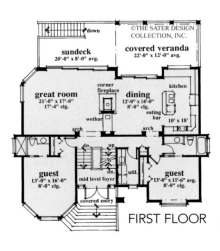
FIRST FLOOR

SECOND FLOOR

THIS RAISED TIDEWATER DESIGN IS WELL-SUITED FOR MANY BUILDING SITUATIONS, with comfortable outdoor areas that encourage year-round living. Horizontal siding and a steeply pitched roof call up a sense of the past, while a smart-space interior redefines the luxury of comfort with up-to-the-minute amenities. A vaulted ceiling highlights the great room, made comfy by a centered fireplace, extensive built-ins, and French doors that let in fresh air and sunlight. The formal dining room opens from the entry hall and features a triple-window view of the side property. A secluded sitting area in the master suite features a wide window and a door to a private area of the rear porch. Two secondary bedrooms share a full bath.

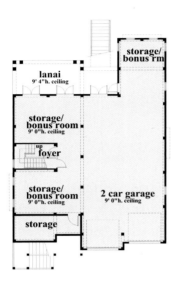

HPK2500048

HOME PLAN

Style: Country

Square Footage: 2,136

Bonus Space: 1,428 sq. ft.

Bedrooms: 3

Bathrooms: 2

Width: 44' - 0"

Depth: 63' - 0"

Foundation: Island Basement

eplans.com

© The Sater Design Collection, Inc.

© Sater Design Collection, Inc.

IMPRESSIVE PILLARS, KEYSTONE LINTEL ARCHES, A COVERED CARPORT, AN ABUNDANCE OF WINDOWS, and an alluring fountain are just a few of the decorative touches of this elegant design. The two-story foyer leads to a two-story great room, which enjoys built-in cabinetry, a two-sided fireplace, and spectacular views to the rear property. To the left of the great room is the dining area, with a wet bar, island kitchen, and nearby bayed breakfast nook. Bedroom 2 boasts a semicircular wall of windows, a full bath, and a walk-in closet. The second-floor master suite is filled with amenities, including a two-sided fireplace.

HOME PLAN

HPK2500049

Style: Mediterranean

Main Level: 2,391 sq. ft.

Second Level: 1,539 sq. ft.

Lower Level: 429 sq. ft.

Total: 4,359 sq. ft.

Bedrooms: 3

Bathrooms: 4 ½

Width: 71' - 0"

Depth: 69' - 0"

Foundation: Island Basement

eplans.com

LOWER LEVEL

MAIN LEVEL

SECOND LEVEL

COASTAL DESIGNS

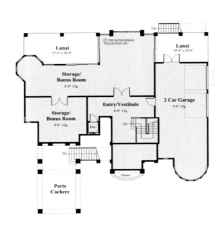

HOME PLAN

HPK2500051

Style: Mediterranean

First Floor: 2,391 sq. ft.

Second Floor: 1,539 sq. ft.

Total: 3,930 sq. ft.

Bedrooms: 3

Bathrooms: 4 ½

Width: 71' - 0"

Depth: 69' - 0"

Foundation: Island Basement

eplans.com

CLASSIC COLUMNS, BEAUTIFUL WINDOWS, AND A GRAND PORTE COCHERE SET OFF THIS DRAMATIC ENTRY. An abundance of windows invite the best views and plenty of sunlight and cool breezes. Decorative columns announce the great room, which enjoys a wall of glass and two sets of sliding doors to separate verandas. The well-equipped kitchen serves a morning bay as well as the formal dining room, which provides a servery for planned events. A secondary suite on the main level offers a sensational bay window. Nearby, a colonnade leads to the study and a quiet space with a window seat. A stylish catwalk on the upper level overlooks the great room and foyer and connects guest quarters to the master suite. The highlight of this private haven is a two-sided fireplace that warms both the bedroom and bath. Separate vanities and a walk-in closet designed for two lend a deep sense of luxury.

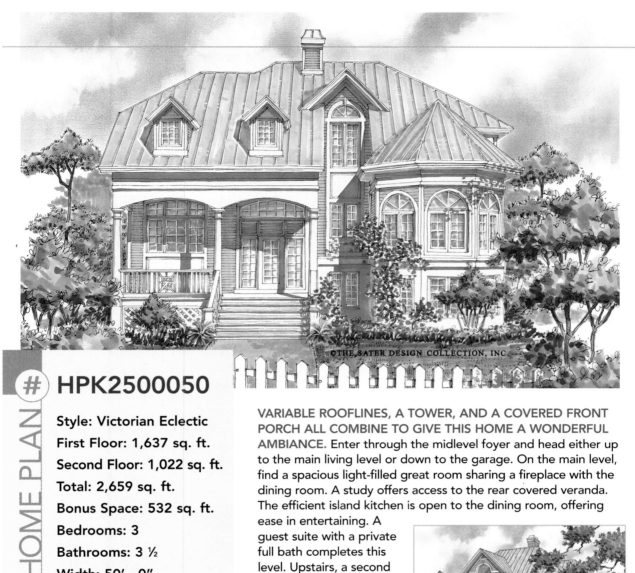

⌗ HPK2500050

Style: Victorian Eclectic

First Floor: 1,637 sq. ft.

Second Floor: 1,022 sq. ft.

Total: 2,659 sq. ft.

Bonus Space: 532 sq. ft.

Bedrooms: 3

Bathrooms: 3 ½

Width: 50' - 0"

Depth: 53' - 0"

Foundation: Pier (same as Piling)

eplans.com

VARIABLE ROOFLINES, A TOWER, AND A COVERED FRONT PORCH ALL COMBINE TO GIVE THIS HOME A WONDERFUL AMBIANCE. Enter through the midlevel foyer and head either up to the main living level or down to the garage. On the main level, find a spacious light-filled great room sharing a fireplace with the dining room. A study offers access to the rear covered veranda. The efficient island kitchen is open to the dining room, offering ease in entertaining. A guest suite with a private full bath completes this level. Upstairs, a second guest suite with its own bath and a deluxe master suite with a covered balcony, sundeck, walk-in closet, and lavish bath are sure to please.

REAR EXTERIOR

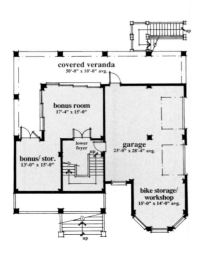

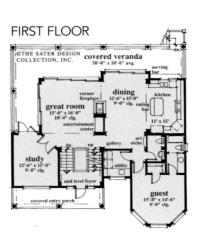

FIRST FLOOR

SECOND FLOOR

LOWER LEVEL

MAIN LEVEL

SECOND LEVEL

HOME PLAN # HPK2500052

Style: Mediterranean

Main Level: 2,491 sq. ft.

Second Level: 1,290 sq. ft.

Lower Level: 358 sq. ft.

Total: 4,139 sq. ft.

Bedrooms: 5

Bathrooms: 4 ½

Width: 62' - 0"

Depth: 67' - 0"

Foundation: Island Basement

eplans.com

ELEMENTS FROM THE VICTORIAN ERA CREATE THIS WONDERFUL FACADE, all decked out with a square tower loft, two-story turret, and charming stickwork. A midlevel landing eases the transition from ground level to the entry and foyer. Grand amenities dress the interior with splendor as cottage charm becomes urbane comfort in the living space. A vaulted ceiling, two-sided fireplace, built-in cabinetry, and a wall of glass bring high vogue to an area that's just right for bare feet. Three sets of sliding glass doors open the interior to the wraparound veranda, where the outdoor kitchen provides a pass-through to the gourmet kitchen. On the main level, Bedroom 4 boasts a private veranda, built-in desk, and a fireplace shared with the great room. A very private secondary suite resides on the upper level with two wardrobes and a private deck. Nearby, a mitered window high-lights the master bedroom, which has its own deck.

© The Sater Design Collection, Inc.

FLORIDA LIVING TAKES OFF IN THIS INVENTIVE DESIGN. A grand room gains attention as a superb entertaining area. A see-through fireplace here connects this room to the dining room. In the study, quiet time is assured—or slip outdoors onto the veranda for some fresh air. A full bath connects the study to the front right bedroom. Another bedroom sits on the opposite side of the house and enjoys its own bath. The kitchen features a large work island and a connecting breakfast nook. Upstairs, the master bedroom suite contains His and Hers baths, a see-through fireplace, and access to an upper deck. A guest bedroom suite is located on the other side of the upper floor.

HOME PLAN #

HPK2500053

Style: New American
First Floor: 2,725 sq. ft.
Second Floor: 1,418 sq. ft.
Total: 4,143 sq. ft.
Bedrooms: 4
Bathrooms: 5 ½
Width: 61' - 4"
Depth: 62' - 0"
Foundation: Pier (same as Piling)

eplans.com

COASTAL DESIGNS

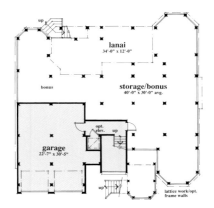

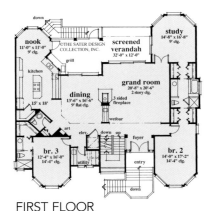

FIRST FLOOR

SECOND FLOOR

FIRST FLOOR

SECOND FLOOR

THE RAISED FRONT PORCH, REACHED BY TWIN STAIRCASES AND ENHANCED BY GRACEFUL PILLARS, dominates the exterior of this wonderful Southern Colonial home. A front dining room is perfect for formal dinner parties, and the spacious great room, with a fireplace and built-in bookshelves, will host many memorable get-togethers. The kitchen has ample counter space and easily serves the sunlit breakfast alcove. Soothing comfort is guaranteed in the master suite, with a walk-in closet, whirlpool tub, and shower with a seat. Upstairs, two bedrooms share a bath. Space is available for a recreation room, a fourth bedroom, and storage in the basement.

HPK2500054

HOME PLAN

Style: Farmhouse
First Floor: 1,542 sq. ft.
Second Floor: 755 sq. ft.
Total: 2,297 sq. ft.
Bedrooms: 3
Bathrooms: 2 ½
Width: 48' - 4"
Depth: 39' - 6"
Foundation: Unfinished Walkout Basement

eplans.com

© William E. Poole Designs, Inc.

© William E. Poole Designs, Inc.

HOME PLAN

HPK2500055

Style: Georgian

First Floor: 1,376 sq. ft.

Second Floor: 695 sq. ft.

Total: 2,071 sq. ft.

Bedrooms: 3

Bathrooms: 2 ½

Width: 47' - 0"

Depth: 49' - 8"

Foundation: Finished Walkout Basement

eplans.com

THE UNIQUE CHARM OF THIS FARMHOUSE BEGINS WITH A FLIGHT OF STEPS AND A WELCOMING, covered front porch. Just inside, the foyer leads to the formal dining room on the left—with easy access to the kitchen—and straight ahead to the great room. Here, a warming fireplace and built-in entertainment center are balanced by access to the rear screened porch. The first-floor master suite provides plenty of privacy; upstairs, two family bedrooms share a full bath. The lower level offers space for a fourth bedroom, a recreation room, and a garage.

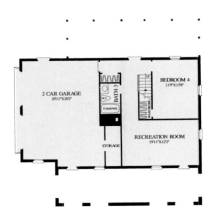

FIRST FLOOR

SECOND FLOOR

SECOND FLOOR

FIRST FLOOR

NOTHING IS MORE SATISFYING AND FULFILLING THAN HOME—and home at Mount Pleasant is the stuff from which dreams are made. Take advantage of the views from the second-story porch of this grand home. Inside, this home considers everyone's needs with private baths in all the bedrooms. The master bedroom boasts His and Her closets, a whirlpool tub, a separate shower, and double sinks. Near the family room (with fireplace), the U-shaped kitchen features a 12-inch bar top and an island. Guests have the option of utilizing the stairs or elevator between floors. The basement is designed with a fifth bedroom, and recreational, mechanical, and storage rooms. A two-car garage protects vehicles from the weather.

HPK2500056

HOME PLAN

Style: Plantation
First Floor: 2,945 sq. ft.
Second Floor: 1,353 sq. ft.
Total: 4,298 sq. ft.
Bedrooms: 4
Bathrooms: 4 ½
Width: 61' - 4"
Depth: 72' - 2"
Foundation: Finished Walkout Basement

eplans.com

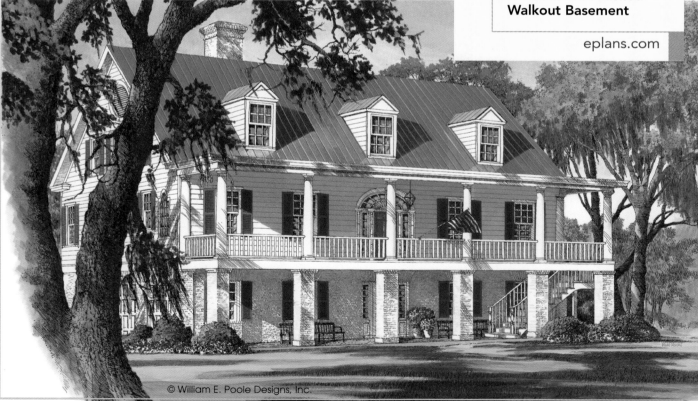

© William E. Poole Designs, Inc.

© William E. Poole Designs, Inc.

HPK2500057

HOME PLAN

Style: Farmhouse

First Floor: 1,554 sq. ft.

Second Floor: 755 sq. ft.

Total: 2,309 sq. ft.

Bonus Space: 869 sq. ft.

Bedrooms: 3

Bathrooms: 2 ½

Width: 57' - 4"

Depth: 39' - 6"

Foundation: Finished Walkout Basement

eplans.com

A WRAPAROUND PORCH WELCOMES YOU TO SIT AWHILE AND ENJOY THE COOL SUMMER BREEZES and adds a warm touch to this three-bedroom home. Inside, the foyer introduces the formal dining room to the left and the spacious great room just ahead. A fireplace, built-in entertainment center, and rear-deck access further enhance the room. The efficient kitchen easily serves the formal dining room as well as the sunny breakfast area. The first-floor master suite is filled with amenities such as a large walk-in closet, a lavish bath, and plenty of privacy. Upstairs, two family bedrooms share a bath. The drive-under garage opens to the recreation room and a possible fourth bedroom.

SECOND FLOOR

FIRST FLOOR

© William E. Poole Designs

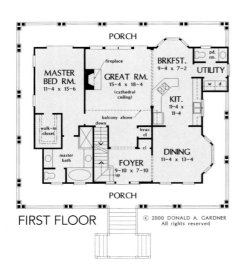

FIRST FLOOR

PORCH

MASTER BED RM.
11-4 x 15-6

fireplace

GREAT RM.
15-4 x 18-4
(cathedral ceiling)

BRKFST.
9-4 x 7-2

UTILITY

pd. rm.

w | d

KIT.
11-4 x 11-4

balcony above

walk-in closet

master bath

down

hvac cl

cl

DINING
11-4 x 13-4

FOYER
9-10 x 7-10 up

PORCH

SECOND FLOOR

great room below

attic storage

attic storage

BED RM.
11-4 x 11-2

down

railing

BED RM.
11-4 x 11-2

cl

cl

bath

cl

cl

attic sto.

foyer below

attic storage

HOME PLAN

HPK2500058

Style: Country

First Floor: 1,368 sq. ft.

Second Floor: 481 sq. ft.

Total: 1,849 sq. ft.

Bedrooms: 3

Bathrooms: 2 ½

Width: 49' - 4"

Depth: 44' - 10"

eplans.com

DO YOU LOVE TO ENTERTAIN OR SIMPLY RELAX OUTDOORS?
This welcoming home features a wide porch that is raised on piers and wraps around the entire house. Grill a burger, read a book, sway on a porch swing in the summer breeze - the options are endless with an abundance of outdoor living space! A stairwell and dining room flank the entry foyer, which leads directly into a two-story great room. Family time is convenient because the eat-in kitchen with an adjacent breakfast nook opens directly to the great room. The master suite occupies the left side of this plan and enjoys private access to the rear porch. Upstairs two bedrooms with a central bath flank the balcony overlooking the great room below.

REAR EXTERIOR

MULTIPLE GABLES, A CENTER DORMER WITH ARCHED CLERESTORY WINDOW, AND A STRIKING FRONT STAIRCASE create visual excitement for this three-bedroom coastal home. Vaulted ceilings in the foyer and great room highlight a dramatic second-floor balcony that connects the two upstairs bedrooms, each with its own bath and private porch. The great room is generously proportioned with built-ins on either side of the fireplace. Private back porches enhance the dining room and the master suite, which boasts His and Her walk-in closets and a magnificent bath with dual vanities, a garden tub, and separate shower.

HOME PLAN

HPK2500059

Style: Country
First Floor: 1,620 sq. ft.
Second Floor: 770 sq. ft.
Total: 2,390 sq. ft.
Bedrooms: 3
Bathrooms: 3 ½
Width: 49' - 0"
Depth: 58' - 8"

eplans.com

FIRST FLOOR

SECOND FLOOR

COASTAL DESIGNS

FIRST FLOOR

BALCONY
13-10 x 5-0

MASTER BED RM.
13-4 x 16-0

walk-in closet

walk-in closet

linen

UTIL.
6-0 x 6-0

master bath

DINING
11-0 x 13-4

KIT.
11-0 x 12-8

GREAT RM.
20-0 x 19-8
(cathedral ceiling)

fireplace

FOYER
6-6 x 4-0

pd. rm.

STUDY
12-0 x 12-0

cl

down

up

PORCH

PORCH

down

down

© 1998 Donald A Gardner, Inc.

SECOND FLOOR

BALCONY
13-10 x 5-0

BED RM.
13-4 x 12-4

cl

lin.

bath

BED RM.
11-0 x 13-4

cl

railing

LOFT
11-2 x 13-8

great room below

arched opening

down

CEDAR SHAKES AND STRIKING GABLES WITH DECORATIVE SCALLOPED INSETS adorn the exterior of this lovely coastal home. The generous great room is expanded by a rear wall of windows, with additional light from transom windows above the front door and a rear clerestory dormer. The kitchen features a pass-through to the great room. The dining room, great room, and study all access an inviting back porch. The master bedroom is a treat with a private balcony, His and Hers walk-in closets, and an impeccable bath. Upstairs, a room-sized loft with an arched opening overlooks the great room below. Two more bedrooms, one with its own private balcony, share a hall bath.

 # HPK2500002

HOME PLAN

Style: Shingle
First Floor: 1,650 sq. ft.
Second Floor: 712 sq. ft.
Total: 2,362 sq. ft.
Bedrooms: 3
Bathrooms: 2 ½
Width: 58' - 10"
Depth: 47' - 4"

eplans.com

©1998 Donald A. Gardner, Inc.

L.B. NATHAN.

© 1999 Donald A. Gardner, Inc.

A NARROW WIDTH AND FRONT AND REAR PORCHES
MAKE THIS HOME PERFECT FOR WATERFRONT LOTS, and
its squared-off design makes it easy to afford. The great room,
kitchen, and breakfast area are all open for a casual and spacious feeling. Numerous windows enhance the area's volume.
Flexible rooms located at the front of the home include a formal
living or dining room and a study or bedroom with optional
entry to the powder room. Upstairs, every bedroom (plus the
master bath) enjoys porch access. The master suite features a
tray ceiling, dual closets, and a sizable bath with linen cabinets.

HOME PLAN

HPK2500060

Style: Neoclassical

First Floor: 1,170 sq. ft.

Second Floor: 1,058 sq. ft.

Total: 2,228 sq. ft.

Bedrooms: 4

Bathrooms: 2 ½

Width: 30' - 0"

Depth: 51' - 0"

eplans.com

FIRST
FLOOR

SECOND FLOOR

COASTAL DESIGNS

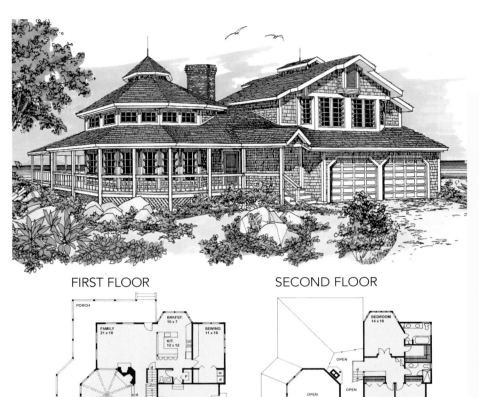

FIRST FLOOR

SECOND FLOOR

HOME PLAN
HPK2500061

Style: Shingle

First Floor: 1,370 sq. ft.

Second Floor: 860 sq. ft.

Total: 2,230 sq. ft.

Bedrooms: 3

Bathrooms: 2 ½

Width: 60' - 0"

Depth: 52' - 0"

Foundation: Unfinished Basement

FIRST FLOOR

SECOND FLOOR

HOME PLAN
HPK2500062

Style: Tidewater

First Floor: 1,073 sq. ft.

Second Floor: 470 sq. ft.

Total: 1,543 sq. ft.

Bedrooms: 4

Bathrooms: 2

Width: 30' - 0"

Depth: 71' - 6"

Foundation: Pier (same as Piling)

DESIGNED FOR THE RELAXING COASTAL LIFESTYLE, this casual beach house aims to please with three well-planned levels. The lower level has French doors to the front for privacy and opens to reveal a carport, covered porch, tons of storage (great for sandy surfboards), and an enclosed entry/utility area. The main level features a two-story living room with a wonderful porch that stretches the length of the house. The kitchen is efficient and easily serves the dining area. The master bedroom has an ample walk-in closet and is conveniently adjacent to a full bath. Upstairs, an additional bedroom has a semiprivate bath and accesses the observation room for amazing ocean views.

HOME PLAN

HPK2500063

Style: Craftsman

First Floor: 832 sq. ft.

Second Floor: 278 sq. ft.

Total: 1,110 sq. ft.

Bedrooms: 2

Bathrooms: 2

Width: 32' - 0"

Depth: 34' - 0"

Foundation: Pier (same as Piling)

eplans.com

COASTAL DESIGNS

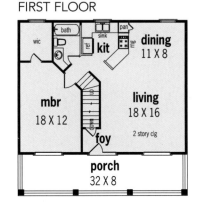

covered porch

entry & utility
18 X 11

sto
18 X 8

carport
34 X 10

WASH DRY

equipment area

FIRST FLOOR

bath

wic

ref

kit

sink

pan

mg

dining
11 X 8

mbr
18 X 12

up

dn

living
18 X 16

foy

2 story clg

porch
32 X 8

SECOND FLOOR

attic space

bath

wic

br 2
12 X 12

dn

open to living below

attic space

observation rm.

attic space

FIRST FLOOR

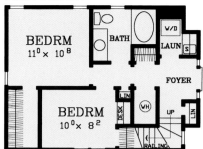

SECOND FLOOR

HOME PLAN

HPK2500064

Style: Contemporary

First Floor: 507 sq. ft.

Second Floor: 438 sq. ft.

Total: 945 sq. ft.

Bedrooms: 2

Bathrooms: 1 ½

Width: 20' - 0"

Depth: 26' - 0"

Foundation: Crawlspace

eplans.com

COMBINE A SHINGLED EXTERIOR AND AN UPSTAIRS DECK AND YOU CAN RECALL THE JOY OF SEASIDE VACATIONS. Let breezes ruffle your hair and ocean spray settle on your skin in this comfortable two-story home. Unique window treatments provide views from every room. The lifestyle is casual, including meals prepared in a kitchen separated from the living room by a snack-bar counter. A powder room and a wet bar complete the upstairs. The first floor houses two bedrooms, a full bath, and a laundry room. A walk-in closet enhances one of the bedrooms that could serve as the master suite. Built-ins make the most of compact space.

HOME PLAN
HPK2500374

Style: Country
First Floor: 1,126 sq. ft.
Second Floor: 616 sq. ft.
Total: 1,742 sq. ft.
Bedrooms: 3
Bathrooms: 2
Width: 64' - 0"
Depth: 34' - 0"
Foundation: Crawlspace, Slab, Unfinished Basement

FIRST FLOOR

SECOND FLOOR

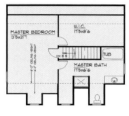

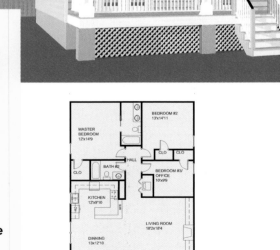

HOME PLAN
HPK2500375

Style: Country
Square Footage: 1,408
Bedrooms: 3
Bathrooms: 2
Width: 32' - 0"
Depth: 50' - 0"
Foundation: Crawlspace

COASTAL DESIGNS

FIRST FLOOR

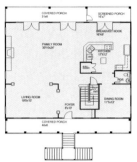

SECOND FLOOR

HOME PLAN
HPK2500066

Style: Tidewater

First Floor: 1,824 sq. ft.

Second Floor: 1,535 sq. ft.

Total: 3,359 sq. ft.

Bedrooms: 3

Bathrooms: 2 ½

Width: 48' - 0"

Depth: 50' - 0"

Foundation: Island Basement

HOME PLAN
HPK2500067

Style: Tidewater

First Floor: 1,193 sq. ft.

Second Floor: 920 sq. ft.

Total: 2,113 sq. ft.

Bedrooms: 3

Bathrooms: 2 ½

Width: 40' - 0"

Depth: 44' - 0"

Foundation: Island Basement

FIRST FLOOR

SECOND FLOOR

HOME PLAN
HPK2500376

Style: Cottage

First Floor: 1,033 sq. ft.

Second Floor: 1,073 sq. ft.

Total: 2,106 sq. ft.

Bedrooms: 3

Bathrooms: 2 ½

Width: 56' - 6"

Depth: 67' - 7"

Foundation: Crawlspace

FIRST
FLOOR

SECOND
FLOOR

HOME PLAN
HPK2500065

Style: Tidewater

Main Level: 1,031 sq. ft.

Second Level: 1,008 sq. ft.

Lower Level: 541 sq. ft.

Total: 2,580 sq. ft.

Bedrooms: 2

Bathrooms: 3 ½

Width: 26' - 0"

Depth: 58' - 0"

Foundation: Island Basement

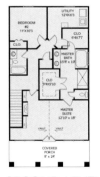

SECOND LEVEL

MAIN LEVEL

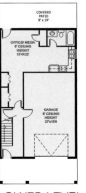

LOWER LEVEL

COASTAL DESIGNS

HOME PLAN
HPK2500068

Style: Tidewater
First Floor: 2,204 sq. ft.
Second Floor: 773 sq. ft.
Total: 2,977 sq. ft.
Bedrooms: 3
Bathrooms: 2 ½
Width: 54' - 0"
Depth: 64' - 0"
Foundation: Island Basement

FIRST FLOOR

SECOND FLOOR

HOME PLAN
HPK2500377

Style: Tidewater
First Floor: 2,204 sq. ft.
Second Floor: 773 sq. ft.
Total: 2,977 sq. ft.
Bedrooms: 3
Bathrooms: 2 ½ + ½
Width: 54' - 0"
Depth: 64' - 0"
Foundation: Island Basement

FIRST FLOOR

SECOND FLOOR

HOME PLAN

HPK2500069

Style: Tidewater

First Floor: 1,681 sq. ft.

Second Floor: 1,810 sq. ft.

Third Floor: 208 sq. ft.

Total: 3,699 sq. ft.

Bedrooms: 5

Bathrooms: 5 ½

Width: 41' - 0"

Depth: 55' - 0"

Foundation: Pier
(same as Piling)

BEDROOM #1
13' x 14'

BEDROOM #2
14'8 x 14'

MEDIA ROOM
18' x 13'

BALCONY

DECK

ELEV

BEDROOM #3
14'4 x 12'3

BEDROOM #4
14'4 x 12'3

BALCONY

FIRST FLOOR

STORAGE

MASTER SUITE
15'9 x 14'

KITCHEN
11' x 17'

BREAKFAST
19' x 12'

ELEV

LIVING ROOM
29' x 20'

BALCONY

SECOND FLOOR

TOWER
14' x 12'

3RD FLOOR DECK
8' X 21'

THIRD FLOOR

HOME PLAN

HPK2500378

Style: Colonial Revival

First Floor: 1,942 sq. ft.

Second Floor: 1,942 sq. ft.

Total: 3,884 sq. ft.

Bedrooms: 5

Bathrooms: 3 ½

Width: 48' - 0"

Depth: 56' - 0"

Foundation: Island
Basement

FIRST FLOOR

8' COVERED PORCH

MASTER
BEDROOM
15'6 x17'2

BREAKFAST
15'6 x13'2

GREAT ROOM
15'8 x24'10

KITCHEN
15'6 x13'10

W.I.C.

W.I.C.

ELEV/

MASTER BATH
15'6 x12'2

UP

PDR

DINING
15'6 x11'8

FOYER

8' COVERED PORCH

SECOND FLOOR

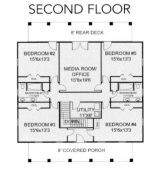

8' REAR DECK

BEDROOM #2
15'6 x13'3

BEDROOM #5
15'6 x13'3

MEDIA ROOM/
OFFICE
15'8 x19'6

BATHROOM

BATHROOM

UTILITY
11'X6'

BEDROOM #3
15'6 x13'3

DOWN

BEDROOM #4
15'6 x13'3

8' COVERED PORCH

COASTAL DESIGNS

Mountain Majesty

Do you prefer the rush of speeding down a mountain slope over the rush of a wave? Or perhaps canoeing across a lake is more your speed? Consider a home with warm interiors, rustic materials, open spaces, and storage for the skis, sleds, and more. A mountain home blends in with its woodsy surroundings and gently curves its way into hillsides. Ideal by a lake or on a peak, Mountain Homes offers designs for every occasion and hilltop location.

A mountain home is unobtrusive and considerate of the area and climate. If your site has a slope, build in a walkout basement rather than unnaturally leveling the ground. This foundation choice is ideal for lakesides, providing a landing zone for muddy feet and wet sporting equipment before entering the main level. If the home is in a region that expects frequent heavy snowfall, a high-pitched roof, like that of an A-frame house, runs the snow off to the ground and minimizes packed weight on the home. Natural materials, often used in Craftsman and cottage-style designs, nestle the home into its location: stone-clad foundations, wood accents, and neutral colors contribute to the welcoming look of a mountain home.

THE RUSTIC STICK TABLE and overhead candle fixture are appropriate furnishings for this wooded setting.

STONE ACCENTS, EARTH TONES, and a walkout basement help this home blend in with its mountain surroundings.

Location is more than the coordinates of a site. If you're on a hillside, you'll want the side of the home with the most windows to face views of the valley and neighboring mountain range for maximum enjoyment. For maximum efficiency, situate the most windows to absorb the most sun for cold climates and away from the sun in warmer areas. This will keep heating and cooling bills low, too.

The look of a mountain home doesn't stop with the exterior. Inside, open layouts invite large gatherings of friends and family. A cathedral ceiling in the great room allows for tall window walls with wider views of the mountains. Choose a rustic stone fireplace to ground the lofty space in warmth. Décor can also derive from natural materials, such as wood and stone, and soft fabrics and furniture will provide comfort on blustery nights by the fire.

The plans in this section could be built anywhere in the country, because their appeal is so universal. But the clean rooflines, rustic building materials, and all the space an active family needs make them truly at home in the mountains.

A FULL-HEIGHT STONE FIREPLACE will warm the interior while windows bring the outdoors in.

MAIN LEVEL

SECOND LEVEL

LOWER LEVEL

HPK2500070

Style: Craftsman

Main Level: 1,268 sq. ft.

Second Level: 931 sq. ft.

Lower Level: 949 sq. ft.

Total: 3,148 sq. ft.

Bedrooms: 4

Bathrooms: 3 ½

Width: 53' - 6"

Depth: 73' - 0"

Foundation: Finished Walkout Basement

eplans.com

HOME PLAN

A COVERED FRONT PORCH PROVIDES A WELCOMING ENTRY FOR THIS CRAFTSMAN DESIGN, which features a stunning, amenity-filled interior. Vaulted ceilings adorn the great room, office, and even the garage; the dining room includes a built-in hutch, and the kitchen boasts a walk-in pantry. Upstairs, the master suite offers a walk-in closet with built-in shelves, along with a private bath that contains a spa tub. Two additional bedrooms also have walk-in closets. A fourth bedroom, a recreation room with a fireplace and wet bar, and a wine cellar reside on the lower level.

REAR EXTERIOR

RIGHT SIDE EXTERIOR

HPK2500071

HOME PLAN #

Style: Cottage
Main Level: 2,464 sq. ft.
Lower Level: 1,887 sq. ft.
Total: 4,351 sq. ft.
Bedrooms: 4
Bathrooms: 3 ½
Width: 59' - 0"
Depth: 81' - 0"
Foundation: Slab, Finished Walkout Basement

eplans.com

HERE IS A GORGEOUS HILLSIDE DESIGN THAT OFFERS AN UNASSUMING FRONT PERSPECTIVE, but behold the side view with its elegant deck flanked by the great room and master bedroom, each with an enormous arch-top window. Inside, the dining room, island kitchen, nook, and great room enjoy an open plan with decorative columns and tray ceilings defining the dining and great rooms. The master suite finds privacy to the right with a luxurious bath. The staircase near the kitchen leads to the lower level where three additional bedrooms are found. The game room offers a built-in media center with a wet bar and wine cellar close at hand.

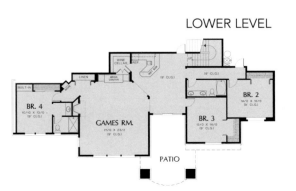

MAIN LEVEL

LOWER LEVEL

MOUNTAIN GETAWAYS

FIRST FLOOR

DINING
10/10 X 13/6 +/-
(9' CLG)

KIT.
13/10 X 13/6

NOOK
10/0 X 10/0
(9' CLG)

UP DN

REF.

PAN

WET BAR

DN

VAULTED
FAMILY
13/4 X 14/8

DEN
13/6 X 12/2
(9' CLG)

VAULTED
LIVING RM
13/0 X 17/10

DECK

SECOND FLOOR

BR. 2
10/0 X 12/6

BR. 3
10/8 X 12/6

LINEN

LINEN

DN

WINDOW SEAT

VAULTED
MASTER
13/8 X 14/8

OPEN TO
LIVING RM
BELOW

STORAGE

CRAWLSPACE

UP

GARAGE

THE CONTEMPORARY LOOK OF THIS MODERN COUNTRY DESIGN is both impressive and unique. Enormous windows brighten and enliven every interior space. The vaulted family room features a fireplace, and a two-sided fireplace warms the formal living and dining rooms. The gourmet island kitchen is open to a nook. Double doors open to a den that accesses a front deck. Upstairs, the master bedroom features a private bath with linen storage and a walk-in closet. Two family bedrooms share a Jack-and-Jill bath. The two-car garage features a storage area on the lower level.

 # HPK2500072

HOME PLAN

Style: New American
First Floor: 1,501 sq. ft.
Second Floor: 921 sq. ft.
Total: 2,422 sq. ft.
Bedrooms: 3
Bathrooms: 2 ½
Width: 52' - 0"
Depth: 36' - 0"
Foundation: Crawlspace

eplans.com

THIS VACATION HOME IS CERTAIN TO BE A FAMILY FAVORITE. The two-story great room boasts a built-in media center, access to a front deck, and a two-sided fireplace shared by the adjacent den. The spacious island kitchen is ideal for entertaining. The second floor houses the master suite, two additional family bedrooms, and a full bath. A workshop and extra storage space in the garage are added bonuses.

HOME PLAN

HPK2500073

Style: Craftsman

First Floor: 1,302 sq. ft.

Second Floor: 960 sq. ft.

Total: 2,262 sq. ft.

Bedrooms: 3

Bathrooms: 2 ½

Width: 40' - 0"

Depth: 40' - 0"

Foundation: Slab

eplans.com

FIRST FLOOR

SECOND FLOOR

MOUNTAIN GETAWAYS

FIRST FLOOR

SECOND FLOOR

HOME PLAN

HPK2500074

Style: New American

First Floor: 1,022 sq. ft.

Second Floor: 813 sq. ft.

Total: 1,835 sq. ft.

Bedrooms: 3

Bathrooms: 2 ½

Width: 36' - 0"

Depth: 33' - 0"

Foundation: Slab

eplans.com

THIS HOME IS QUITE APPEALING, WITH ITS STEEPLY SLOPING ROOFLINES AND LARGE SUNBURST AND MULTIPANE WINDOWS. The plan not only accommodates a narrow lot, but it also fits a sloping site. The angled corner entry gives way to a two-story living room with a tiled hearth. The dining room shares an interesting angled space with this area and offers easy service from the efficient kitchen. Double doors in the family room lead to a refreshing balcony. A powder room and laundry room complete the main level. Upstairs, a vaulted master bedroom has a private bath; two other bedrooms share a bath.

HOME PLAN

HPK2500075

Style: Craftsman

First Floor: 1,106 sq. ft.

Second Floor: 872 sq. ft.

Total: 1,978 sq. ft.

Bedrooms: 3

Bathrooms: 2 ½

Width: 38' - 0"

Depth: 35' - 0"

Foundation: Slab, Unfinished Basement

eplans.com

ALTHOUGH THIS HOME EVOKES THE CHARACTER OF NORTHWEST ARCHITECTURE, it will be a winner in any neighborhood. From the foyer, the two-story living room is just a couple of steps up and features a through-fireplace. The U-shaped kitchen has a cooktop work island, an adjacent nook, and easy access to the formal dining room. A spacious family room shares the fireplace with the living room, is enhanced by built-ins, and offers a quiet deck for stargazing. The upstairs consists of two family bedrooms sharing a full bath and a vaulted master suite complete with a walk-in closet and sumptuous bath. A two-car, drive-under garage has plenty of room for storage.

MOUNTAIN GETAWAYS

FIRST FLOOR

SECOND FLOOR

LOWER LEVEL

MAIN LEVEL

SECOND LEVEL

DRAMATIC BALCONIES AND SPECTACULAR WINDOW TREATMENTS enhance this stunning luxury home. Inside, a through-fireplace warms the formal living room and a restful den. Both living spaces open to a balcony that invites quiet reflection on starry nights. The banquet-sized dining room is easily served from the adjacent kitchen. Here, space is shared with an eating nook that provides access to the rear grounds and a family room with a corner fireplace—perfect for casual gatherings. The upper level contains two family bedrooms and a luxurious master suite that enjoys its own private balcony. The basement accommodates a shop and a bonus room for future development.

HPK2500076

HOME PLAN

Style: Mediterranean
Main Level: 1,989 sq. ft.
Second Level: 1,349 sq. ft.
Lower Level: 105 sq. ft.
Total: 3,443 sq. ft.
Bonus Space: 487 sq. ft.
Bedrooms: 3
Bathrooms: 2 ½
Width: 63' - 0"
Depth: 48' - 0"
Foundation: Finished Walkout Basement

eplans.com

Photos by: Bob Greenspan. This home, as shown in photographs, may differ from the actual blueprints. For more detailed information, please check the floor plans carefully.

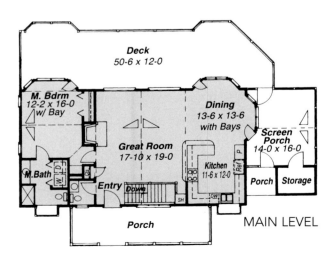

REAR EXTERIOR

A BEAUTIFUL HALF-CIRCLE WINDOW TOPS A COVERED FRONT PORCH on this fine three-bedroom home. Inside, the main-level amenities start with the large, open great room and a warming fireplace. A uniquely shaped dining room is adjacent to the efficient kitchen, which offers a small bay window over the sink. The deluxe master suite is complete with a cathedral ceiling, sitting bay and private bath with laundry facilities. On the lower level, a two-car garage shelters the family fleet, while two bedrooms—or make one a study/home office—share a full hall bath.

HOME PLAN

HPK2500077

Style: Country
Main Level: 1,128 sq. ft.
Lower Level: 604 sq. ft.
Total: 1,732 sq. ft.
Bedrooms: 3
Bathrooms: 2 ½
Width: 59' - 0"
Depth: 28' - 0"
Foundation: Finished Walkout Basement

eplans.com

MOUNTAIN GETAWAYS

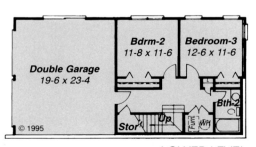

Deck
50-6 x 12-0

M. Bdrm
12-2 x 16-0
w/ Bay

M.Bath

Dining
13-6 x 13-6
with Bays

Great Room
17-10 x 19-0

Screen Porch
14-0 x 16-0

Kitchen
11-6 x 12-0

Entry

Porch

Storage

Porch

MAIN LEVEL

Double Garage
19-6 x 23-4

Bdrm-2
11-8 x 11-6

Bedroom-3
12-6 x 11-6

Bth-2

Stor

© 1995

LOWER LEVEL

MAIN LEVEL

LOWER LEVEL

LOOKING A BIT LIKE A MOUNTAIN RESORT, this fine rustic-style home is sure to be the envy of your neighborhood. Upon entering through the elegant front door, find an open staircase to the right and a spacious great room directly ahead. Here, a fireplace and a wall of windows give a cozy welcome. A lavish master suite begins with a sitting room, complete with a fireplace, and continues to a private porch, large walk-in closet, and sumptuous bedroom. The gourmet kitchen adjoins a sunny dining room that offers access to a screened porch.

HPK2500078

HOME PLAN

Style: Craftsman
Main Level: 3,040 sq. ft.
Lower Level: 1,736 sq. ft.
Total: 4,776 sq. ft.
Bedrooms: 5
Bathrooms: 4 ½ + ½
Width: 106' - 5"
Depth: 104' - 2"

eplans.com

REAR EXTERIOR

HOME PLAN

HPK2500079

Style: Craftsman

Main Level: 2,151 sq. ft.

Lower Level: 1,150 sq. ft.

Total: 3,301 sq. ft.

Bedrooms: 4

Bathrooms: 3

Width: 83' - 0"

Depth: 74' - 4"

eplans.com

TWIN DORMERS, SHINGLED SIDING, AND A STONE CHIMNEY PRODUCE A RUSTIC, Craftsman look for this four-bedroom mountain retreat. Exposed beams span the vaulted ceiling, controlling the height of the great room and kitchen. Nearby, two decks, a screened porch, and a spacious patio provide plenty of room for outdoor entertaining and seasonal enjoyment. High-end amenities abound, such as the master suiteís deep walk-ins and garden-side tub. A second suite on the main floor is reserved for guests.

MAIN LEVEL

LOWER LEVEL

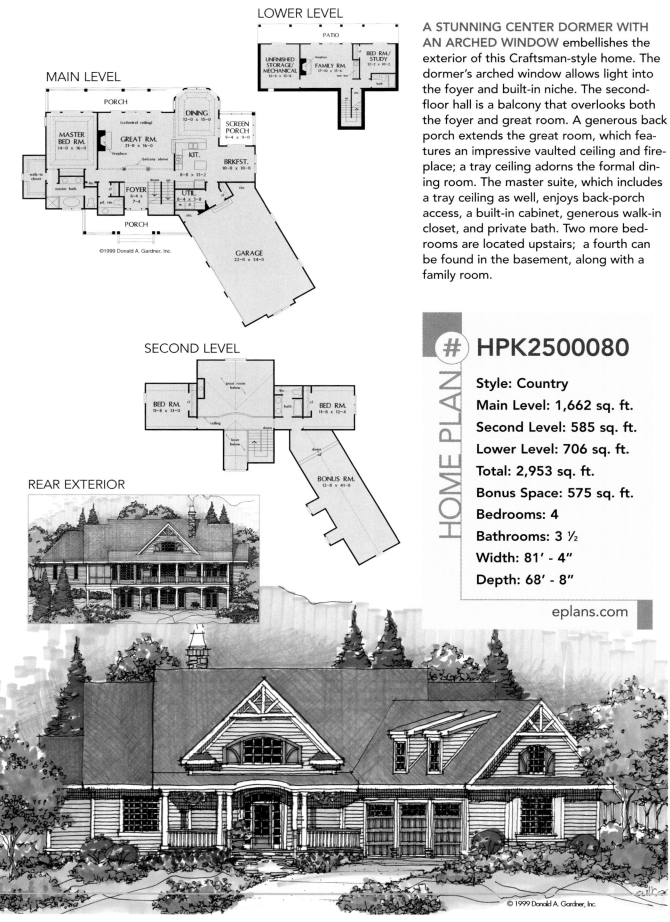

LOWER LEVEL

PATIO

UNFINISHED STORAGE/ MECHANICAL
13-4 x 15-8

FAMILY RM.
17-10 x 15-6

fireplace

wet bar

BED RM./ STUDY
12-2 x 10-2

bath

sto.

MAIN LEVEL

PORCH

(cathedral ceiling)

DINING
12-0 x 15-0

SCREEN PORCH
9-4 x 9-0

MASTER BED RM.
14-0 x 16-0

GREAT RM.
21-0 x 16-0

fireplace   balcony above

KIT.
8-8 x 13-2

BRKFST.
10-0 x 10-0

walk-in closet

master bath

lin.

FOYER
6-4 x 7-4

pd. rm.

down up

UTIL.
8-4 x 5-8

w   d

cl

sto.

cl   sto.

PORCH

©1999 Donald A. Gardner, Inc.

GARAGE
22-0 x 34-0

SECOND LEVEL

BED RM.
11-8 x 13-0

great room below

bath

lin.

cl

BED RM.
11-8 x 12-4

d

railing

foyer below

down

down

BONUS RM.
12-8 x 41-0

REAR EXTERIOR

A STUNNING CENTER DORMER WITH AN ARCHED WINDOW embellishes the exterior of this Craftsman-style home. The dormer's arched window allows light into the foyer and built-in niche. The second-floor hall is a balcony that overlooks both the foyer and great room. A generous back porch extends the great room, which features an impressive vaulted ceiling and fireplace; a tray ceiling adorns the formal dining room. The master suite, which includes a tray ceiling as well, enjoys back-porch access, a built-in cabinet, generous walk-in closet, and private bath. Two more bedrooms are located upstairs; a fourth can be found in the basement, along with a family room.

HPK2500080

HOME PLAN

Style: Country

Main Level: 1,662 sq. ft.

Second Level: 585 sq. ft.

Lower Level: 706 sq. ft.

Total: 2,953 sq. ft.

Bonus Space: 575 sq. ft.

Bedrooms: 4

Bathrooms: 3 ½

Width: 81' - 4"

Depth: 68' - 8"

eplans.com

© 1999 Donald A. Gardner, Inc.

©1999 Donald A. Gardner, Inc.

HPK2500081

Style: Bungalow

Main Level: 1,734 sq. ft.

Second Level: 546 sq. ft.

Lower Level: 788 sq. ft.

Total: 3,068 sq. ft.

Bonus Space: 381 sq. ft.

Bedrooms: 4

Bathrooms: 3 ½

Width: 60' - 8"

Depth: 68' - 0"

eplans.com

MULTIPLE GABLES, CEDAR SHAKES, STUCCO, AND STONE PROVIDE PLENTY OF ENCHANTMENT for the exterior of this hillside home. Craftsman character abounds inside as well as out, evidenced by the home's functional floor plan. Built-ins flank the great room's fireplace for convenience, and a rear deck extends living space outdoors. The exceptionally well-designed kitchen features an island cooktop and an adjacent breakfast bay. The master suite, also with a bay window, enjoys two walk-in closets and a delightful bath with dual vanities. Two upstairs bedrooms are divided by an impressive balcony that overlooks the foyer and great room.

REAR EXTERIOR

MAIN LEVEL

SECOND LEVEL

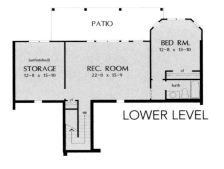

LOWER LEVEL

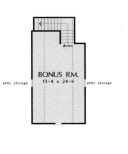

© 1999 Donald A. Gardner, Inc.

HOME PLAN
HPK2500082

Style: French Country
Main Level: 1,901 sq. ft.
Lower Level: 1,075 sq. ft.
Total: 2,976 sq. ft.
Bedrooms: 4
Bathrooms: 3
Width: 64' - 0"
Depth: 62' - 4"

LOWER LEVEL

MAIN LEVEL

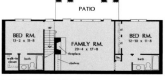

LOWER LEVEL

MAIN LEVEL

HOME PLAN
HPK2500083

Style: Craftsman
Main Level: 3,213 sq. ft.
Lower Level: 1,070 sq. ft.
Total: 2,143 sq. ft.
Bedrooms: 4
Bathrooms: 4
Width: 73' - 9"
Depth: 60' - 0"

HOME PLAN
HPK2500084

Style: Craftsman

First Floor: 2,506 sq. ft.

Second Floor: 1,135 sq. ft.

Total: 3,641 sq. ft.

Bedrooms: 3

Bathrooms: 4 ½

Width: 108' - 0"

Depth: 80' - 0"

Foundation: Unfinished Walkout Basement

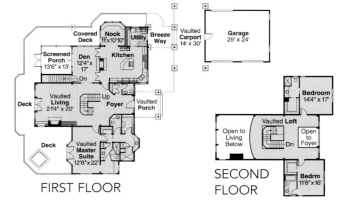

FIRST FLOOR

SECOND FLOOR

HOME PLAN
HPK2500085

Style: Prairie

First Floor: 2,254 sq. ft.

Second Floor: 609 sq. ft.

Total: 2,863 sq. ft.

Bonus Space: 575 sq. ft.

Bedrooms: 3

Bathrooms: 2 ½

Width: 80' - 0"

Depth: 54' - 10"

Foundation: Crawlspace

FIRST FLOOR

SECOND FLOOR

MOUNTAIN GETAWAYS

MAIN LEVEL

LOWER LEVEL

THIS CHARMING RANCH HOME GETS ITS INSPIRATION FROM CLASSIC FARMHOUSES of long ago. Eight columns grace the facade, creating a porch area perfect for enjoying a cool summer evening. As you enter, find a formal dining room to the left and a second bedroom/den to the right—both with cathedral ceilings. Straight ahead, the great room has an impressive view of the backyard through a wall of windows. The kitchen features an eat-in island and flows easily into the nook. An adjacent sunroom has French doors that open to a large wood deck. The master suite features a unique tray ceiling, large walk-in closet, and spa tub. On the lower level, a spacious recreation room with wet bar and three additional bedrooms with walk-in closets serve all your entertainment needs.

HPK2500086

HOME PLAN

Style: Ranch

Main Level: 2,614 sq. ft.

Lower Level: 1,827 sq. ft.

Total: 4,441 sq. ft.

Bedrooms: 5

Bathrooms: 4 ½

Width: 80' - 4"

Depth: 91' - 8"

Foundation: Finished Basement

eplans.com

IMPRESSIVE AMENITIES DELIGHT IN THIS LOVELY HILLSIDE HOME. Inventive room shapes add a contemporary feel. The kitchen boasts abundant counter space, an island snack bar, a walk-in pantry, and access to the rear covered deck. A fireplace in the master suite adds ambiance and warmth. The study is a potential home office or an ideal guest suite, complete with an adjacent full bath. On the lower level, enjoy the family room equipped with a wet bar for casual entertaining. The exercise room is an added bonus.

MAIN LEVEL

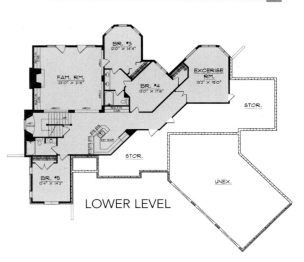

LOWER LEVEL

MOUNTAIN GETAWAYS

FIRST FLOOR

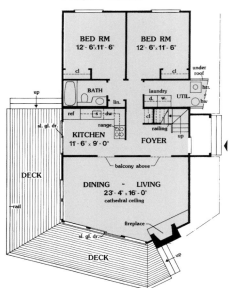

SECOND FLOOR

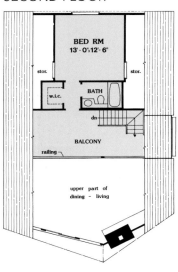

HPK2500088

Style: A-Frame

First Floor: 1,016 sq. ft.

Second Floor: 400 sq. ft.

Total: 1,416 sq. ft.

Bedrooms: 3

Bathrooms: 2

Width: 24' - 0"

Depth: 44' - 4"

Foundation: Crawlspace, Slab, Unfinished Basement

eplans.com

THIS CLEVERLY MODIFIED HOME COMBINES A DRAMATIC EXTERIOR with an exciting interior that offers a commanding view through a vast expanse of windows. The central foyer leads to the spacious living/dining room on the left, which features a soaring cathedral ceiling and stone fireplace. Just ahead is the kitchen with sliding glass doors opening onto the wraparound deck. Two bedrooms and a bath are located at the rear; another bedroom and bath reside upstairs. The broad balcony overlooking the living room serves as a lounge or extra guest room. Natural wood siding and shingles and plank flooring add to the rustic effect.

THIS CHALET PLAN IS ENHANCED BY A STEEP GABLE ROOF, SCALLOPED FASCIA BOARDS, and fieldstone chimney detail. The front-facing deck and covered balcony add to outdoor living spaces. The fireplace is the main focus in the living room. The bedroom on the first floor enjoys access to a full hall bath. A storage/mudroom at the back of the plan is perfect for keeping skis and boots. Two additional bedrooms and a half-bath occupy the second floor. The master bedroom provides a walk-in closet. Three storage areas are also found on the second floor.

HOME PLAN # **HPK2500089**

Style: Cottage

First Floor: 672 sq. ft.

Second Floor: 401 sq. ft.

Total: 1,073 sq. ft.

Bedrooms: 3

Bathrooms: 1 ½

Width: 24' - 0"

Depth: 36' - 0"

Foundation: Crawlspace, Unfinished Basement

eplans.com

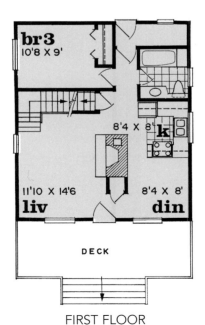

FIRST FLOOR

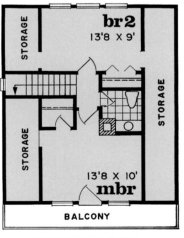

SECOND FLOOR

MOUNTAIN GETAWAYS

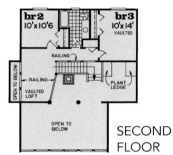

HOME PLAN

HPK2500090

Style: A-Frame

First Floor: 1,157 sq. ft.

Second Floor: 638 sq. ft.

Total: 1,795 sq. ft.

Bedrooms: 3

Bathrooms: 2 ½

Width: 36' - 0"

Depth: 40' - 0"

Foundation: Crawlspace, Unfinished Basement

FIRST FLOOR

SECOND FLOOR

HOME PLAN

HPK2500091

Style: A-Frame

First Floor: 616 sq. ft.

Second Floor: 300 sq. ft.

Total: 916 sq. ft.

Bedrooms: 2

Bathrooms: 1

Width: 22' - 0"

Depth: 28' - 0"

Foundation: Crawlspace

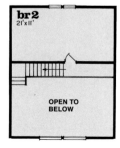

FIRST FLOOR

SECOND FLOOR

HPK2500092

Style: A-Frame

First Floor: 1,042 sq. ft.

Second Floor: 456 sq. ft.

Total: 1,498 sq. ft.

Bedrooms: 3

Bathrooms: 2

Width: 36' - 0"

Depth: 35' - 8"

Foundation: Crawlspace, Unfinished Basement

eplans.com

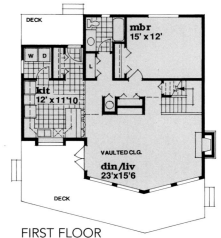

FIRST FLOOR

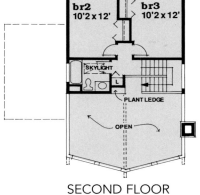

SECOND FLOOR

WITH A DECK TO THE FRONT, THIS VACATION HOME WON'T MISS OUT ON ANY OUTDOOR FUN. The living and dining rooms are dominated by a window wall that takes advantage of the view. A high vaulted ceiling and wood-burning fireplace create a warm atmosphere. The U-shaped kitchen, with an adjoining laundry room, is open to the dining room with a pass-through counter. Note the deck beyond the kitchen and the full wall closet by the laundry. The master bedroom to the rear utilizes a full bath with a large linen closet. Two family bedrooms upstairs share a full bath that includes a skylight.

HOME PLAN

HPK2500093

Style: A-Frame

First Floor: 1,375 sq. ft.

Second Floor: 284 sq. ft.

Total: 1,659 sq. ft.

Bedrooms: 3

Bathrooms: 2

Width: 58' - 0"

Depth: 32' - 0"

Foundation: Crawlspace, Unfinished Basement

eplans.com

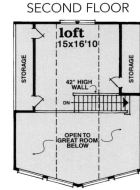

FIRST FLOOR

br2 10'2x10'
br3 10'2x10'
W.I.C.
VAULTED mbr 13'6x12'4
W D
WOOD STOVE
DN
UP
VAULTED din 10'x12'4
k 10'x12'4
grt rm 23'x13'8 VAULTED
DECK

SECOND FLOOR

loft 15x16'10
STORAGE
STORAGE
42" HIGH WALL
DN
OPEN TO GREAT ROOM BELOW

AN EXPANSIVE WINDOW WALL ACROSS THE GREAT ROOM OF THIS HOME ADDS A SPECTACULAR VIEW and accentuates the high ceiling. The open kitchen shares an eating bar with the dining room and features a convenient "U" shape. Sliding glass doors in the dining room lead to the deck. Two family bedrooms sit to the back of the plan and share the use of a full bath. The master suite provides a walk-in closet and private bath. The loft on the upper level adds living or sleeping space.

HOME PLAN
HPK2500094

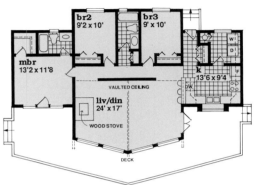

Style: A-Frame

Square Footage: 1,292

Bedrooms: 3

Bathrooms: 2

Width: 52' - 0"

Depth: 34' - 0"

Foundation: Crawlspace

HOME PLAN
HPK2500095

Style: A-Frame

Square Footage: 1,495

Bedrooms: 3

Bathrooms: 2

Width: 58' - 6"

Depth: 33' - 0"

Foundation: Crawlspace

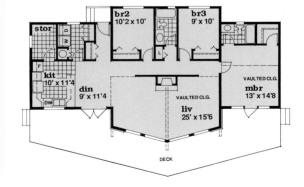

MOUNTAIN GETAWAYS

FIRST FLOOR

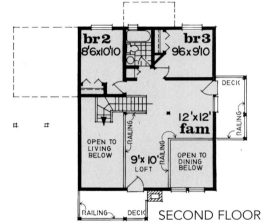

SECOND FLOOR

STONE AND SIDING WORK TOGETHER TO COMPLEMENT THIS COZY CHALET-STYLE DESIGN. The vaulted living and dining rooms, with exposed beam ceilings, are open to the loft above. A spacious wood storage area is found off the living room to feed the warm hearth inside. The kitchen features a pass-through counter to the dining area and leads to a laundry room with work bench. The master suite is on the first floor and has a private patio and bath. An additional half-bath is located in the main hall. The second floor holds a family room with desk and two family bedrooms with shared bath.

HPK2500096

HOME PLAN

Style: A-Frame

First Floor: 1,036 sq. ft.

Second Floor: 630 sq. ft.

Total: 1,666 sq. ft.

Bedrooms: 3

Bathrooms: 2 ½

Width: 45' - 6"

Depth: 44' - 0"

Foundation: Crawlspace

eplans.com

A COVERED VERANDA WITH COVERED DECK ABOVE
OPENS THROUGH FRENCH DOORS to the living/dining area
of this vacation cottage. A masonry fireplace with a wood storage bin warms this area. A modified U-shaped kitchen serves
the dining room, and a laundry room is just across the hall near
a side veranda. The master bedroom is on the first floor and
has the use of a full bath. Sliding glass doors in the master
bedroom and the living room lead to still another veranda. The
second floor has two family bedrooms, a full bath, a family
room with a balcony overlooking the living room and dining
room, a fireplace, and double doors leading to a patio. A large
storage area on this level adds convenience.

HOME PLAN

HPK2500097

Style: A-Frame
First Floor: 1,094 sq. ft.
Second Floor: 576 sq. ft.
Total: 1,670 sq. ft.
Bedrooms: 3
Bathrooms: 2
Width: 43' - 0"
Depth: 35' - 4"
Foundation: Crawlspace

eplans.com

MOUNTAIN GETAWAYS

FIRST FLOOR

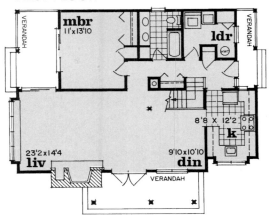

SECOND FLOOR

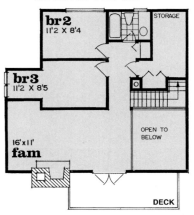

HOME PLAN

FIRST FLOOR

SECOND FLOOR

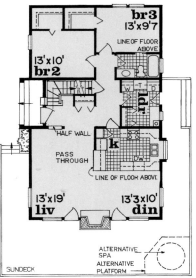

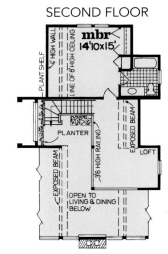

(#) HPK2500098

Style: A-Frame

First Floor: 1,235 sq. ft.

Second Floor: 543 sq. ft.

Total: 1,778 sq. ft.

Bedrooms: 3

Bathrooms: 2

Width: 27' - 6"

Depth: 46' - 0"

Foundation: Crawlspace, Unfinished Basement

eplans.com

AN EXPANSIVE SUN DECK WITH AN OPTIONAL SPA WRAPS AROUND THIS DESIGN to highlight outdoor living. Tall windows accent the vaulted ceiling in the living and dining rooms. Both areas are warmed by a central fireplace flanked by doors to the deck. A U-shaped kitchen is open to the dining room. Two bedrooms with walk-in closets sit to the back of the first floor and share the use of a full bath. The master suite dominates the upper level and has a full bath and large wall closet. Note the laundry room and service entrance on the first floor.

HOME PLAN
HPK2500099

Style: Cottage

First Floor: 893 sq. ft.

Second Floor: 408 sq. ft.

Total: 1,301 sq. ft.

Bedrooms: 3

Bathrooms: 2

Width: 28' - 0"

Depth: 32' - 0"

Foundation: Unfinished Basement

FIRST FLOOR

SECOND FLOOR

HOME PLAN
HPK2500100

Style: Cottage

First Floor: 1,069 sq. ft.

Second Floor: 809 sq. ft.

Total: 1,878 sq. ft.

Bedrooms: 3

Bathrooms: 2

Width: 34' - 0"

Depth: 34' - 0"

Foundation: Unfinished Basement

FIRST FLOOR

SECOND FLOOR

FIRST FLOOR

SECOND FLOOR

HOME PLAN

HPK2500101

Style: Bungalow

First Floor: 908 sq. ft.

Second Floor: 576 sq. ft.

Total: 1,484 sq. ft.

Bedrooms: 3

Bathrooms: 2

Width: 26' - 0"

Depth: 48' - 0"

Foundation: Finished Walkout Basement

eplans.com

PICTURE YOURSELF DRIVING UP TO THE LAKE AFTER A LONG WEEK AT WORK and pulling into the driveway of this gorgeous vacation home. In the foyer, you can hang your coat in the closet and store the toys for the kids. Days are naturally lit by sunlight streaming in through the abundant fenestration throughout the home, but be sure to enjoy the view off the screened porch as well. With a full kitchen at your disposal, you can create a meal to be enjoyed either leisurely at the island or more formally in the dining room. Curl up with a good book and a glass of wine and enjoy the glow of the wood-burning fireplace in the family room, or invite friends over for a movie. They can stay over in the first-floor bedroom with nearby full bath. Then retreat upstairs where you can tuck the kids into their room and fall fast asleep in yours.

HOME PLAN

HPK2500102

Style: Bungalow

First Floor: 1,024 sq. ft.

Second Floor: 456 sq. ft.

Total: 1,480 sq. ft.

Bedrooms: 2

Bathrooms: 2

Width: 32' - 0"

Depth: 40' - 0"

Foundation: Finished Walkout Basement

eplans.com

PILLARS, A LARGE FRONT PORCH, AND PLENTY OF WINDOW VIEWS LEND A CLASSIC FEEL to this lovely country cottage. Inside, the entry room has a coat closet and an interior entry door to eliminate drafts. The light-filled L-shaped kitchen lies conveniently near the entrance. A large room adjacent to the kitchen serves as a dining and living area where a fireplace adds warmth. A master suite boasts a walk-in closet and full bath. The second floor holds a loft, a second bedroom, and a full bath.

FIRST FLOOR

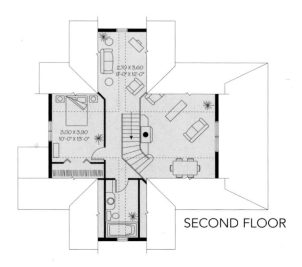

SECOND FLOOR

FIRST FLOOR

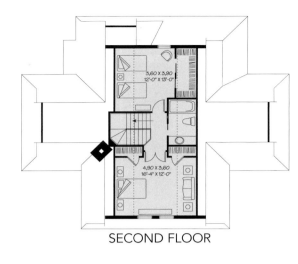

SECOND FLOOR

THIS COMFORTABLE VACATION DESIGN PROVIDES TWO LEVELS OF RELAXING FAMILY SPACE. The main level offers a spacious wrapping front porch and an abundance of windows, filling interior spaces with the summer sunshine. A two-sided fireplace warms the living room/dining room combination and a master bedroom that features a roomy walk-in closet. Nearby, the hall bath offers a relaxing whirlpool tub. The kitchen is open and features an island snack bar and pantry storage. A cozy sunroom accesses the wrapping deck. Upstairs, two additional bedrooms feature ample closet space and share a second-floor bath.

HOME PLAN

 # HPK2500103

Style: **Country**

First Floor: **1,212 sq. ft.**

Second Floor: **620 sq. ft.**

Total: **1,832 sq. ft.**

Bedrooms: **3**

Bathrooms: **2**

Width: **38' - 0"**

Depth: **40' - 0"**

Foundation: **Finished Walkout Basement**

eplans.com

SITUATE THIS HOUSE BY THE SEA AND YOU'VE GOT YOURSELF THE ULTIMATE WATERFRONT RETREAT. Three levels of spacious living mean ample room for everyone, and extra storage provides a place to put seasonal equipment. Enter from the main level to find a grand family room. Nearby, a secluded sunroom makes an excellent den or home office. A snack-bar island in the open kitchen seats five, or meals may be enjoyed in the bayed dining area. The master suite reigns on this level and boasts a private deck and palatial bath. Upstairs, a bedroom loft suite overlooks the family room. The lower level offers two bedrooms, a gathering room with a fireplace, and a large laundry room.

HOME PLAN # HPK2500104

Style: Country
Main Level: 1,434 sq. ft.
Second Level: 524 sq. ft.
Lower Level: 1,434 sq. ft.
Total: 3,392 sq. ft.
Bedrooms: 4
Bathrooms: 3 ½
Width: 72' - 0"
Depth: 42' - 0"
Foundation: Finished Walkout Basement

eplans.com

LOWER LEVEL

MAIN LEVEL

SECOND LEVEL

FIRST FLOOR

SECOND FLOOR

(#) HPK2500105

Style: Bungalow

First Floor: 1,232 sq. ft.

Second Floor: 987 sq. ft.

Total: 2,219 sq. ft.

Bedrooms: 3

Bathrooms: 3 ½

Width: 67' - 0"

Depth: 40' - 0"

Foundation: Unfinished Walkout Basement

eplans.com

AS A COZY MOUNTAIN CABIN OR A REFRESHING LAKE RETREAT, this comfy home is designed for privacy and total relaxation. Highlighting the home is a gourmet kitchen with a cooktop island and an adjoining snack bar for casual meals. A dining room is nearby and opens to the spacious gathering room with a fireplace and side-porch access. A grand master suite uses unique angles and a luxury bath to add subtle style. Up the central stairs, a bedroom enjoys a full bath and quiet loft reading area. Above the garage (but accessed from the interior), apartment-style sleeping quarters include a separate bedroom and living area and a full bath.

HPK2500106

Style: Craftsman

First Floor: 856 sq. ft.

Second Floor: 581 sq. ft.

Total: 1,437 sq. ft.

Bedrooms: 3

Bathrooms: 1 ½

Width: 44' - 0"

Depth: 26' - 0"

Foundation: Unfinished Walkout Basement

eplans.com

A STANDING-SEAM METAL ROOF, HORIZONTAL SIDING, AND A MASSIVE DECK combine to create a mosaic of parallel lines on this rustic two-story home. Sunlight spills into the great room through four beautiful clerestory windows. A generous L-shaped kitchen with a work island adjoins the dining area. A bedroom and powder room are neatly tucked behind the staircase that leads to the second-floor sleeping quarters. Upstairs, a loft allows plenty of space for a computer in kick-off-your-shoes comfort.

FIRST FLOOR

SECOND FLOOR

HOME PLAN
HPK2500107

Style: Contemporary
First Floor: 1,078 sq. ft.
Second Floor: 794 sq. ft.
Total: 1,872 sq. ft.
Bedrooms: 3
Bathrooms: 2
Width: 36' - 0"
Depth: 34' - 0"
Foundation: Unfinished Basement

FIRST FLOOR

SECOND FLOOR

HOME PLAN
HPK2500108

Style: Contemporary
First Floor: 975 sq. ft.
Second Floor: 622 sq. ft.
Total: 1,597 sq. ft.
Bedrooms: 3
Bathrooms: 2
Width: 38' - 0"
Depth: 30' - 0"
Foundation: Unfinished Basement

FIRST FLOOR

SECOND FLOOR

HOME PLAN

HPK2500109

Style: Contemporary
Main Level: 790 sq. ft.
Second Level: 299 sq. ft.
Lower Level: 787 sq. ft.
Total: 1,876 sq. ft.
Bedrooms: 3
Bathrooms: 2
Width: 32' - 4"
Depth: 24' - 4"
Foundation: Unfinished Walkout Basement

LOWER LEVEL

MAIN LEVEL

SECOND LEVEL

HOME PLAN

HPK2500110

Style: Shed
First Floor: 2,357 sq. ft.
Second Floor: 170 sq. ft.
Total: 2,527 sq. ft.
Bedrooms: 3
Bathrooms: 2 ½
Width: 66' - 0"
Depth: 44' - 0"
Foundation: Slab

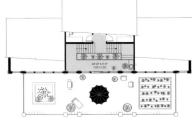

FIRST FLOOR

SECOND FLOOR

MOUNTAIN GETAWAYS

FIRST FLOOR

SECOND FLOOR

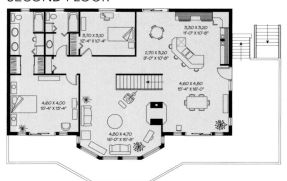

FOUR-SEASON LIVING IN THE MOUNTAINS OR BY A LAKE, this home is a perfect place to enjoy the view. A wraparound deck takes advantage of the weather and increases living and dining space. The lower level provides a family room with fireplace, two family bedrooms, large storage room, laundry room, and a full bath. Upstairs, the main living areas include a bright open kitchen with snack-bar island, breakfast area, and a dining room with see-through fireplace to the living room. The master suite is outfitted with sliders to access the deck, private bath, and closet space. Another secondary bedroom sits just off the kitchen and near a full hall bath.

HOME PLAN

 # HPK2500111

Style: Contemporary

First Floor: 1,470 sq. ft.

Second Floor: 1,634 sq. ft.

Total: 3,104 sq. ft.

Bedrooms: 4

Bathrooms: 3

Width: 62' - 0"

Depth: 36' - 0"

Foundation: Unfinished Walkout Basement

eplans.com

THIS BEAUTIFUL CHALET VACATION HOME ABOUNDS WITH VIEWS OF THE OUTDOORS AND PROVIDES A GRAND DECK, creating additional living space. With its entry on the lower level, you'll find two family bedrooms that share a full bath, an office/study, and a family room with a warming fireplace. There's an extra room here that could be a third family bedroom or perhaps a library or study. Upstairs, a great room with a cathedral ceiling shares a through-fireplace with the formal dining room. Conveniently nearby is the kitchen, which boasts an island work area/snack bar and an informal dining area. On the upper level is the master suite with its own private bath. Also on this floor, a fourth bedroom and another full bath would certainly accommodate weekend or overnight guests.

HOME PLAN

 # HPK2500112

Style: Contemporary
First Floor: 1,470 sq. ft.
Second Floor: 1,635 sq. ft.
Total: 3,105 sq. ft.
Bedrooms: 4
Bathrooms: 3
Width: 62' - 0"
Depth: 36' - 0"
Foundation: Finished Walkout Basement

eplans.com

FIRST FLOOR

SECOND FLOOR

HOME PLAN
HPK2500113

Style: Craftsman
First Floor: 1,602 sq. ft.
Second Floor: 1,948 sq. ft.
Total: 3,550 sq. ft.
Bedrooms: 4
Bathrooms: 3 ½
Width: 40' - 0"
Depth: 60' - 0"
Foundation: Crawlspace

FIRST FLOOR

SECOND FLOOR

HOME PLAN
HPK2500114

Style: Craftsman
Main Level: 1,405 sq. ft.
Second Level: 1,348 sq. ft.
Lower Level: 42 sq. ft.
Total: 2,795 sq. ft.
Bedrooms: 3
Bathrooms: 2 ½
Width: 32' - 0"
Depth: 52' - 6"
Foundation: Crawlspace

LOWER LEVEL

MAIN LEVEL

SECOND LEVEL

FIRST FLOOR

SECOND FLOOR

HOME PLAN
HPK2500115

Style: Craftsman
First Floor: 3,005 sq. ft.
Second Floor: 1,030 sq. ft.
Total: 4,035 sq. ft.
Bedrooms: 4
Bathrooms: 3
Width: 66' - 9"
Depth: 93' - 6"
Foundation: Crawlspace

HOME PLAN
HPK2500116

Style: Craftsman
Main Level: 2,285 sq. ft.
Second Level: 1,726 sq. ft.
Lower Level: 368 sq. ft.
Total: 4,379 sq. ft.
Bedrooms: 4
Bathrooms: 2 ½
Width: 59' - 0"
Depth: 58' - 6"
Foundation: Crawlspace

LOWER LEVEL

MAIN LEVEL

SECOND LEVEL

MOUNTAIN GETAWAYS

HOME PLAN
HPK2500117

Style: Craftsman
Main Level: 1,630 sq. ft.
Second Level: 1,460 sq. ft.
Lower Level: 130 sq. ft.
Total: 3,220 sq. ft.
Bedrooms: 3
Bathrooms: 2 ½
Width: 40' - 0"
Depth: 55' - 6"
Foundation: Crawlspace

LOWER LEVEL   MAIN LEVEL   SECOND LEVEL

HOME PLAN
HPK2500118

Style: Craftsman
Main Level: 1,685 sq. ft.
Second Level: 1,490 sq. ft.
Lower Level: 200 sq. ft.
Total: 3,375 sq. ft.
Bedrooms: 3
Bathrooms: 2 ½
Width: 37' - 0"
Depth: 58' - 0"
Foundation: Crawlspace

LOWER LEVEL   MAIN LEVEL   SECOND LEVEL

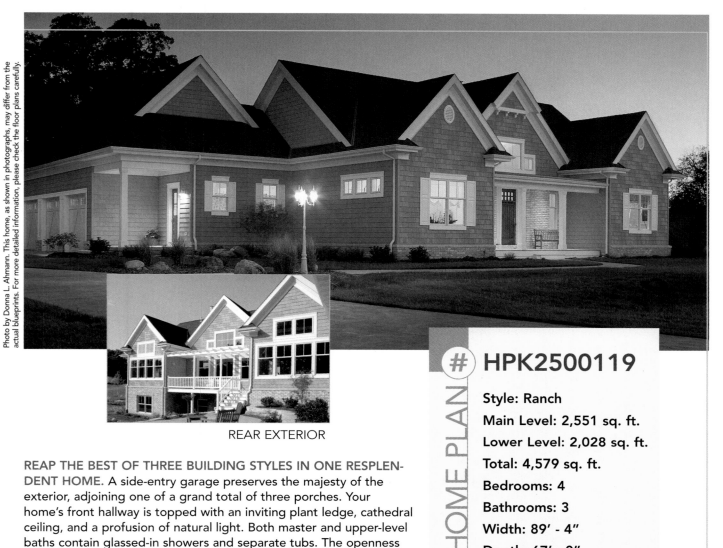

REAR EXTERIOR

REAP THE BEST OF THREE BUILDING STYLES IN ONE RESPLEN-
DENT HOME. A side-entry garage preserves the majesty of the
exterior, adjoining one of a grand total of three porches. Your
home's front hallway is topped with an inviting plant ledge, cathedral
ceiling, and a profusion of natural light. Both master and upper-level
baths contain glassed-in showers and separate tubs. The openness
and functionality of the kitchen area is highlighted by the walk-in
pantry, snack bar, and prep island, and leads to your formal dining
room. The great room and master suite perpetuate the feeling of
self-contained luxury. The top floor is reserved for bedrooms three
and four, more entertaining (impress with recreation and media
rooms), and storage. Leave the bustle inside as you escape to your
private patio/deck through the master suite, or gaze through a
series of arched windows with expansive rear and front views.

HOME PLAN

HPK2500119

Style: Ranch
Main Level: 2,551 sq. ft.
Lower Level: 2,028 sq. ft.
Total: 4,579 sq. ft.
Bedrooms: 4
Bathrooms: 3
Width: 89' - 4"
Depth: 67' - 0"
Foundation: Finished
Basement

eplans.com

MOUNTAIN GETAWAYS

MAIN LEVEL

LOWER LEVEL

RELAX IN THIS SWEET-FACED BUNGALOW FEATURING CRAFTSMAN DETAILS and charm. The main floor is open and modern without any wasted space. The large kitchen is set to the front of the plan with the dining and family areas just a few steps away. The master suite offers a full bath and walk-in closet. The screened porch and adjoining deck make this cottage live larger than its modest square footage. The lower level provides guests with two secondary bedrooms, a full bath, and a game room.

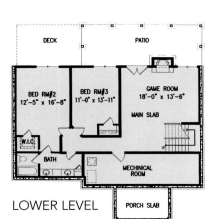

MAIN LEVEL

LOWER LEVEL

HOME PLAN

HPK2500120

Style: Bungalow

Main Level: 1,288 sq. ft.

Lower Level: 1,242 sq. ft.

Total: 2,530 sq. ft.

Bedrooms: 3

Bathrooms: 2 ½

Width: 44' - 0"

Depth: 30' - 0"

Foundation: Finished Walkout Basement

eplans.com

HPK2500121

Style: Craftsman

Main Level: 1,451 sq. ft.

Lower Level: 2,035 sq. ft.

Total: 3,486 sq. ft.

Bedrooms: 4

Bathrooms: 3 ½

Width: 56' - 0"

Depth: 65' - 0"

Foundation: Finished Walkout Basement

eplans.com

THIS CHARMING VACATION RETREAT WILL FEEL LIKE HOME IN THE MOUNTAINS as well as by a wooded lakefront. With a covered deck, screened porch, and spacious patio, this home is designed for lovers of the outdoors. Inside, a comfy, rustic aura dominates. On the main level, a lodge-like living area with an extended-hearth fireplace and snack bar dominates. A library, easy-to-use kitchen, and enchanting master suite are also located on this floor. Downstairs, there are two more bedrooms, a huge recreation room, a hobby room (or make it into another bedroom), and lots of storage space.

MAIN LEVEL

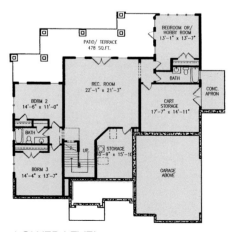

LOWER LEVEL

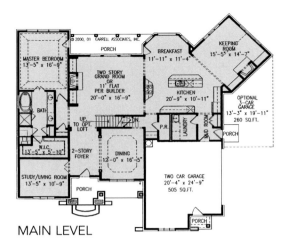

MAIN LEVEL

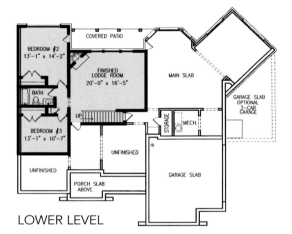

LOWER LEVEL

AN EYE-CATCHING SHED DORMER IS BOTH LOVELY AND FUNCTIONAL, bringing light into the foyer. A mudroom is the perfect casual entry off the garage, right next to the main-level laundry and optional third-car garage. The open kitchen works with the keeping, breakfast, and grand rooms. A study—or living room—and formal dining room flank the foyer for entertaining guests.

HOME PLAN

HPK2500122

Style: Craftsman

Main Level: 2,171 sq. ft.

Lower Level: 919 sq. ft.

Total: 3,090 sq. ft.

Bedrooms: 3

Bathrooms: 2 ½

Width: 68' - 3"

Depth: 60' - 11"

Foundation: Finished Walkout Basement

eplans.com

HPK2500123

Style: Bungalow

Main Level: 2,160 sq. ft.

Lower Level: 919 sq. ft.

Total: 3,079 sq. ft.

Bedrooms: 3

Bathrooms: 2 ½

Width: 68' - 3"

Depth: 60' - 11"

Foundation: Finished Walkout Basement

eplans.com

MAIN LEVEL

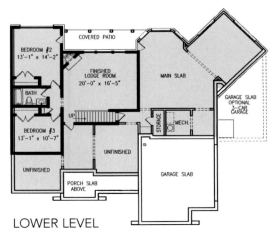

LOWER LEVEL

A WARM CRAFTSMAN EXTERIOR SHOWCASES CEDAR SHINGLES AND THICK PILLARS. The main level is an inviting arrangement of casual and formal spaces. The open kitchen is positioned between the keeping room and grand room and features a breakfast bay. The first-floor master suite enjoys porch access and a private bath. A lower level provides secondary bedrooms and a spacious lodge room.

MOUNTAIN GETAWAYS

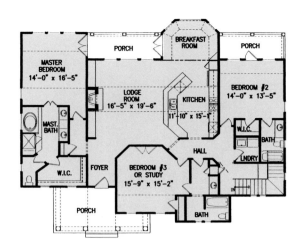

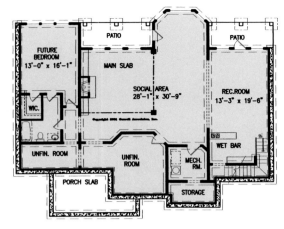

A CHARMING COUNTRY COTTAGE ADDS CURB APPEAL TO ANY NEIGHBORHOOD. The island kitchen easily serves the adjoining lodge room, and the breakfast room offers a bayed view of the backyard and access to a rear porch. The master bathroom is equipped with a dual-sink vanity, garden tub, walk-in closet, private toilet, and shower. Two additional bedrooms each have a full bath. The basement is available for future expansion.

HOME PLAN

HPK2500124

Style: Cottage

Square Footage: 2,086

Bedrooms: 3

Bathrooms: 3

Width: 57' - 6"

Depth: 46' - 6"

Foundation: Unfinished Basement

eplans.com

Christine Canova 2/02

HPK2500125

Style: French Country

Main Level: 3,615 sq. ft.

Lower Level: 2,803 sq. ft.

Total: 6,418 sq. ft.

Bedrooms: 4

Bathrooms: 3 ½ + ½

Width: 98' - 0"

Depth: 94' - 0"

Foundation: Finished Basement

eplans.com

A COMBINATION OF STONE, SIDING, AND MULTIPLE ROOFLINES CREATES A COTTAGE FEEL to this large home. Inside, the master suite opens from a short hallway and enjoys a private fireplace, access to the rear covered porch, a spacious walk-in closet, compartmented toilet, separate shower, garden tub, and dual vanities. The gourmet kitchen includes an island cooktop, snack bar, access to the covered porch, and conveniently serves the adjoining dining room and lodge room. Two additional family bedrooms share a full bath in the basement and a guest suite is located upstairs near the front door.

MAIN LEVEL

LOWER LEVEL

CRAFTSMAN FEATURES, SUCH AS THE LOW-PITCHED ROOF, OVER-HANGING EAVES, SQUARE COLUMNS, AND RUSTIC MATERIALS, suit this home for many American neighborhoods as well as vacation settings. The empty-nester layout provides for a spacious and central gathering area with great outdoor spaces accessible at the top and left of the plan. The guest room at the front of the home may usually serve as a study. Homeowners will love the hard-working utility room near the kitchen, available as a laundry room, office, pantry, or mudroom.

MAIN LEVEL

LOWER LEVEL

HOME PLAN

(#) HPK2500126

Style: Bungalow

Main Level: 2,026 sq. ft.

Lower Level: 1,387 sq. ft.

Total: 3,413 sq. ft.

Bonus Space: 107 sq. ft.

Bedrooms: 4

Bathrooms: 4 ½

Width: 102' - 0"

Depth: 84' - 6"

Foundation: Finished Walkout Basement

eplans.com

© Stephen Fuller, Inc.

© Stephen Fuller, Inc.

HPK2500127

Style: Craftsman

Main Level: 2,388 sq. ft.

Lower Level: 2,159 sq. ft.

Total: 4,547 sq. ft.

Bonus Space: 312 sq. ft.

Bedrooms: 4

Bathrooms: 3 ½

Width: 90' - 0"

Depth: 33' - 0"

Foundation: Unfinished Walkout Basement

eplans.com

THIS SPACIOUS HOME WITH INTERESTING ANGLES IS PERFECT FOR A HILLSIDE LOT. Board-and-batten and shake siding give a casual feel, while expansive windows provide natural light. On the main level, a kitchen adds convenience on one side of the plan while, on the opposite side of the room, a fireplace and chimney reach the ceiling. Overhead beams combined with tongue-and-groove paneling detail the ceiling for a rustic vacation feel. The master bedroom occupies an entire side of the home and opens to a private balcony. There's a nice choice of optional living space on the lower level. Bedrooms can double as office or study spaces, and a spacious center room with a bar is perfect for entertaining. Or take the entertaining outside to a lower-level lanai with fireplace or veranda with food prep area.

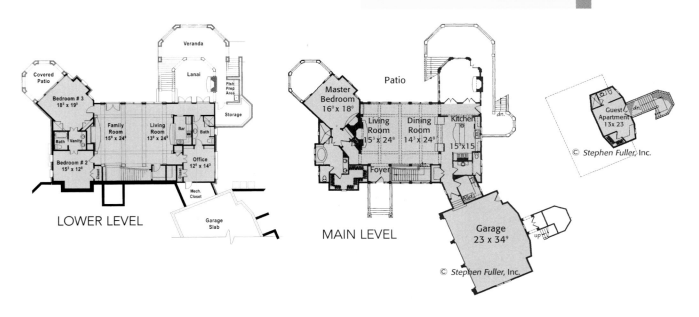

LOWER LEVEL

MAIN LEVEL

© Stephen Fuller, Inc.

MOUNTAIN GETAWAYS

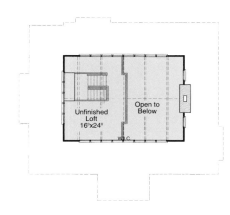

RIGHT SIDE EXTERIOR

HPK2500128

HOME PLAN

Style: Bungalow

Square Footage: 2,019

Bonus Space: 368 sq. ft.

Bedrooms: 3

Bathrooms: 2

Width: 56' - 0"

Depth: 56' - 3"

Foundation: Crawlspace

eplans.com

THIS DESIGN TAKES INSPIRATION FROM THE CASUAL FISHING CABINS of the Pacific Northwest and interprets it for modern livability. It offers three options for a main entrance. One door opens to a mud porch, where a small hall leads to a galley kitchen and the vaulted great room. Two French doors on the side porch open into a dining room with bay-window seating. Another porch entrance opens directly into the great room, which is centered around a massive stone fireplace and accented with a wall of windows. The secluded master bedroom features a bath with a clawfoot tub and twin pedestal sinks, as well as a separate shower and walk-in closet. Two more bedrooms share a bath. An unfinished loft overlooks the great room.

HOME PLAN

HPK2500129

Style: Bungalow
First Floor: 872 sq. ft.
Second Floor: 734 sq. ft.
Total: 1,606 sq. ft.
Bedrooms: 3
Bathrooms: 3
Width: 40' - 0"
Depth: 29' - 6"
Foundation: Crawlspace

SIDING, SHINGLES, AND A STONE CHIMNEY GIVE RUSTIC CHARM TO THIS COZY COTTAGE. The living room, with a fireplace, built-in shelves and a wall of windows, opens to the covered side porch. In the kitchen you will find plenty of work space, and the kitchen sink overlooks the living area. The first-floor bedroom adjoins a full bath. The master suite—with a private bath and His and Her closets—reside with a family bedroom upstairs. An upper hall leads to a full bath and an ample wardrobe with storage.

FIRST FLOOR

SECOND FLOOR

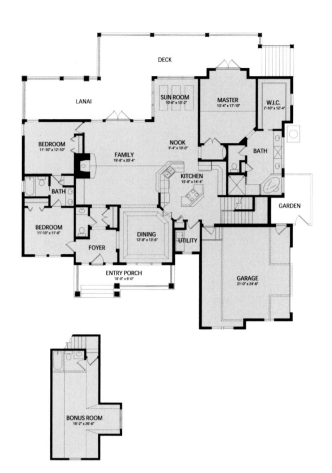

FINE DETAILS LIKE THE SHED DORMER, OPEN MILLWORK ACCENTS, an arched entry, and a standing-seam roof will make this home a neighborhood favorite. A split-bedroom floor plan positions the family bedrooms to the left with a compartmented bath between them. The family room, with fireplace and built-ins, is a generous and open space that works with the huge island kitchen, bright sunroom, and breakfast nook. A more formal dining space is found to the right of the foyer. Seclusion is just one amenity the master suite boasts; others include an oversized walk-in closet, super bath, and French doors to the deck.

HOME PLAN

HPK2500130

Style: Craftsman

Square Footage: 2,326

Bonus Space: 358 sq. ft.

Bedrooms: 3

Bathrooms: 2 ½

Width: 64' - 0"

Depth: 72' - 4"

Foundation: Unfinished Basement

eplans.com

THIS SENSIBLE PLAN FLOUTS TRADITION AND DELIVERS HIGH-END AMENITIES in a well-balanced design. A full-sized formal dining room, featuring a tray ceiling, enables homeowners to host elegant dinners made to perfection in the gourmet kitchen. The combined space of the great room, breakfast nook, and sun room is enhanced even further by the lanai and deck. Homeowners will know just how pleasing this home can be as they retire each night to a deluxe master suite. The bedroom features exclusive access to the deck, and a private garden beautifies the corner whirlpool tub.

HPK2500131

Style: Craftsman

Square Footage: 2,326

Bonus Space: 358 sq. ft.

Bedrooms: 3

Bathrooms: 2 ½

Width: 64' - 0"

Depth: 72' - 4"

Foundation: Finished Walkout Basement

eplans.com

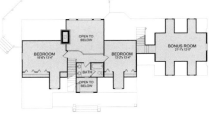

FIRST FLOOR

SECOND FLOOR

HOME PLAN #

HPK2500132

Style: Log House

First Floor: 1,799 sq. ft.

Second Floor: 709 sq. ft.

Total: 2,508 sq. ft.

Bonus Space: 384 sq. ft.

Bedrooms: 3

Bathrooms: 2 ½

Width: 77' - 4"

Depth: 41' - 4"

Foundation: Unfinished Walkout Basement

HOME PLAN #

HPK2500133

Style: Craftsman

First Floor: 1,799 sq. ft.

Second Floor: 709 sq. ft.

Total: 2,508 sq. ft.

Bonus Space: 384 sq. ft.

Bedrooms: 3

Bathrooms: 2 ½

Width: 77' - 4"

Depth: 41' - 4"

Foundation: Unfinished Walkout Basement

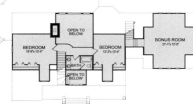

FIRST FLOOR

SECOND FLOOR

HPK2500134

Style: Country

First Floor: 1,799 sq. ft.

Second Floor: 709 sq. ft.

Total: 2,508 sq. ft.

Bonus Space: 384 sq. ft.

Bedrooms: 3

Bathrooms: 2 ½

Width: 77' - 4"

Depth: 41' - 4"

Foundation: Unfinished Walkout Basement

eplans.com

CRAFTSMAN DETAILS HELP CREATE A RUSTIC RETREAT PERFECT FOR THE MOUNTAINS OR LAKESIDE. A formal dining room brings a touch of class to more formal settings. A modern approach to casual living groups the family room, eating nook, and kitchen into a highly efficient and open space. Nestled to the left, the master suite includes a super bath and oversized walk-in closet. The second floor is home to two family bedrooms and a full bath. Above the garage, flexible bonus space is offered.

FIRST FLOOR

SECOND FLOOR

HOME PLAN

HPK2500135

Style: Log House

First Floor: 2,589 sq. ft.

Second Floor: 981 sq. ft.

Total: 3,570 sq. ft.

Bedrooms: 4

Bathrooms: 3 ½

Width: 70' - 8"

Depth: 61' - 10"

Foundation: Crawlspace

FIRST FLOOR

SECOND FLOOR

HOME PLAN

HPK2500136

Style: Craftsman

First Floor: 2,589 sq. ft.

Second Floor: 981 sq. ft.

Total: 3,570 sq. ft.

Bedrooms: 4

Bathrooms: 3 ½

Width: 70' - 8"

Depth: 61' - 10"

Foundation: Crawlspace

FIRST FLOOR

SECOND FLOOR

THE HORIZONTAL SIDING OF THIS FACADE EVOKES A SENSE OF CHARM AND COMFORT similar to a log cabin. The covered porch opens to a foyer, flanked by a study on the left and the dining room on the right. Beyond the foyer sits the living room, complete with a fireplace and double-door access to the large rear deck. To the right of the living room, a second fireplace in the family room warms the large country kitchen, the nearby utility room, and the office. An island snack bar in the kitchen conveniently serves the family room. On the opposite side of the floor plan, the master suite offers a private entrance to the rear deck, His and Hers walk-in closets, a dual sink vanity, a compartmented toilet, a separate shower, and a garden tub. Upstairs, three family bedrooms, each with a walk-in closet, share two full baths.

HOME PLAN # HPK2500003

Style: Craftsman
First Floor: 2,589 sq. ft.
Second Floor: 981 sq. ft.
Total: 3,570 sq. ft.
Bedrooms: 4
Bathrooms: 3 ½
Width: 70' - 8"
Depth: 61' - 10"
Foundation: Crawlspace

eplans.com

FIRST FLOOR

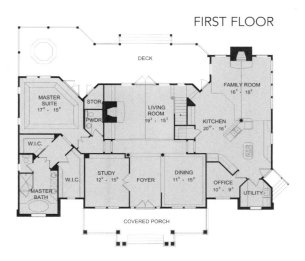

SECOND FLOOR

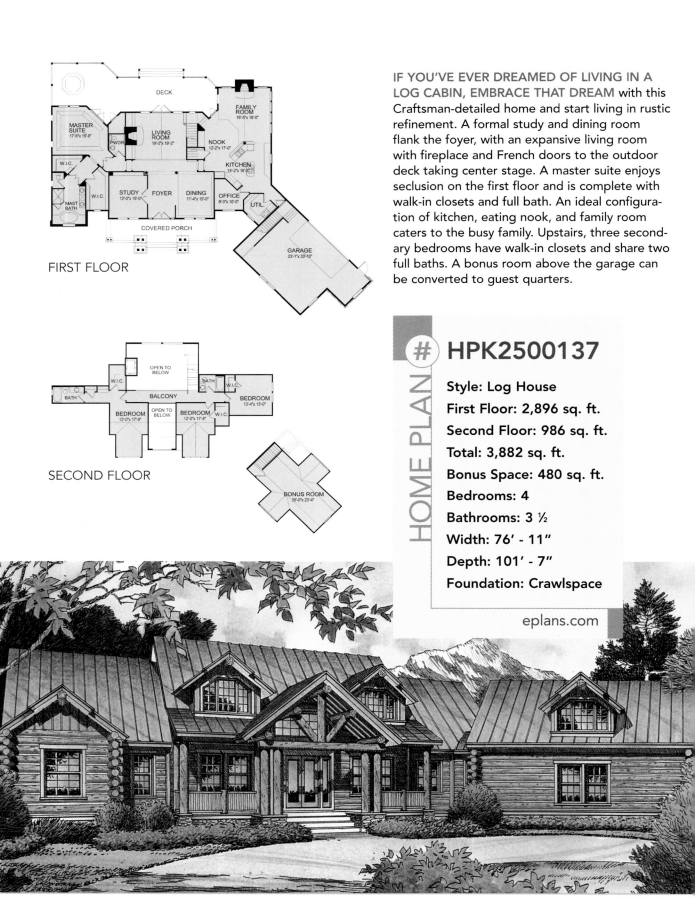

FIRST FLOOR

DECK

MASTER SUITE 17'-6"x 15'-8"

PWDR

LIVING ROOM 19'-2"x 19'-2"

NOOK 12'-2"x 17'-0"

FAMILY ROOM 16'-5"x 18'-0"

KITCHEN 14'-2"x 16'-0"

W.I.C.

MAST BATH

W.I.C.

STUDY 12'-0"x 15'-0"

FOYER

DINING 11'-4"x 15'-0"

OFFICE 9'-0"x 10'-0"

UTIL.

COVERED PORCH

GARAGE 23'-1"x 33'-10"

SECOND FLOOR

OPEN TO BELOW

W.I.C.

BATH

BATH

W.I.C.

BALCONY

BEDROOM 13'-4"x 13'-0"

BEDROOM 12'-0"x 17'-8"

OPEN TO BELOW

BEDROOM 12'-0"x 17'-8"

W.I.C.

BONUS ROOM 26'-0"x 23'-4"

IF YOU'VE EVER DREAMED OF LIVING IN A LOG CABIN, EMBRACE THAT DREAM with this Craftsman-detailed home and start living in rustic refinement. A formal study and dining room flank the foyer, with an expansive living room with fireplace and French doors to the outdoor deck taking center stage. A master suite enjoys seclusion on the first floor and is complete with walk-in closets and full bath. An ideal configuration of kitchen, eating nook, and family room caters to the busy family. Upstairs, three secondary bedrooms have walk-in closets and share two full baths. A bonus room above the garage can be converted to guest quarters.

HOME PLAN

HPK2500137

Style: Log House

First Floor: 2,896 sq. ft.

Second Floor: 986 sq. ft.

Total: 3,882 sq. ft.

Bonus Space: 480 sq. ft.

Bedrooms: 4

Bathrooms: 3 ½

Width: 76' - 11"

Depth: 101' - 7"

Foundation: Crawlspace

eplans.com

HPK2500138

HOME PLAN #

Style: Craftsman
First Floor: 2,896 sq. ft.
Second Floor: 986 sq. ft.
Total: 3,882 sq. ft.
Bonus Space: 480 sq. ft.
Bedrooms: 4
Bathrooms: 3 ½
Width: 76' - 11"
Depth: 101' - 7"
Foundation: Crawlspace

eplans.com

STONE AND WOOD SIDING, BORROWED FROM NATURE, lend this home design a woodsy resort style. Windows, transoms, and French doors allow plenty of light and the surrounding view to fill the home. A spacious foyer introduces the dining room and private study. To the rear, the great room is outfitted with a fireplace, built-ins, and an expansive deck just beyond French doors. A trio of warm, casual spaces—the oversized kitchen, eating nook, and family room—creates an incredibly livable combination. A home office is tucked behind the kitchen for privacy. Three secondary bedrooms are positioned upstairs, giving the master suite plenty of seclusion on the first floor.

MOUNTAIN GETAWAYS

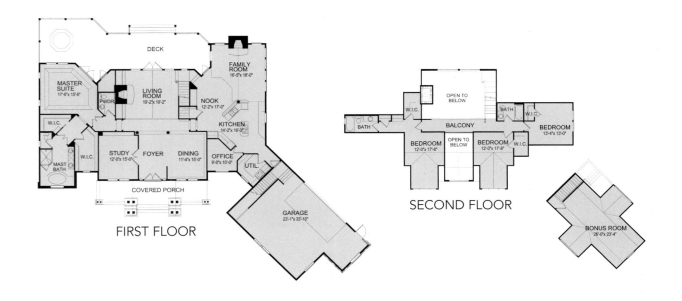

FIRST FLOOR

SECOND FLOOR

PERFECT WINTER GETAWAY HOME!

This retreat includes all the comforts of home; formal dining area, private study, cozy living room, gourmet kitchen, and open family room. The quiet master suite will relax and pamper the homeowner with a large super bath, dual walk-in closets, and French doors to the deck. The second level gives the family privacy with three bedrooms and two full baths. Above the garage, a bonus room will make comfortable guest quarters.

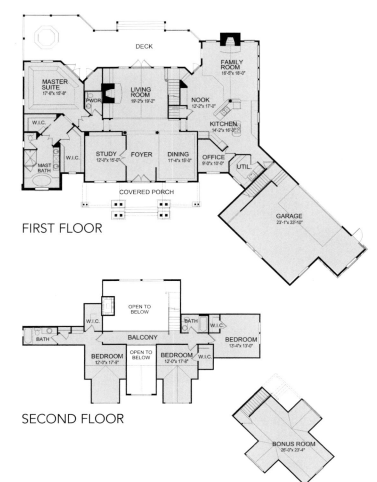

FIRST FLOOR

SECOND FLOOR

BONUS ROOM
26'-0"x 23'-4"

HOME PLAN

HPK2500139

Style: Craftsman
First Floor: 2,896 sq. ft.
Second Floor: 986 sq. ft.
Total: 3,882 sq. ft.
Bonus Space: 480 sq. ft.
Bedrooms: 4
Bathrooms: 3 ½
Width: 76' - 11"
Depth: 101' - 7"
Foundation: Crawlspace

eplans.com

HPK2500140

Style: Craftsman

Square Footage: 2,816

Bonus Space: 290 sq. ft.

Bedrooms: 4

Bathrooms: 4 ½ + ½

Width: 94' - 0"

Depth: 113' - 6"

Foundation: Slab

eplans.com

A STRIKING FRONT-FACING GABLE, BOLD COLUMNS, AND VARYING ROOFLINES set this design apart from the rest. An angled entry leads to the foyer, flanked on one side by the dining room with a tray ceiling and on the other by a lavish master suite. This suite is enhanced with a private bath, two large walk-in closets, a garden tub, a compartmented toilet and bidet, and access to the covered patio. The parlor also enjoys rear-yard views. The vaulted ceilings provide a sense of spaciousness from the breakfast nook and kitchen to the family room. A laundry room and pantry are accessible from the kitchen area. Two family bedrooms reside on the right side of the plan; each has its own full bath and both are built at interesting angles. An upstairs, vaulted bonus room includes French doors opening to a second-floor sundeck.

LOWER LEVEL

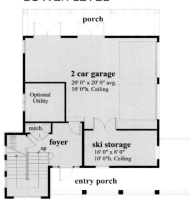

MAIN LEVEL

SECOND LEVEL

HPK2500141

Style: Craftsman

Main Level: 874 sq. ft.

Second Level: 880 sq. ft.

Lower Level: 242 sq. ft.

Total: 1,754 sq. ft.

Bedrooms: 3

Bathrooms: 2 ½

Width: 34' - 0"

Depth: 43' - 0"

Foundation: Unfinished Walkout Basement

eplans.com

A MAGNIFICENT TURRET PROVIDES A GREAT ACCENT TO THE WELL-CRAFTED LOOK of this historic exterior. French doors open the main-level living areas to the outside. Built-in cabinetry frames the massive fireplace, which warms the decor and atmosphere. Arches and columns help define the interior space, lending a sense of privacy to the dining area—a stunning space with views and access to the covered porch. On the upper level, two secondary bedrooms share a full bath. Double doors lead to the master retreat.

© Sater Design Collection, Inc.

© Sater Design Collection, Inc.

ⓘ HPK2500142

Style: New American

First Floor: 1,342 sq. ft.

Second Floor: 511 sq. ft.

Total: 1,853 sq. ft.

Bedrooms: 3

Bathrooms: 2

Width: 44' - 0"

Depth: 40' - 0"

Foundation: Unfinished Basement

eplans.com

FIRST FLOOR

SECOND FLOOR

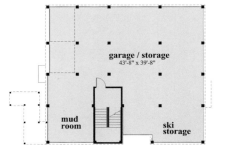

MATCHSTICK DETAILS AND A CAREFUL BLEND OF STONE AND SIDING lend a special style and spirit to this stately retreat. Multipane windows take in the scenery and deck out the refined exterior of this cabin-style home, designed for a life of luxury. An open foyer shares its natural light with the great room—a bright reprieve filled with its own outdoor light. Dinner guests may wander from the coziness of the hearth space into the crisp night air through lovely French doors. The master retreat is an entire wing of the main level.

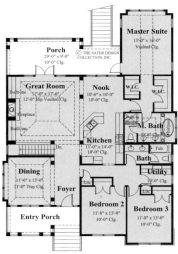

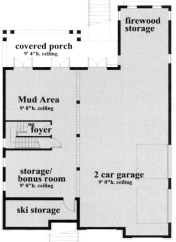

THE HORIZONTAL LINES AND STRAIGHTFORWARD DETAILS OF THIS RUSTIC PLAN borrow freely from the Arts and Crafts style, with a dash of traditional warmth. At the heart of the home, the kitchen and nook bring people together for easy meals and conversation. Clustered sleeping quarters ramble across the right wing and achieve privacy and convenience for the homeowners. The master suite is all decked out with a wall of glass, two walk-in closets, and generous dressing space. On the lower level, a mud area leads in from a covered porch, and the two-car garage leaves plenty of room for bicycles.

HOME PLAN

HPK2500143

Style: **New American**

Square Footage: **2,137**

Bedrooms: **3**

Bathrooms: **2**

Width: **44' - 0"**

Depth: **63' - 0"**

Foundation: **Unfinished Walkout Basement**

eplans.com

© Sater Design Collection, Inc.

STONEWORK AND ELEMENTS OF CRAFTSMAN STYLE MAKE A STRONG STATEMENT but are partnered here with a sweet disposition. Sidelights and transoms enrich the elevation and offer a warm welcome to a well-accoutered interior with up-to-the-minute amenities. A wealth of windows allows gentle breezes to flow through the living space, and French doors extend an invitation to enjoy the rear covered porch. Nearby, a well-organized kitchen offers a pass-through to the great room and service to the formal dining room through a convenient butler's pantry. Upstairs, the master suite sports a private sitting area that opens to an upper deck through French doors. The upper-level gallery provides an overlook to the great room and connects the master retreat with a secondary bedroom that opens to the deck.

HOME PLAN

HPK2500144

Style: Country

First Floor: 1,542 sq. ft.

Second Floor: 971 sq. ft.

Total: 2,513 sq. ft.

Bedrooms: 3

Bathrooms: 3

Width: 46' - 0"

Depth: 51' - 0"

Foundation: Island Basement

eplans.com

FIRST FLOOR

SECOND FLOOR

FIRST FLOOR

SIDING AND SHINGLES GIVE THIS HOME A CRAFTSMAN LOOK while columns and gables suggest a more traditional style. The foyer opens to a short flight of stairs that leads to the great room, which features a lovely coffered ceiling, a fireplace, built-ins, and French doors to the rear veranda. To the left, the open island kitchen has a pass-through to the great room and easy service to the dining bay. The secluded master suite features two walk-in closets, a luxurious bath, and veranda access. Upstairs, two family bedrooms have their own full baths and share a loft area.

HOME PLAN # HPK2500145

Style: New American

First Floor: 2,096 sq. ft.

Second Floor: 892 sq. ft.

Total: 2,988 sq. ft.

Bedrooms: 3

Bathrooms: 3 ½

Width: 56' - 0"

Depth: 54' - 0"

Foundation: Unfinished Walkout Basement

eplans.com

SECOND FLOOR

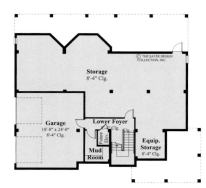

©The Sater Design Collection, Inc.

©The Sater Design Collection, Inc.

HOME PLAN

HPK2500146

Style: Craftsman

Main Level: 2,146 sq. ft.

Second Level: 952 sq. ft.

Lower Level: 187 sq. ft.

Total: 3,285 sq. ft.

Bedrooms: 3

Bathrooms: 3 ½

Width: 52' - 0"

Depth: 65' - 4"

Foundation: Unfinished Walkout Basement

eplans.com

MAIN LEVEL

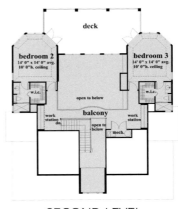

SECOND LEVEL

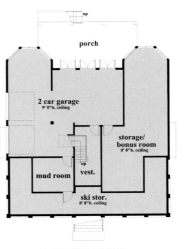

LOWER LEVEL

TALL WINDOWS WRAP THIS NOBLE EXTERIOR WITH DAZZLING DETAILS and allow plenty of natural light inside. A wraparound porch sets a casual but elegant pace for the home, with space for rockers and swings. Well-defined formal rooms are placed just off the foyer. A host of French doors opens the great room to an entertainment porch and inspiring views. Even formal meals take on the ease and comfort of a mountain region in the stunning open dining room. Nearby, a gourmet kitchen packed with amenities serves any occasion.

LOWER LEVEL

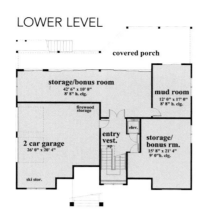

MAIN LEVEL

SECOND LEVEL

HPK2500147

HOME PLAN

Style: New American

Main Level: 2,039 sq. ft.

Second Level: 1,426 sq. ft.

Lower Level: 374 sq. ft.

Total: 3,465 sq. ft.

Bedrooms: 3

Bathrooms: 4

Width: 56' - 0"

Depth: 54' - 0"

Foundation: Unfinished Basement

eplans.com

THIS FABULOUS MOUNTAIN HOME BEGINS WITH A STUNNING TRANSOM that tops a classic paneled door and sets off a host of windows brightening the facade. Inside, a three-sided fireplace and wet bar invite entertaining on any scale, from grand to cozy. The gourmet of the family will easily prepare meals in a well-equipped kitchen. A wide window overlooks the outdoor kitchen area of the patio, which includes a rinsing sink and outdoor grill. An upper level dedicated to the master retreat boasts a wide deck where, on a clear day, the beauty of natural light splashes this room with a sense of the outdoors and mingles with the crackle of the fireplace. Private baths for two provide separate amenities, including an exercise area and a knee-space vanity. Separate garages on the lower level lead to an entry vestibule with both an elevator and stairs.

CLIMATE IS A KEY COMPONENT OF ANY MOUNTAIN RETREAT, and outdoor living is an integral part of its design. This superior cabin features open and covered porches. A mix of matchstick details and rugged stone sets off this lodge-house facade, concealing a well-defined interior. Windows line the breakfast bay and brighten the kitchen, which features a center cooktop island. A door leads out to a covered porch with a summer kitchen. The upper level features a secluded master suite with a spacious bath beginning with a double walk-in closet and ending with a garden view of the porch. A two-sided fireplace extends warmth to the whirlpool spa-style tub.

HOME PLAN # HPK2500148

Style: Craftsman

Main Level: 2,391 sq. ft.

Second Level: 1,539 sq. ft.

Lower Level: 429 sq. ft.

Total: 3,930 sq. ft.

Bedrooms: 3

Bathrooms: 4 ½

Width: 71' - 0"

Depth: 69' - 0"

Foundation: Island Basement

eplans.com

LOWER LEVEL

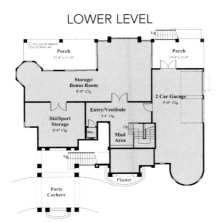

MAIN LEVEL

SECOND LEVEL

A Cottage of One's Own

What if you're not looking to build a second home on a beach or mountainside? What if you're planning to downsize and simply move to a new neighborhood closer to the grandkids? Many plans tend to be location-specific, but ideal homebuilding sites aren't always found in the mountains or by the shore. The homes in our Cottage Country section serve multiple purposes, tastes, styles, and needs, and could be just the type of home you're looking for.

The term "cottage country" encompasses many small homes of various influences. It commonly describes dormered designs with wide front porches clad in vinyl siding, but it can also describe a brick-faced home with a vaulted entry or a European home of stone and stucco. Even some Craftsman and bungalow homes could be considered country cottages. So, no matter what your taste in style is, your taste in homes may be of the cottage country persuasion.

One of the wonderful things about a cottage country home is that it can be

COUNTRY FURNISHINGS and neutral color schemes are good choices for a cottage-style home.

any shape or size yet still maintain its quaint appeal. Your future intentions for the home, however, could very much dictate whether you build a two-story farmhouse or a one-story gingerbread gem. If you plan to use the home for family weekend getaways, more space allows everyone to have the privacy they so desire in a home away from home. If you plan to retire to your new cottage, keep in mind what your future needs may be. Single-level living is kinder to the joints than climbing flights of stairs. And wide rooms and doorways make maneuvering a wheelchair or other medical equipment much less burdensome.

Cottages are often furbished in distressed wood and floral fabrics. This is a common interior design decision for traditionally country homes, but this section includes other

NESTED GABLES AND A WRAPPING PORCH are familiar cottage elements. The oversized front-facing window is a more modern touch.

styles as well. Clerestory dormers can highlight white-painted wooden furnishings and brighten formal dining or living rooms, and a wide rear window may overlook a back porch of wicker rockers from the great room. But Victorian-era tables and chairs could decorate an English countryside design, while plenty of built-ins and comfy couches can adorn the rooms of a bungalow in the woods. Such versatility makes it easy to make a cottage country home uniquely yours.

A WHOLE-HOUSE AUDIO SYSTEM (note the speakers) adds contemporary function to this historically minded family room.

OPTIONAL LAYOUT

FIRST FLOOR

SECOND FLOOR

HOME PLAN

HPK2500149

Style: Cottage

First Floor: 1,001 sq. ft.

Second Floor: 466 sq. ft.

Total: 1,467 sq. ft.

Bonus Space: 292 sq. ft.

Bedrooms: 3

Bathrooms: 2 ½

Width: 42' - 0"

Depth: 42' - 0"

Foundation: Crawlspace, Slab, Unfinished Walkout Basement

eplans.com

ARCHED TRANSOMS SET OFF BY KEYSTONES ADD THE FINAL DETAILS to the traditional exterior of this home. The foyer opens to a vaulted family room, which includes a warm fireplace and leads to a two-story dining area with built-in plant shelves and to a U-shaped kitchen with an angled countertop and spacious pantry. Down the hall, the abundant master suite boasts a tray ceiling and can be found in its own secluded area. Upstairs, two additional bedrooms are found sharing a full bath—note both bedrooms have French doors. An optional bonus room with a walk-in closet is included in this plan.

HOME PLAN

HPK2500150

Style: Cottage

Square Footage: 1,546

Bedrooms: 3

Bathrooms: 2

Width: 37' - 0"

Depth: 65' - 5"

Foundation: Slab

HOME PLAN

HPK2500151

Style: Cottage

Square Footage: 1,124

Bedrooms: 3

Bathrooms: 2

Width: 43' - 4"

Depth: 31' - 6"

Foundation: Unfinished Walkout Basement

COTTAGE COUNTRY

THE STRIKING COMBINATION OF WOOD FRAMING, SHINGLES, AND GLASS CREATES THE EXTERIOR OF THIS CLASSIC COTTAGE. The foyer opens to the main-level layout. To the left of the foyer is a study with a warming hearth and vaulted ceiling; to the right is a formal dining room. A great room with an attached breakfast area sits to the rear near the kitchen. A guest room is nestled in the rear of the plan for privacy. The master suite provides an expansive tray ceiling, a glass sitting area, and easy passage to the outside deck. Upstairs, two bedrooms are accompanied by a loft for a quiet getaway.

HOME PLAN (#) HPK2500152

Style: New American

First Floor: 2,070 sq. ft.

Second Floor: 790 sq. ft.

Total: 2,860 sq. ft.

Bedrooms: 4

Bathrooms: 3 ½

Width: 58' - 4"

Depth: 54' - 10"

Foundation: Finished Walkout Basement

eplans.com

FIRST FLOOR

SECOND FLOOR

FIRST FLOOR

SECOND FLOOR

HOME PLAN

HPK2500153

Style: French Country

First Floor: 1,724 sq. ft.

Second Floor: 700 sq. ft.

Total: 2,424 sq. ft.

Bedrooms: 3

Bathrooms: 2 ½

Width: 47' - 10"

Depth: 63' - 8"

Foundation: Finished Walkout Basement

eplans.com

ALL THE CHARM OF GABLES, STONEWORK, AND MULTILEVEL ROOFLINES combine to create this home. To the left of the foyer, you will see the dining room highlighted by a tray ceiling. This room and the living room flow together to form one large entertainment area. The gourmet kitchen holds a work island and adjoining octagonal breakfast room. The great room is a fantastic living space, featuring a pass-through wet bar, a fireplace, and bookcases. The master suite enjoys privacy at the rear of the home. An open-rail loft above the foyer leads to two additional bedrooms with walk-in closets, private vanities, and a shared bath.

FIRST FLOOR

Deck

Master Bedroom
13³ x 18³

Breakfast
10⁶ x 11⁰

Great Room
17⁹ x 16⁹

Kitchen
10⁶ x 15⁹

Study
11³ x 12⁶

Dining Room
12⁰ x 12³

Porch

© Stephen Fuller, Inc.

Two Car Garage
20³ x 24³

©Stephen Fuller

SECOND FLOOR

Bedroom #2
10⁶ x 14⁰

Bedroom #3
12⁰ x 12⁶

© Stephen Fuller, Inc.

Bedroom #4
11⁰ x 22⁰

REAR EXTERIOR

THIS HOME IS A TRUE SOUTHERN ORIGINAL. INSIDE, the spacious foyer leads directly to a vaulted great room with a handsome fireplace. The dining room, just off the foyer, features a dramatic vaulted ceiling. The kitchen offers both storage and large work areas opening up to the breakfast room. At the rear of the home, you will find the master bedroom with its garden bath, His and Hers vanities, and oversized closet. The second floor provides three additional bedrooms with a shared bath and a balcony overlook.

HOME PLAN

HPK2500154

Style: French Country

First Floor: 1,944 sq. ft.

Second Floor: 1,055 sq. ft.

Total: 2,999 sq. ft.

Bedrooms: 4

Bathrooms: 3 ½

Width: 51' - 6"

Depth: 72' - 0"

Foundation: Finished Walkout Basement

eplans.com

HOME PLAN

HPK2500155

Style: French Country

First Floor: 1,900 sq. ft.

Second Floor: 890 sq. ft.

Total: 2,790 sq. ft.

Bedrooms: 4

Bathrooms: 2 ½

Width: 63' - 0"

Depth: 51' - 0"

Foundation: Finished Walkout Basement

eplans.com

FIRST FLOOR

SECOND FLOOR

A PERFECT BLEND OF STUCCO AND STACKED STONE SETS OFF KEYSTONES, transoms, and arches in this French Country facade to inspire an elegant spirit. The foyer is flanked by the spacious dining room and study, which is accented by a vaulted ceiling and a fireplace. A great room with a full wall of glass connects the interior with the outdoors. A first-floor master suite offers both style and intimacy with a coffered ceiling and a secluded bath.

COTTAGE COUNTRY

FIRST FLOOR

- SITTING
  10-4 X 4-0
  10 FT CLG
- MASTER BEDROOM
  15-8 X 15-6
  11 FT TRAY CLG
- COVERED PORCH
- BRKFST ROOM
  12-8 X 11-0
  10 FT CLG
- FAMILY ROOM
  15-4 X 19-0
  10 FT CLG
  FP
- MASTER BATH
  10 FT CLG
- KITCHEN
- LIVING ROOM
  19-2 X 15-6
  VAULTED TO 2 STORY
  12-8 X 15-4
  10 FT CLG
- UTIL
- BATH 2
- BEDROOM 2
  12-6 X 12-6
  10 FT CLG
- FOYER
  2 STORY
  CLG
- DINING ROOM
  12-0 X 14-0
  10 FT CLG
- PWDR
- STORAGE
- PORCH
- 3 CAR GARAGE
- Larry E. Belk Designs

EUROPEAN ACCENTS SHAPE THE EXTERIOR OF THIS STRIKING FAMILY HOME. Inside, the foyer is open to the dining room on the right and the living room straight ahead. Here, two sets of double doors open to the rear covered porch. Casual areas of the home include a family room warmed by a fireplace and an island kitchen open to a bayed breakfast room. The first-floor master retreat is a luxurious perk, which offers a bayed sitting area, a whirlpool bath, and large His and Hers walk-in closets. The first-floor bedroom—with its close proximity to the master suite—is perfect for a nursery or home office. Upstairs, two more family bedrooms boast walk-in closets and share a bath. Future space is available just off the game room.

HPK2500156

HOME PLAN

Style: French Country

First Floor: 2,654 sq. ft.

Second Floor: 1,013 sq. ft.

Total: 3,667 sq. ft.

Bedrooms: 4

Bathrooms: 3 ½

Width: 75' - 4"

Depth: 74' - 2"

Foundation: Crawlspace, Slab, Unfinished Basement

eplans.com

SECOND FLOOR

- BEDROOM 4
  13-6 X 16-4
- ATTIC
- OPEN TO BELOW
- BATH 3
- GAME ROOM
  14-6 X 17-6
- OPEN TO BELOW
- BEDROOM 3
  11-6 X 13-6
- EXPANDABLE
  12-0 X 16-0
  8 FT CLG
- 5 FT KNEE WALL
- 5 FT KNEE WALL

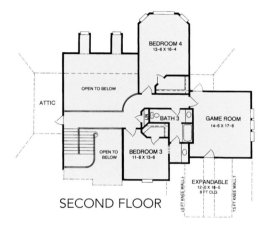

FIRST FLOOR

MASTER BEDRM
13-4 X 16-4
10 FT TRAY CLG

BRKFST ROOM
11-4 X 13-0
10 FT TRAY CLG

PORCH

KITCHEN
16-6 X 13-4
9 FT CLG

MASTER BATH

GREAT ROOM
17-0 X 20-6
10 FT TRAY CLG

DESK

PAN

BATH 2

STORAGE

UTIL
11-4 X 8-0
9 FT CLG

GARAGE

DINING ROOM
12-6 X 13-4
10 FT CLG

FOYER
2 STORY CLG

ARCH

BEDROOM 2
12-6 X 13-6
9 FT CLG

PORCH

© Larry E. Belk Designs

SECOND FLOOR

ATTIC

EXPANDABLE AREA
17-4 X 18-0

BEDROOM 4
13-4 X 10-4

BATH 3

OPEN TO
FOYER BELOW

BEDROOM 3
13-0 X 11-6

PLANT LEDGE

HOME PLAN

(#) HPK2500157

Style: Country

First Floor: 2,028 sq. ft.

Second Floor: 558 sq. ft.

Total: 2,586 sq. ft.

Bonus Space: 272 sq. ft.

Bedrooms: 4

Bathrooms: 3

Width: 64' - 10"

Depth: 61' - 0"

Foundation: Crawlspace, Slab, Unfinished Basement

eplans.com

DOUBLE COLUMNS AND AN ARCH-TOP CLERESTORY WINDOW create an inviting entry to this fresh interpretation of traditional style. Decorative columns and arches open to the formal dining room and to the octagonal great room, which has a 10-foot tray ceiling. The U-shaped kitchen looks over an angled counter to a breakfast bay that brings in the outdoors and shares a through-fireplace with the great room. A sitting area and a lavish bath set off the secluded master suite. A nearby secondary bedroom with its own bath could be used as a guest suite. Upstairs, two family bedrooms share a full bath and a hall that leads to an expandable area.

COTTAGE COUNTRY

FIRST FLOOR

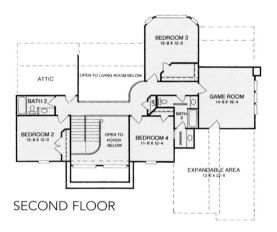

SECOND FLOOR

FLOWER BOXES, ARCHES, AND MULTIPANE WINDOWS COMBINE TO CREATE THE ELEGANT FACADE of this four-bedroom home. Inside, the two-story foyer introduces a formal dining room to its right and leads to a two-story living room that is filled with light. An efficient kitchen has a bayed breakfast room and shares a snack bar with a cozy family room. Located on the first floor for privacy, the master suite is graced with a luxurious bath. Upstairs, three secondary bedrooms share two full baths and access a large game room. For future growth there is an expandable area accessed through the game room.

HOME PLAN

(#) HPK2500158

Style: New American

First Floor: 1,919 sq. ft.

Second Floor: 1,190 sq. ft.

Total: 3,109 sq. ft.

Bonus Space: 286 sq. ft.

Bedrooms: 4

Bathrooms: 3 ½

Width: 64' - 6"

Depth: 55' - 10"

Foundation: Crawlspace, Slab, Unfinished Basement

eplans.com

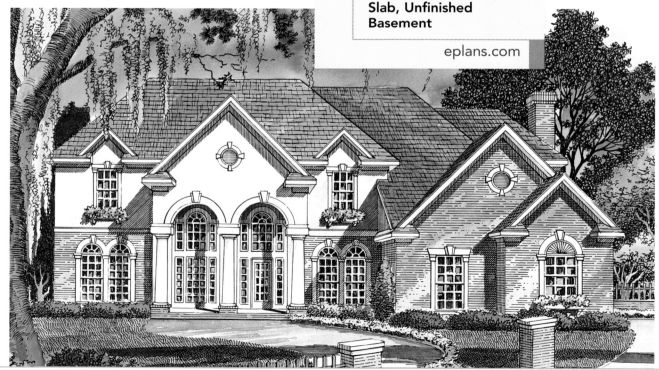

DESIGNED FOR UTMOST LIVABILITY, THIS ENGLISH MINI-ESTATE IS FULL OF CHARM. A turret entrance leads to the vaulted foyer and the great room beyond. An adjacent kitchen features a 42-inch breakfast bar, a walk-in pantry, and a planning desk. The spacious, multiwindowed breakfast room allows access to the octagonal porch perfect for outdoor dining. Located on the first floor, the master suite includes a relaxing master bath and an enormous walk-in closet. The second floor holds an additional bedroom and a full bath. A large expandable area is available off the balcony and can be used for storage or finished for additional living space.

HOME PLAN

HPK2500159

Style: Tudor
First Floor: 1,276 sq. ft.
Second Floor: 378 sq. ft.
Total: 1,654 sq. ft.
Bedrooms: 2
Bathrooms: 2 ½
Width: 54' - 4"
Depth: 53' - 10"
Foundation: Crawlspace, Slab

eplans.com

FIRST FLOOR

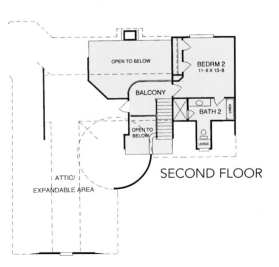

SECOND FLOOR

REMINISCENT OF THE POPULAR TOWNHOUSES OF THE PAST, this fine clapboard home is perfect for urban or riverfront living. Two balconies grace the second floor—one at the front and one on the side. A two-way fireplace between the formal living and dining rooms provides visual impact. Built-in bookcases flank an arched opening between these rooms. A pass-through from the kitchen to the dining room simplifies serving, and a walk-in pantry provides storage. On the second floor, the master bedroom opens to a large balcony, and the relaxing master bath is designed with a separate shower and an angled whirlpool tub. Two secondary bedrooms and a full bath are located at the rear of the plan.

HOME PLAN

HPK2500160

Style: **Neoclassical**

First Floor: **904 sq. ft.**

Second Floor: **1,058 sq. ft.**

Total: **1,962 sq. ft.**

Bedrooms: **3**

Bathrooms: **2 ½**

Width: **22' - 0"**

Depth: **74' - 0"**

Foundation: **Crawlspace, Slab**

eplans.com

FIRST FLOOR

SECOND FLOOR

A SIX-PANEL DOOR WITH AN ARCHED TRANSOM MAKES AN IMPRESSIVE ENTRY. Upon entering the foyer, find the formal dining room to the right. The great room comes complete with a cozy fireplace and built-ins. On the far left of the home, two bedrooms share a full bath and a linen closet. The kitchen and breakfast room provide ample space for the family to enjoy meals together. The rear porch is accessible from a rear bedroom and from an angled door between the great room and breakfast room. In the master bedroom, two walk-in closets provide plenty of space, and two separate vanities make dressing less crowded.

 # HPK2500161

Style: Federal - Adams

Square Footage: 2,046

Bedrooms: 3

Bathrooms: 2 ½

Width: 68' - 2"

Depth: 57' - 4"

Foundation: Crawlspace, Slab, Unfinished Basement

eplans.com

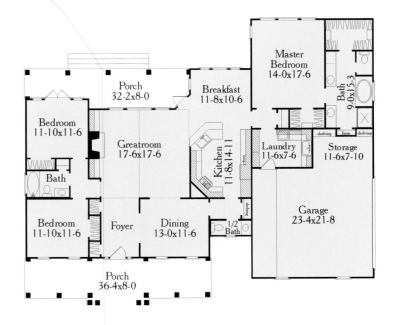

Bedroom 11-10x11-6

Bath

Bedroom 11-10x11-6

Porch 32-2x8-0

Greatroom 17-6x17-6

Kitchen 11-8x14-11

Foyer

Dining 13-0x11-6

Porch 36-4x8-0

Breakfast 11-8x10-6

Master Bedroom 14-0x17-6

Bath 9-0x15-3

Laundry 11-6x7-6

shelving linen shelving

Storage 11-6x7-10

1/2 Bath

Garage 23-4x21-8

COTTAGE COUNTRY

FIRST FLOOR

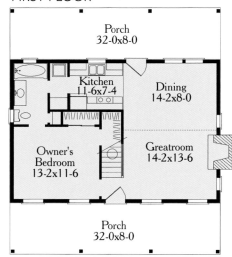

Porch
32-0x8-0

Kitchen
11-6x7-4

Dining
14-2x8-0

Owner's
Bedroom
13-2x11-6

Greatroom
14-2x13-6

Porch
32-0x8-0

SECOND FLOOR

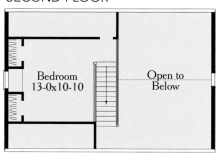

Bedroom
13-0x10-10

Open to
Below

THIS COMPACT DESIGN OFFERS A HOST OF EXTRAS, beginning with its charming exterior. Wide, country-style porches grace both the front and back of this cozy home. The focus of the interior centers on the open living area with a vaulted ceiling. Split into a great room and dining room, this area includes a large, warming fireplace and lots of windows for outdoor viewing and increased natural lighting. The fully equipped kitchen is located near the rear porch for convenient outdoor dining. The master bedroom finishes the first floor. An extra bedroom upstairs includes two closets. Storage space is located in the eaves.

HPK2500162

HOME PLAN

Style: Country

First Floor: 720 sq. ft.

Second Floor: 203 sq. ft.

Total: 923 sq. ft.

Bedrooms: 2

Bathrooms: 1

Width: 32' - 0"

Depth: 38' - 6"

Foundation: Crawlspace, Slab, Unfinished Basement

eplans.com

HOME PLAN

HPK2500163

Style: Farmhouse

Square Footage: 2,090

Bedrooms: 3

Bathrooms: 2 ½

Width: 84' - 6"

Depth: 64' - 0"

Foundation: Crawlspace

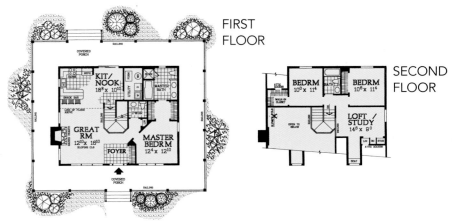

HOME PLAN

HPK2500164

Style: Farmhouse

First Floor: 1,093 sq. ft.

Second Floor: 603 sq. ft.

Total: 1,696 sq. ft.

Bedrooms: 3

Bathrooms: 2 ½

Width: 52' - 0"

Depth: 46' - 0"

Foundation: Crawlspace

FIRST FLOOR

SECOND FLOOR

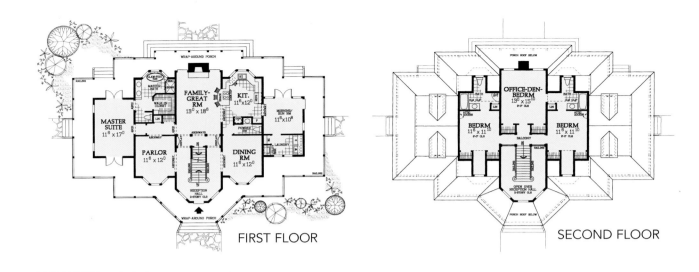

FIRST FLOOR

SECOND FLOOR

HOME PLAN

HPK2500165

Style: Victorian Eclectic

First Floor: 1,752 sq. ft.

Second Floor: 906 sq. ft.

Total: 2,658 sq. ft.

Bedrooms: 4

Bathrooms: 3 ½

Width: 74' - 0"

Depth: 51' - 7"

Foundation: Unfinished Basement

eplans.com

DELIGHTFULLY PROPORTIONED AND SUPERBLY SYMMETRICAL, THIS VICTORIAN FARMHOUSE has lots of curb appeal. The wrap-around porch offers rustic columns and railings, and broad steps present easy access to the front, rear, and side yards. Archways, display niches, and columns help define the great room, which offers a fireplace framed by views to the rear property. A formal parlor and a dining room flank the reception hall, and each offers a bay window. The master suite boasts two sets of French doors to the wraparound porch and a private bath with a clawfoot tub, twin lavatories, a walk-in closet, and a stall shower. Upstairs, a spacious office/den adjoins two family bedrooms and can serve as a guest room.

THIS QUAINT, COUNTRY-STYLE COTTAGE would make a fine vacation retreat. Balusters and columns deck out the wraparound porch, and the glass-paneled entry offers an elegant welcome. With a cozy fireplace and plenty of views in the great room, the interior is warmed by more than just heat—it enjoys a charming sense of the outdoors. The spacious great room provides an area for good conversation and plenty of relaxation. A well-organized kitchen has its own door to the wraparound porch. Upstairs, two bedrooms—each with a private bathroom—complete the plan.

HPK2500166

Style: Country
First Floor: 586 sq. ft.
Second Floor: 486 sq. ft.
Total: 1,072 sq. ft.
Bedrooms: 2
Bathrooms: 2 ½
Width: 40' - 0"
Depth: 40' - 0"
Foundation: Crawlspace

eplans.com

FIRST FLOOR

SECOND FLOOR

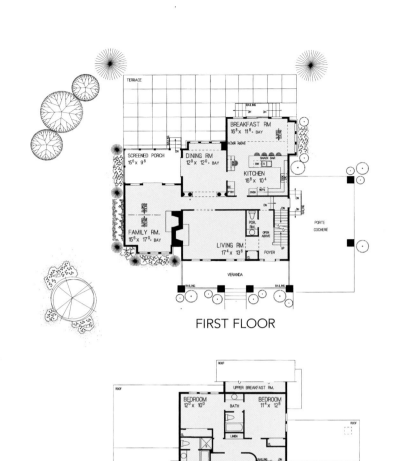

FIRST FLOOR

SECOND FLOOR

COZY LIVING ABOUNDS IN THIS COMFORTABLE TWO-STORY BUNGALOW. Enter the foyer and find a spacious living room with a fireplace to the left. The bayed family room features a fireplace and entry to a screened porch. Upstairs, secondary bedrooms offer ample closet space and direct access to a shared bath. The master suite contains a large walk-in closet, a double-bowl vanity, and a compartmented shower and toilet.

HPK2500167

HOME PLAN

Style: Craftsman

First Floor: 1,482 sq. ft.

Second Floor: 885 sq. ft.

Total: 2,367 sq. ft.

Bedrooms: 3

Bathrooms: 2 ½

Width: 64' - 0"

Depth: 50' - 0"

Foundation: Unfinished Basement

eplans.com

THE MASSIVE HIPPED ROOF OF THIS HOME CREATES AN IMPRESSIVE FACADE, and varying roof planes and projecting gables further enhance appeal. A central foyer routes traffic efficiently to the sleeping, formal, and informal zones of the house. Note the sliding glass doors that provide access to outdoor living facilities. A built-in china cabinet and planter unit are fine decor features. In the angular kitchen, a high ceiling and efficient work design set the pace. The conversation room may act as a multipurpose room. Sleeping quarters take off in the spacious master suite with a tray ceiling and sliding doors to the rear yard. Two sizable bedrooms accommodate family members or guests.

HOME PLAN

 # HPK2500168

Style: New American
Square Footage: 2,881
Bedrooms: 3
Bathrooms: 2 ½
Width: 77' - 11"
Depth: 73' - 11"
Foundation: Unfinished Basement

eplans.com

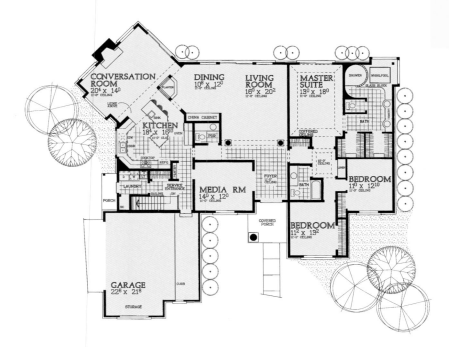

HOME PLAN

 # HPK2500169

Style: **Cottage**

Square Footage: **1,389**

Bedrooms: **3**

Bathrooms: **2**

Width: **44' - 8"**

Depth: **54' - 6"**

Foundation: **Slab**

eplans.com

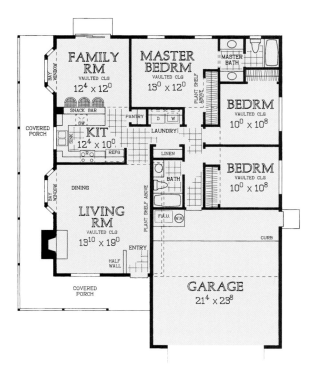

TWO EXTERIORS, ONE FLOOR PLAN—WHAT MORE COULD YOU ASK? Simple rooflines and an inviting porch enhance the floor plan. A formal living room has a warming fireplace and a delightful bay window. The U-shaped kitchen shares a snack bar with the bayed family room. Note the sliding glass doors to the rear yard here. Three bedrooms include two family bedrooms served by a full bath and a lovely master suite with its own private bath.

HOME PLAN

HPK2500170

Style: Farmhouse

First Floor: 1,099 sq. ft.

Second Floor: 535 sq. ft.

Total: 1,634 sq. ft.

Bedrooms: 3

Bathrooms: 2

Width: 44' - 8"

Depth: 41' - 4"

Foundation: Crawlspace, Unfinished Basement

FIRST FLOOR

SECOND FLOOR

OPTIONAL LAYOUT

HOME PLAN

HPK2500171

Style: Country

Square Footage: 1,360

Bedrooms: 3

Bathrooms: 2

Width: 64' - 0"

Depth: 38' - 0"

Foundation: Crawlspace, Unfinished Basement

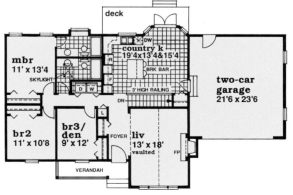

THIS CAPE COD DESIGN IS ENHANCED WITH SHINGLES, STONE DETAILING, AND MUNTIN WINDOWS. The entry is flanked on the left by a bedroom/den, perfect for overnight guests or as a cozy place to relax. The hearth-warmed great room enjoys expansive views of the rear deck area. The dining room is nestled next to the island kitchen, which boasts plenty of counter space. The master bedroom is positioned at the rear of the home for privacy and accesses its own bath. Two family bedrooms and a spacious games room complete the finished basement.

MAIN LEVEL

HOME PLAN

HPK2500172

Style: Cottage

Main Level: 1,544 sq. ft.

Lower Level: 1,018 sq. ft.

Total: 2,562 sq. ft.

Bedrooms: 4

Bathrooms: 3

Width: 40' - 0"

Depth: 60' - 0"

Foundation: Finished Walkout Basement

eplans.com

LOWER LEVEL

HPK2500173

Style: Cottage

Main Level: 1,230 sq. ft.

Lower Level: 769 sq. ft.

Total: 1,999 sq. ft.

Bedrooms: 3

Bathrooms: 2 ½

Width: 40' - 0"

Depth: 52' - 6"

Foundation: Finished Walkout Basement

eplans.com

HOME PLAN

MAIN LEVEL

DECK

VAULTED
MASTER
16/2 X 13/0

SCISSOR VAULTED
LIVING/DINING
15/2 X 20/2

D. W.

LIN.

PAN.

GARAGE
19/6 X 20/0

REF.

DEN
11/0 X 10/0
(10' CLG.)

DN.

LOWER LEVEL

BR. 2
10/6 X 12/8

BR. 3
10/8 X 11/0

REC. RM.
14/10 X 12/8

CRAWLSPACE

UP

STORAGE

THIS PETITE COUNTRY COTTAGE DESIGN IS ENHANCED WITH ALL THE MODERN AMENITIES. Inside, through a pair of double doors, the family den is illuminated by a large window. The kitchen, which features efficient pantry space, opens to the living/dining area. This spacious room is highlighted by a scissor vaulted ceiling, and features a warming fireplace and nook space. The living/dining room also overlooks a large rear deck, which is accessed through a back door. Secluded on the ground level for extra privacy, the vaulted master bedroom includes a private full bath and a walk-in closet. A laundry room, two-car garage, and powder room all complete this floor. Downstairs, two additional family bedrooms share a hall bath. The recreation room is an added bonus. Extra storage space is also available on this floor.

HOME PLAN

HPK2500174

Style: Cottage
Square Footage: 1,580
Bedrooms: 3
Bathrooms: 2 ½
Width: 50' - 0"
Depth: 48' - 0"
Foundation: Crawlspace

HOME PLAN

HPK2500175

Style: Bungalow
Square Footage: 1,275
Bedrooms: 3
Bathrooms: 2
Width: 40' - 0"
Depth: 58' - 0"
Foundation: Crawlspace

FIRST FLOOR

COVD PORCH

NOOK
11-0 x 11-0

KITCHEN
15-0 x 15-0

FAMILY
15-6 x 17-0

DINING
11-0 x 15-0

UTILITY

LIVING
13-0 x 17-0

UP

PDR

FOYER

DEN
11-0 x 15-0

3-CAR GARAGE
25-0 x 31-0

COVD PORCH

SECOND FLOOR

SITTING
11-0 x 11-0

MSTR BEDRM
13-6 x 17-2

WIC

MSTR BATH

DN

LANDING

BA 2

BEDRM 2
11-4 x 12-2

OPEN

HALL

WIC

BEDRM 3
11-0 x 13-2

BA 3

BONUS
15-0 x 13-2

GUEST BEDRM
13-0 x 13-6

HPK2500176

Style: Craftsman
First Floor: 1,735 sq. ft.
Second Floor: 1,855 sq. ft.
Total: 3,590 sq. ft.
Bedrooms: 4
Bathrooms: 3 ½
Width: 74' - 0"
Depth: 72' - 0"
Foundation: Crawlspace

HOME PLAN

eplans.com

REAR EXTERIOR

SHINGLES AND STONE BLEND SEAMLESSLY to create a striking facade worthy of any upscale neighborhood. The interior reveals an open floor plan distinguished by a variety of room shapes and upgraded amenities. Four fireplaces, including one on the covered porch, add to the rustic ambiance of this Craftsman home. The family bedrooms are housed on the second floor, highlighted by the impressive master suite. The spacious sitting room boasts an octagonal view of the backyard and beyond.

COTTAGE COUNTRY

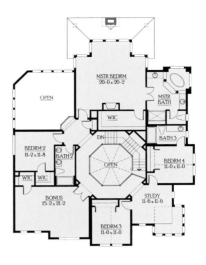

FIRST FLOOR

SECOND FLOOR

WIDE COLUMNS, EXPOSED EAVES, AND SQUARE WINDOWS reveal the Craftsman influence of this home. Inside, a circular layout places the formal rooms toward the front of the plan and informal rooms toward the rear. All revolve around a central rotunda formed by a curving staircase to the second floor. Here, a wall of windows refreshes the rear-facing master bedroom with natural light. A master bath is equipped with a corner tub, standing shower, and compartmented toilet. The walk-in closet is behind the bedroom's fireplace. Down the hall and around the rotunda, three more bedrooms share two full baths, a bonus room, and a study with a balcony.

REAR EXTERIOR

HPK2500177

Style: Craftsman
First Floor: 2,000 sq. ft.
Second Floor: 2,084 sq. ft.
Total: 4,084 sq. ft.
Bedrooms: 4
Bathrooms: 3 ½
Width: 66' - 6"
Depth: 74' - 0"
Foundation: Crawlspace

eplans.com

HOME PLAN

HPK2500178

Style: Craftsman

First Floor: 1,230 sq. ft.

Second Floor: 1,190 sq. ft.

Total: 2,420 sq. ft.

Bedrooms: 4

Bathrooms: 2 ½

Width: 62' - 0"

Depth: 42' - 0"

Foundation: Crawlspace

FIRST FLOOR

SECOND FLOOR

HOME PLAN

HPK2500179

Style: Craftsman

First Floor: 1,450 sq. ft.

Second Floor: 1,470 sq. ft.

Total: 2,920 sq. ft.

Bedrooms: 3

Bathrooms: 2 ½

Width: 65' - 0"

Depth: 54' - 0"

Foundation: Crawlspace

FIRST FLOOR

SECOND FLOOR

COTTAGE COUNTRY

HOME PLAN #

HPK2500180

Style: Craftsman

First Floor: 1,400 sq. ft.

Second Floor: 1,482 sq. ft.

Total: 2,882 sq. ft.

Bedrooms: 3

Bathrooms: 2 ½

Width: 40' - 0"

Depth: 61' - 6"

Foundation: Crawlspace

FIRST FLOOR

SECOND FLOOR

HOME PLAN #

HPK2500181

Style: Craftsman

First Floor: 1,239 sq. ft.

Second Floor: 1,168 sq. ft.

Total: 2,407 sq. ft.

Bedrooms: 4

Bathrooms: 2 ½

Width: 50' - 0"

Depth: 40' - 0"

Foundation: Crawlspace

FIRST FLOOR

SECOND FLOOR

HOME PLAN
HPK2500182

Style: Craftsman
First Floor: 1,085 sq. ft.
Second Floor: 1,045 sq. ft.
Total: 2,130 sq. ft.
Bedrooms: 3
Bathrooms: 2 ½
Width: 48' - 0"
Depth: 38' - 0"
Foundation: Crawlspace

FIRST FLOOR

SECOND FLOOR

HOME PLAN
HPK2500183

Style: Craftsman
First Floor: 1,100 sq. ft.
Second Floor: 1,054 sq. ft.
Total: 2,154 sq. ft.
Bedrooms: 3
Bathrooms: 2 ½
Width: 58' - 0"
Depth: 40' - 0"
Foundation: Crawlspace

FIRST FLOOR

SECOND FLOOR

COTTAGE COUNTRY

THIS LOVELY COUNTRY DESIGN FEATURES A STUNNING WRAPPING PORCH and plenty of windows to provide the interior with natural light. The living room boasts a centered fireplace that helps to define this spacious open area. A nine-foot ceiling on the first floor adds a sense of spaciousness and light. The casual living room leads outdoors to a rear porch. Upstairs, four bedrooms cluster around a central hall. The master suite sports a walk-in closet and a deluxe bath with an oval tub and a separate shower.

FIRST FLOOR

SECOND FLOOR

HPK2500184

HOME PLAN

Style: Country

First Floor: 1,060 sq. ft.

Second Floor: 1,039 sq. ft.

Total: 2,099 sq. ft.

Bedrooms: 4

Bathrooms: 2 ½

Width: 50' - 8"

Depth: 39' - 4"

Foundation: Unfinished Basement

eplans.com

HPK2500185

Style: Country

First Floor: 1,319 sq. ft.

Second Floor: 1,107 sq. ft.

Total: 2,426 sq. ft.

Bedrooms: 3

Bathrooms: 2 ½

Width: 52' - 0"

Depth: 46' - 8"

Foundation: Unfinished Basement

eplans.com

THE TRADITIONAL CHARM OF THIS FAMILY HOME OFFERS A DISTINCT AMERICAN FLAVOR. Horizontal siding and a quaint wraparound front porch are sure signs of country styling. To the left of the foyer, the home office is a quiet retreat. To the right is a combined living and dining room area. The gourmet kitchen features a snack bar overlooking the rear porch and is open to a casual family area with a fireplace. A two-car garage, laundry room, and half-bath complete the first floor. Upstairs, the master suite offers a private bath and massive walk-in closet.

FIRST FLOOR

SECOND FLOOR

COTTAGE COUNTRY

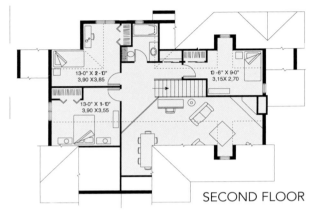

FIRST FLOOR

SECOND FLOOR

PERFECT FOR WATERFRONT PROPERTY, the home is designed for great views from the rear of the plan. Inside, open planning can be found in the living room, which offers a corner fireplace for cool evenings and blends beautifully into the dining and kitchen areas. For chores and storage, the laundry room is conveniently nestled between the kitchen and the two-car garage. The master suite features a walk-through closet and sumptuous bath. Upstairs, three uniquely shaped bedrooms share a full bath.

HOME PLAN

HPK2500186

Style: Cottage

First Floor: 1,347 sq. ft.

Second Floor: 690 sq. ft.

Total: 2,037 sq. ft.

Bedrooms: 4

Bathrooms: 2

Width: 55' - 0"

Depth: 41' - 0"

Foundation: Unfinished Basement

eplans.com

FRONT EXTERIOR

STONE-AND-WOOD SIDING ECHO THE GREAT OUTDOORS IN THIS DESIGN. A small porch is perfect for dusting off the snow and stargazing on dark winter nights. Inside, a fireplace warms up the living room. The kitchen provides an area for a dining table, plenty of work space, and storage with a corner window sink. The master bedroom has a spacious walk-in closet and has a full bath with a dual-sink vanity. On the second level, two family bedrooms share a full bath and the loft overlook to the living room.

FRONT EXTERIOR

HOME PLAN

HPK2500187

Style: Craftsman
First Floor: 1,108 sq. ft.
Second Floor: 517 sq. ft.
Total: 1,625 sq. ft.
Bedrooms: 3
Bathrooms: 2
Width: 36' - 0"
Depth: 36' - 0"
Foundation: Unfinished Basement

eplans.com

COTTAGE COUNTRY

FIRST FLOOR

SECOND FLOOR

FIRST FLOOR

THIS CHARMING COUNTRY TRADITIONAL HOME PROVIDES A WELL-LIT HOME OFFICE harbored in a beautiful bay with three windows. The second-floor bay brightens the master bath, which has a double-bowl vanity, a step-up tub, and a dressing area. The living and dining rooms share a two-sided fireplace. The gourmet kitchen has a cooktop island counter and enjoys outdoor views through sliding glass doors in the breakfast area. A sizable bonus room above the two-car garage can be developed into hobby space or a recreation room.

HOME PLAN

HPK2500188

Style: Victorian Eclectic

First Floor: 1,044 sq. ft.

Second Floor: 892 sq. ft.

Total: 1,936 sq. ft.

Bonus Space: 228 sq. ft.

Bedrooms: 3

Bathrooms: 2 ½

Width: 58' - 0"

Depth: 43' - 6"

Foundation: Unfinished Basement

eplans.com

SECOND FLOOR

COUNTRY FINESSE AND STYLISH CHARM PRESENT A LOVELY SIDING-AND-STONE EXTERIOR. The rear of the house encourages outdoor relaxation with abundant porches, an elegant bayed turret, and a graceful curved stairway cascading from the second-floor porch to the rear patio. Inside, the family room is warmed by a large fireplace and the dining room is illuminated by the spectacular turret bay. The first-floor master suite is enchanting with a walk-in closet and a private bath. Upstairs, two family bedrooms share a full hall bath and a study loft area.

FRONT EXTERIOR

HOME PLAN

HPK2500189

Style: Craftsman

First Floor: 1,301 sq. ft.

Second Floor: 652 sq. ft.

Total: 1,953 sq. ft.

Bonus Space: 342 sq. ft.

Bedrooms: 3

Bathrooms: 2 ½

Width: 58' - 0"

Depth: 55' - 0"

Foundation: Unfinished Basement

eplans.com

FIRST FLOOR

SECOND FLOOR

COTTAGE COUNTRY

FIRST FLOOR

SECOND FLOOR

THIS MODERN FARMHOUSE BLENDS WELL INTO A MOUNTAIN OR SEASIDE SETTING. The wrapping front porch welcomes you inside to a foyer flanked by a dining room and study. The octagonal great room features a fireplace and three sets of double doors to the rear porch. The gourmet kitchen serves a bayed nook. The master suite offers two walk-in closets.

HOME PLAN

HPK2500190

Style: French Country
First Floor: 1,874 sq. ft.
Second Floor: 901 sq. ft.
Total: 2,775 sq. ft.
Bonus Space: 424 sq. ft.
Bedrooms: 3
Bathrooms: 3 ½
Width: 90' - 6"
Depth: 61' - 0"
Foundation: Crawlspace

eplans.com

© Sater Design Collection, Inc.

AN ENCHANTING CENTER GABLE ANNOUNCES A GRACEFUL, HONEST ARCHITECTURE that's at home with the easygoing nature of this coastal design. A columned porch and romantic fretwork lend balance and proportion outside. The great room, featuring double doors, arches, a built-in entertainment center, and a warming fireplace, is the heart of this home. The kitchen is adjoined to the dining room (with French doors) by an eating bar and provides a walk-in pantry. The foyer stairs lead to a master suite with a spacious bedroom and a lavish private bath.

REAR EXTERIOR

HOME PLAN #HPK2500191

Style: Mediterranean
First Floor: 1,007 sq. ft.
Second Floor: 869 sq. ft.
Total: 1,876 sq. ft.
Bedrooms: 3
Bathrooms: 3
Width: 43' - 8"
Depth: 53' - 6"
Foundation: Unfinished Basement

eplans.com

FIRST FLOOR

SECOND FLOOR

GRACEFUL DORMERS TOP A WELCOMING COVERED PORCH THAT IS ENHANCED BY VICTORIAN DETAILS on this fine three-bedroom home. Inside, the foyer leads past the formal dining room back to the spacious two-story great room. Here, a fireplace, built-ins, and outdoor access make any gathering special. The nearby kitchen features a work island, a pantry, a serving bar, and an adjacent bayed breakfast area. Located on the first floor for privacy, the master suite is designed to pamper. Upstairs, two family bedrooms share a hall bath. Note the bonus space above the two-car garage.

HOME PLAN

(#) HPK2500192

Style: Cottage

First Floor: 1,819 sq. ft.

Second Floor: 638 sq. ft.

Total: 2,457 sq. ft.

Bonus Space: 385 sq. ft.

Bedrooms: 3

Bathrooms: 2 ½

Width: 47' - 4"

Depth: 82' - 8"

Foundation: Crawlspace, Unfinished Basement

eplans.com

FIRST FLOOR

SECOND FLOOR

© 1996 William E. Poole Designs, Inc.

© 1996 William E. Poole Designs, Inc.

HOME PLAN

(#) HPK2500193

Style: Cottage

Square Footage: 2,151

Bonus Space: 814 sq. ft.

Bedrooms: 3

Bathrooms: 2

Width: 61' - 0"

Depth: 55' - 8"

Foundation: Crawlspace, Unfinished Basement

eplans.com

COUNTRY FLAVOR IS WELL ESTABLISHED ON THIS FINE THREE-BEDROOM HOME. The covered front porch welcomes friends and family alike to the foyer, where the formal dining room opens to the left. The vaulted ceiling in the great room enhances the wall of windows with backyard views. An efficient kitchen blends well with the bayed breakfast area. The secluded master suite offers a walk-in closet and a lavish bath; on the other side of the home, two family bedrooms share a full bath. Upstairs, an optional fourth bedroom is available for guests or in-laws and provides access to a large recreation room.

FIRST FLOOR

SECOND FLOOR

IMAGINE DRIVING UP TO THIS COTTAGE BEAUTY AT THE END OF A LONG WEEK. The long wraparound porch, hipped rooflines, and shuttered windows will transport you. Inside, the foyer is flanked by a living room on the left and a formal dining room on the right. Across the gallery hall, the hearth-warmed family room will surely become the hub of the home. To the right, the spacious kitchen boasts a worktop island counter, ample pantry space, and a breakfast area. A short hallway opens to the utility room and the two-car garage. The master suite takes up the entire left wing of the home, with an elegant private bath and a seemingly endless walk-in closet. Upstairs, three more bedrooms reside, sharing two full baths. Expandable future space awaits on the right.

HOME PLAN

HPK2500194

Style: Farmhouse
First Floor: 2,142 sq. ft.
Second Floor: 960 sq. ft.
Total: 3,102 sq. ft.
Bonus Space: 327 sq. ft.
Bedrooms: 4
Bathrooms: 3 ½
Width: 75' - 8"
Depth: 53' - 0"
Foundation: Crawlspace

eplans.com

ELEGANT COUNTRY—THAT'S ONE WAY TO DESCRIBE THIS ATTRACTIVE THREE-BEDROOM HOME. Inside, comfort is the theme, with the formal dining room flowing into the U-shaped kitchen and casual dining place in the sunny breakfast area. The spacious, vaulted great room offers a fireplace and built-ins. The first-floor master suite is complete with a walk-in closet, a whirlpool tub, and a separate shower. Upstairs, the sleeping quarters include two family bedrooms with private baths and walk-in closets.

HOME PLAN

HPK2500195

Style: Farmhouse
First Floor: 1,704 sq. ft.
Second Floor: 734 sq. ft.
Total: 2,438 sq. ft.
Bonus Space: 479 sq. ft.
Bedrooms: 3
Bathrooms: 3 ½
Width: 50' - 0"
Depth: 82' - 6"
Foundation: Crawlspace

eplans.com

FIRST FLOOR

SECOND FLOOR

COTTAGE COUNTRY

©1997 William E Poole Designs, Inc.

HOME PLAN
HPK2500196

Style: Farmhouse

First Floor: 1,776 sq. ft.

Second Floor: 643 sq. ft.

Total: 2,419 sq. ft.

Bonus Space: 367 sq. ft.

Bedrooms: 4

Bathrooms: 3

Width: 61' - 8"

Depth: 74' - 4"

Foundation: Crawlspace, Unfinished Basement

FIRST FLOOR

SECOND FLOOR

HOME PLAN
HPK2500197

Style: Federal - Adams

Square Footage: 2,777

Bonus Space: 424 sq. ft.

Bedrooms: 3

Bathrooms: 2 ½

Width: 75' - 6"

Depth: 60' - 2"

Foundation: Crawlspace, Unfinished Basement

© 1995 William E Poole Designs, Inc.

©1997 William E Poole Designs, Inc.

SOMEWHAT RUSTIC IN NATURE, THIS DELIGHTFUL ONE-AND-A-HALF STORY HOME offers charm with elements borrowed from the Stick style of the mid-19th Century. The interior offers a very modern, open floor plan that allows freedom of movement from room to room. The central staircase is the hub from which the living spaces radiate. The formal dining room is at the front with elegant columns and the spacious great room is at the rear. The angled kitchen with its island work space adjoins the sunny breakfast area to the left where a short hall leads to the two-car garage and a secondary staircase leads to the future rec room. On the right, the master suite finds privacy being separated from the family bedrooms that reside on the second floor.

HOME PLAN

HPK2500198

Style: Country

First Floor: 1,712 sq. ft.

Second Floor: 668 sq. ft.

Total: 2,380 sq. ft.

Bonus Space: 573 sq. ft.

Bedrooms: 3

Bathrooms: 2 ½

Width: 86' - 0"

Depth: 50' - 2"

Foundation: Crawlspace, Unfinished Basement

eplans.com

FIRST FLOOR

SECOND FLOOR

COTTAGE COUNTRY

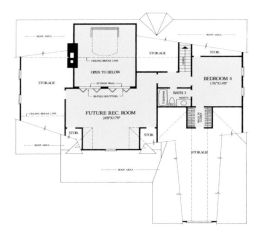

THIS HOME MAINTAINS TRUE COUNTRY AMBIANCE while achieving a very modern layout. Shuttered windows and porch details add charm to the facade. Enter the large foyer to find a formal dining room to the right and a sophisticated gallery hall straight ahead. The great room lies just beyond, complete with built-in shelves, a fireplace, and views of the rear property. The adjacent bayed breakfast nook is open to a counter-filled kitchen. Two family bedrooms share a full bath; the stunning master suite enjoys its own luxurious bath on the right. Upstairs, a wealth of future expansion space awaits.

HPK2500199

HOME PLAN

Style: Cottage

Square Footage: 2,151

Bonus Space: 786 sq. ft.

Bedrooms: 3

Bathrooms: 2

Width: 61' - 0"

Depth: 55' - 8"

Foundation: Crawlspace, Unfinished Basement

eplans.com

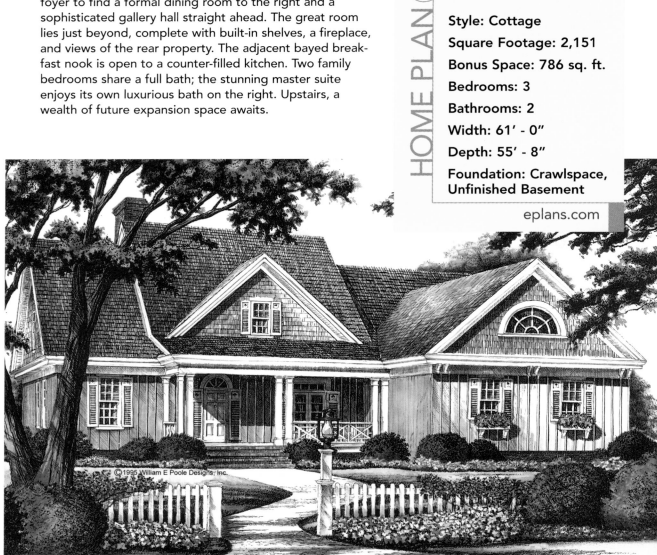

©1997 William E Poole Designs, Inc.

HOME PLAN

(#) HPK2500200

Style: Cottage

First Floor: 1,601 sq. ft.

Second Floor: 667 sq. ft.

Total: 2,268 sq. ft.

Bonus Space: 378 sq. ft.

Bedrooms: 3

Bathrooms: 2 ½

Width: 83' - 4"

Depth: 39' - 8"

Foundation: Crawlspace, Unfinished Basement

eplans.com

FIRST FLOOR

SECOND FLOOR

A WELCOMING WRAPAROUND PORCH

IS INVITING, with all the charm of a true country cottage. The great room will be the heart of the home; an enchanting extended-hearth fireplace and convenient built-in entertainment center will draw them in—sliding glass doors to the rear property will usher them out. The sunny breakfast area flows into the kitchen and effortlessly continues to the formal dining room. The master suite includes a lavish bath with a whirlpool tub and a generous walk-in closet. Two upstairs bedrooms share a full bath. Future space on the second floor is ready for your imagination.

COTTAGE COUNTRY

WOOD SIDING, MUNTIN WINDOW DORMERS, AND A DOUBLE-DECKER PORCH exemplify Southern Country style in this welcoming plan. Slide off your porch swing and enter through the foyer, flanked by the bayed living room and dining room. The family room flows effortlessly into the breakfast area and the kitchen, complete with an island. The master bedroom wows with a closet designed for a true clotheshorse. Three upstairs bedrooms enjoy access to the upper porch and space for a future recreation room.

FIRST FLOOR

SECOND FLOOR

HOME PLAN

(#) HPK2500201

Style: **Neoclassical**

First Floor: **1,995 sq. ft.**

Second Floor: **1,062 sq. ft.**

Total: **3,057 sq. ft.**

Bonus Space: **459 sq. ft.**

Bedrooms: **4**

Bathrooms: **3 ½**

Width: **71' - 0"**

Depth: **57' - 4"**

Foundation: **Unfinished Basement**

eplans.com

© 1996 William E. Poole Designs, Inc.

HOME PLAN

#

HPK2500202

Style: Cottage

First Floor: 1,075 sq. ft.

Second Floor: 994 sq. ft.

Total: 2,069 sq. ft.

Bonus Space: 382 sq. ft.

Bedrooms: 3

Bathrooms: 2 ½

Width: 56' - 4"

Depth: 35' - 4"

Foundation: Crawlspace, Unfinished Basement

eplans.com

THIS ROMANTIC GETAWAY PUTS CHARM INTO ISLAND LIVING. A double-decker terrace and rear porch extend the living space to the outdoors. Views from every room keep the home light and open. The great room sports a fireplace and is within steps of the island kitchen/breakfast room combination. The dining room is to the left of the foyer, which makes entertaining a breeze. Upstairs, two family bedrooms share a compartmented bath with dual vanities. The master suite is indulged with a private bath and a spacious His and Hers walk-in closet.

COTTAGE COUNTRY

FIRST FLOOR

SECOND FLOOR

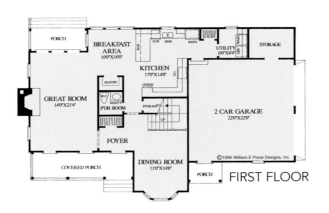

FIRST FLOOR

SECOND FLOOR

WITH ALL OF THE SLEEPING QUARTERS LOCATED ON THE SECOND FLOOR, the first floor is ideal for family interaction and entertaining. The great room sits between the front and rear porches and opens to the adjacent breakfast area and kitchen. The bay-windowed dining room provides an option for formal meals. On the second floor, the master bedroom boasts a whirlpool tub, compartmented shower and toilet, and a dual-sink vanity. Two family bedrooms share a full bath. Future expansion space completes this plan.

HPK2500203

HOME PLAN

Style: Cottage
First Floor: 1,047 sq. ft.
Second Floor: 976 sq. ft.
Total: 2,023 sq. ft.
Bonus Space: 318 sq. ft.
Bedrooms: 3
Bathrooms: 2 ½
Width: 58' - 0"
Depth: 37' - 4"
Foundation: Crawlspace, Unfinished Basement

eplans.com

© 1995 William E Poole Designs, Inc.

(#) HPK2500204

Style: Farmhouse

First Floor: 1,913 sq. ft.

Second Floor: 997 sq. ft.

Total: 2,910 sq. ft.

Bonus Space: 377 sq. ft.

Bedrooms: 4

Bathrooms: 3 ½

Width: 63' - 0"

Depth: 59' - 4"

Foundation: Crawlspace, Unfinished Basement

eplans.com

THIS ENCHANTING FARMHOUSE BRINGS THE PAST TO LIFE WITH PLENTY OF MODERN AMENITIES. An open-flow kitchen/breakfast area and family room combination is the heart of the home, opening up to the screened porch and offering the warmth of a fireplace. For more formal occasions, the foyer is flanked by a living room on the left and a dining room on the right. An elegant master bedroom, complete with a super-sized walk-in closet, is tucked away quietly behind the garage. Three more bedrooms reside upstairs, along with two full baths and a future recreation room.

FIRST FLOOR

SECOND FLOOR

FIRST FLOOR

SECOND FLOOR

HOME PLAN

(#) HPK2500205

Style: Farmhouse

First Floor: 2,099 sq. ft.

Second Floor: 1,260 sq. ft.

Total: 3,359 sq. ft.

Bonus Space: 494 sq. ft.

Bedrooms: 4

Bathrooms: 3 ½

Width: 68' - 4"

Depth: 54' - 0"

Foundation: Crawlspace

eplans.com

THIS COLONIAL HOME GETS A VICTORIAN TREATMENT WITH AN EXPANSIVE COVERED PORCH complete with a gazebo-like terminus. Inside, the impressive foyer is flanked by the living room and the formal dining room. The spacious island kitchen is ideally situated between the dining room and the sunny breakfast area. Completing the living area, the family room includes a fireplace, built-ins, and a generous view. The lavish master suite resides on the far right with a private bath and a huge walk-in closet. A second master suite is found on the upper level, along with two additional bedrooms that share a full bath.

© William E. Poole Designs, Inc.

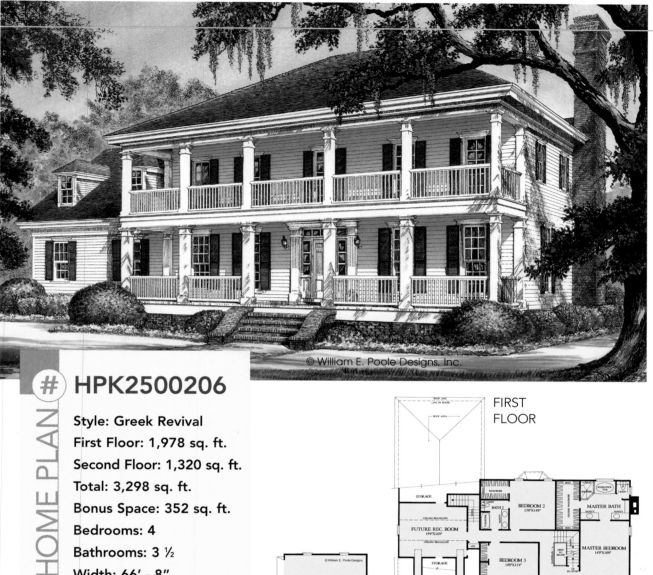

© William E. Poole Designs, Inc.

HPK2500206

HOME PLAN

Style: Greek Revival

First Floor: 1,978 sq. ft.

Second Floor: 1,320 sq. ft.

Total: 3,298 sq. ft.

Bonus Space: 352 sq. ft.

Bedrooms: 4

Bathrooms: 3 ½

Width: 66' - 8"

Depth: 62' - 0"

Foundation: Crawlspace

eplans.com

FIRST FLOOR

SECOND FLOOR

THE WIDE, HIPPED ROOF OF THIS CLASSIC SOUTHERN PLANTATION HOME DEMONSTRATES THE INFLUENCE OF CREOLE CONVENTIONS. Shady porches protect the front rooms from the southern sun and provide pleasant places to sit and enjoy the evening breezes. The traditional center-hall plan features formal living and dining rooms flanking the foyer, while the rear of the home is modern as can be, with an open arrangement of family room, breakfast nook, and kitchen. A grand fireplace, built-in cabinetry, and conveniences like a walk-in pantry and planning desk in the kitchen are every homeowner's dream. Upstairs are two spacious bedrooms and a bath, as well as the sumptuous master suite.

COTTAGE COUNTRY

FIRST FLOOR

SECOND FLOOR

THIS DESIGN INCORPORATES VICTORIAN TOUCHES with the masterful use of a turret and a gazebo. With a wealth of windows, this home never lacks natural light. Inside, a variety of room shapes offer interesting appeal. The family room is centrally located with a fireplace and a built-in entertainment center on the left wall. The island kitchen features a built-in desk, abundant counter space, and a butler's pantry. A separate utility room houses the washer/dryer, fold-down ironing board, and sink. The second floor houses the sleeping quarters, including the lavish master suite, complete with a private sitting area and fireplace, and three additional family bedrooms sharing two full baths.

HOME PLAN

HPK2500207

Style: Queen Anne

First Floor: 1,480 sq. ft.

Second Floor: 1,651 sq. ft.

Total: 3,131 sq. ft.

Bedrooms: 4

Bathrooms: 3 ½

Width: 67' - 5"

Depth: 61' - 5"

Foundation: Crawlspace

eplans.com

©1993 William E Poole Designs, Inc.

© 1996 William E Poole Designs, Inc.

THIS CHARMING VICTORIAN COTTAGE BRINGS TO MIND THE SIMPLER DAYS OF YESTERYEAR and artfully blends in the amenities of today. Enter from a covered porch to find an open foyer. The living room is on the right and flows easily into the dining room for effortless entertaining. The kitchen is appointed with a servingbar to the two-story bayed breakfast nook, which leads into the hearth-warmed family room. The master suite completes this level with a fabulous spa bath and plenty of closet space. The upper level hosts three bedrooms that share a quiet sitting room and access to an expansive recreation room.

HOME PLAN

HPK2500208

Style: Victorian Eclectic

First Floor: 1,809 sq. ft.

Second Floor: 944 sq. ft.

Total: 2,753 sq. ft.

Bonus Space: 440 sq. ft.

Bedrooms: 4

Bathrooms: 3 ½

Width: 54' - 4"

Depth: 59' - 0"

Foundation: Crawlspace, Unfinished Basement

eplans.com

FIRST FLOOR

© 1996 William E Poole Designs, Inc.

SECOND FLOOR

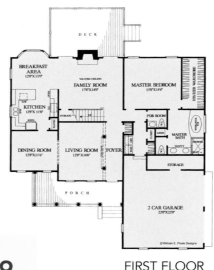

FIRST FLOOR

SECOND FLOOR

HOME PLAN

HPK2500209

Style: Greek Revival

First Floor: 1,714 sq. ft.

Second Floor: 683 sq. ft.

Total: 2,397 sq. ft.

Bonus Space: 287 sq. ft.

Bedrooms: 3

Bathrooms: 2 ½

Width: 53' - 8"

Depth: 56' - 8"

Foundation: Crawlspace

eplans.com

DESIGNED FOR OLD-FASHIONED COMFORT, THIS TWO-STORY HOME has plenty of modern amenities. The front covered porch and rear deck extend the living space outward, creating a sense of roominess. The family room, furnished with a fireplace, flows smoothly into the breakfast bay and kitchen. A front living room and formal dining area offer convenient space for entertaining. The resplendent master suite comes with a walk-in closet, dual-sink vanity, and separate tub and shower. Two bedrooms on the second floor share a bath and loft. Extra space can be developed into a recreation room. Access to the two-car garage is through the laundry.

©2006 William E Poole Designs, Inc

A NEOCLASSICAL MASTERPIECE, this design is a sight to behold. The front veranda and accompanying stairway curve to create a welcome entrance for guests. The traditional layout places the dining room and study/library on either side of a center foyer. Directly ahead, the great room offers French-door access to the rear porch and a pass-through to the breakfast area, kitchen, and neighboring workspace. Also near the great room, the master suite is located on the first floor away from the remaining bedrooms, which all reside upstairs along with two full baths.

HPK2500210

HOME PLAN

Style: Neoclassical
First Floor: 2,411 sq. ft.
Second Floor: 1,207 sq. ft.
Total: 3,618 sq. ft.
Bonus Space: 691 sq. ft.
Bedrooms: 4
Bathrooms: 4 ½ + ½
Width: 84' - 2"
Depth: 93' - 4"
Foundation: Crawlspace

eplans.com

FIRST FLOOR

SECOND FLOOR

HOME PLAN

HPK2500211

Style: Country

Square Footage: 1,737

Bedrooms: 3

Bathrooms: 2

Width: 65' - 10"

Depth: 59' - 8"

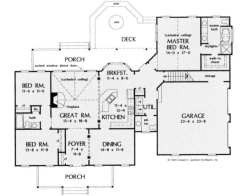

HOME PLAN

HPK2500212

Style: Country

Square Footage: 1,864

Bonus Space: 420 sq. ft.

Bedrooms: 3

Bathrooms: 2 ½

Width: 71' - 0"

Depth: 56' - 4"

USING MATERIALS THAT COMBINE THE RUGGED FRONTIER WITH STATELY ELEGANCE, this home has a grand, majestic facade. Four towering columns frame the dramatic barrel-vaulted entrance and clerestories mimic the arched theme. Cedar shake, stone, and siding complement a metal roof over the front porch. The two-story foyer has impressive views of the study, dining room, living room, and balcony. Cathedral ceilings top the family room and master bedroom and a vaulted ceiling tops the living room. Built-ins, three fireplaces, and a walk-in pantry add special touches. The master suite on the first floor and two family bedrooms upstairs each boast private baths and walk-in closets. A library and flexible bonus space round out the second level.

HOME PLAN

HPK2500213

Style: French Country

First Floor: 2,766 sq. ft.

Second Floor: 881 sq. ft.

Total: 3,647 sq. ft.

Bonus Space: 407 sq. ft.

Bedrooms: 3

Bathrooms: 3 ½

Width: 92' - 5"

Depth: 71' - 10"

eplans.com

COTTAGE COUNTRY

FIRST FLOOR

SECOND FLOOR

SCREEN PORCH
20-8 x 9-6
(cathedral ceiling)

DECK

PORCH

© 1997 DONALD A. GARDNER
All rights reserved

GARAGE
21-0 x 20-8

BRKFST.
10-8 x 9-8

UTIL.
7-6 x 7-10

w d

storage

MASTER BED RM.
12-8 x 17-2

fireplace

GREAT RM.
15-4 x 19-4
(cathedral ceiling)

balcony above

KIT.
13-0 x 13-6

walk-in closet

up

master bath

lin.

bath

up

lin.

BED RM./ STUDY
12-8 x 11-4

cl

cl

FOYER
13-0 x 8-10
(vaulted ceiling)

DINING
12-8 x 12-8

PORCH

FIRST FLOOR

great room below

attic storage

railing

balcony

attic storage

BED RM.
12-8 x 12-0

d

d

bath

down

BED RM.
12-8 x 12-0

d

d

attic storage

foyer below

attic storage

BONUS RM.
12-0 x 20-8

down

down

SECOND FLOOR

© 1997 Donald A. Gardner Architects, Inc.

A LOVELY ARCH-TOP WINDOW AND A WRAP-AROUND PORCH set off this country exterior. Inside, formal rooms open off the foyer, which leads to a spacious great room. This living area provides a fireplace and access to a screened porch with a cathedral ceiling. Bay windows allow natural light into the breakfast area and formal dining room. The master suite features a spacious bath and access to a private area of the rear porch. Two second-floor bedrooms share a bath and a balcony hall that offers an overlook to the great room.

**HPK2500214**

HOME PLAN

Style: Farmhouse

First Floor: 1,743 sq. ft.

Second Floor: 555 sq. ft.

Total: 2,298 sq. ft.

Bonus Space: 350 sq. ft.

Bedrooms: 4

Bathrooms: 3

Width: 77' - 11"

Depth: 53' - 2"

eplans.com

© 1993 Donald A. Gardner Architects, Inc.

HOME PLAN

HPK2500215

Style: Farmhouse

First Floor: 1,618 sq. ft.

Second Floor: 570 sq. ft.

Total: 2,188 sq. ft.

Bonus Space: 495 sq. ft.

Bedrooms: 3

Bathrooms: 2 ½

Width: 87' - 0"

Depth: 57' - 0"

eplans.com

THE FOYER AND GREAT ROOM IN THIS MAGNIFICENT FARMHOUSE have Palladian window dormers to allow natural light to illuminate the house. The spacious great room boasts a fireplace, cabinets, and bookshelves. The second-floor balcony overlooks the great room. The kitchen with a cooking island is conveniently located between the dining room and the breakfast room with an open view of the great room. A generous master bedroom has plenty of closet space as well as an expansive master bath. A bonus room over the garage allows for expansion.

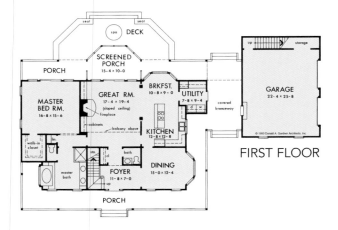

FIRST FLOOR

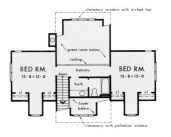

SECOND FLOOR

EYE-CATCHING TWIN CHIMNEYS DOMINATE THE EXTERIOR OF THIS GRAND DESIGN, but on closer approach you will delight in the covered porch with decorated pediment and the tall windows across the front of the house. A long hallway separates the family room, with a fireplace, from the rest of the house. A large U-shaped kitchen features an island work center and direct access to the sunny breakfast room and the formal dining room. A study/living room (with an optional second fireplace) completes the first floor. Upstairs, you'll find a well-appointed master suite, two family bedrooms, and a bonus room over the garage.

FIRST FLOOR

© 1996 Donald A. Gardner Architects, Inc.

SECOND FLOOR

HPK2500216

Style: Country

First Floor: 1,428 sq. ft.

Second Floor: 1,067 sq. ft.

Total: 2,495 sq. ft.

Bonus Space: 342 sq. ft.

Bedrooms: 3

Bathrooms: 2 ½

Width: 74' - 0"

Depth: 64' - 8"

eplans.com

HOME PLAN

© 1996 Donald A. Gardner Architects, Inc.

HOME PLAN
HPK2500217

Style: Country
First Floor: 1,002 sq. ft.
Second Floor: 336 sq. ft.
Total: 1,338 sq. ft.
Bedrooms: 3
Bathrooms: 2
Width: 36' - 8"
Depth: 44' - 8"

FIRST FLOOR

SECOND FLOOR

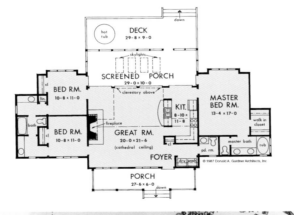

HOME PLAN
HPK2500218

Style: Country
Square Footage: 1,426
Bedrooms: 3
Bathrooms: 2 ½
Width: 67' - 6"
Depth: 36' - 8"

COTTAGE COUNTRY

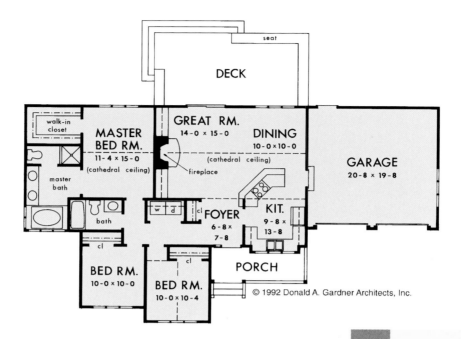

walk-in closet

MASTER BED RM.
11-4 × 15-0
(cathedral ceiling)

master bath

bath

cl

GREAT RM.
14-0 × 15-0

fireplace

(cathedral ceiling)

DINING
10-0 × 10-0

(cathedral ceiling)

GARAGE
20-8 × 19-8

w d

cl

FOYER
6-8 ×
7-8

KIT.
9-8 ×
13-8

BED RM.
10-0 × 10-0

cl

BED RM.
10-0 × 10-4

PORCH

DECK

seat

© 1992 Donald A. Gardner Architects, Inc.

THIS ECONOMICAL PLAN MAKES AN IMPRESSIVE VISUAL STATEMENT with its comfortable and well-proportioned appearance. The entrance foyer leads to all areas of the house. The great room, dining area, and kitchen are all open to one another, allowing visual interaction. The great room and dining area share a dramatic cathedral ceiling and feature a grand fireplace flanked by bookshelves and cabinets. The master suite has a cathedral ceiling, walk-in closet, and bath with double-bowl vanity, whirlpool tub, and shower. Two family bedrooms and a full hall bath complete this cozy home.

HPK2500219

Style: Country
Square Footage: 1,287
Bedrooms: 3
Bathrooms: 2
Width: 66' - 4"
Depth: 48' - 0"

HOME PLAN #

eplans.com

© 1992 Donald A. Gardner Architects, Inc.

B .NATI

© 1996 Donald A. Gardner Architects, Inc.

THIS COUNTRY HOME PRESENTS AN ELEGANT FACADE WITH GRACIOUS WINDOWS. The foyer opens to a great room and provides access to the bedrooms, and the great room features a fireplace and open access to the dining room. The efficient L-shaped kitchen provides an entrance to the dining room. The master bedroom features a cathedral ceiling in the bedroom and sports a large walk-in closet and a full bath. Two additional bedrooms complete this adorable home, one of which also has a cathedral ceiling. Above the two-car garage, a bonus room offers skylights and attic storage.

©1998 Donald A. Gardner Architects, Inc.

HOME PLAN

HPK2500221

Style: Craftsman

Square Footage: 1,544

Bonus Space: 320 sq. ft.

Bedrooms: 3

Bathrooms: 2

Width: 63' - 0"

Depth: 43' - 0"

© 1997 Donald A. Gardner Architects, Inc.

HOME PLAN

HPK2500222

Style: Country

Square Footage: 1,517

Bonus Space: 287 sq. ft.

Bedrooms: 3

Bathrooms: 2

Width: 61' - 4"

Depth: 48' - 6"

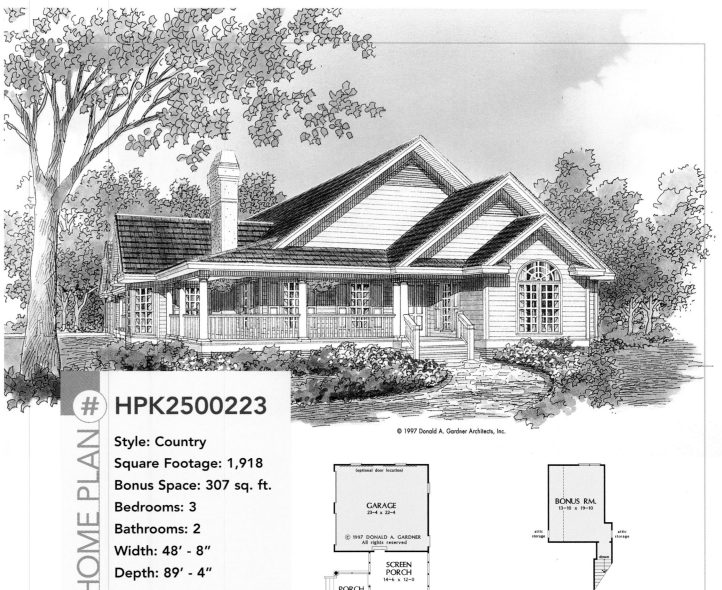

© 1997 Donald A. Gardner Architects, Inc.

HOME PLAN

(#) # HPK2500223

Style: Country
Square Footage: 1,918
Bonus Space: 307 sq. ft.
Bedrooms: 3
Bathrooms: 2
Width: 48' - 8"
Depth: 89' - 4"

eplans.com

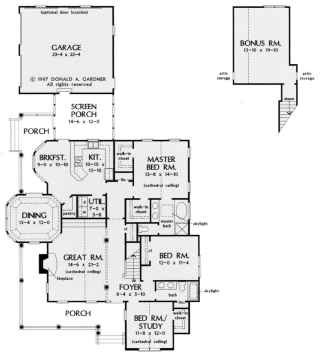

A WRAPAROUND FRONT PORCH, THREE GABLES, and a circle-top window lend elegance to this plan. Columns define the entry to the vaulted great room, which features a fireplace and built-in cabinets. The octagonal dining room presents a tray ceiling and opens to the side porch. The kitchen and breakfast bay are open and conveniently access the pantry, laundry room, and screened porch. The vaulted master bedroom offers two walk-in closets and a private bath brightened by a skylight. Two secondary bedrooms share a bath. The upstairs bonus room could be a fourth bedroom in the future.

HOME PLAN #

HPK2500224

Style: Country

Square Footage: 1,498

Bedrooms: 3

Bathrooms: 2

Width: 59' - 8"

Depth: 46' - 8"

HOME PLAN #

HPK2500225

Style: Country

Square Footage: 1,652

Bonus Space: 367 sq. ft.

Bedrooms: 3

Bathrooms: 2

Width: 64' - 4"

Depth: 51' - 0"

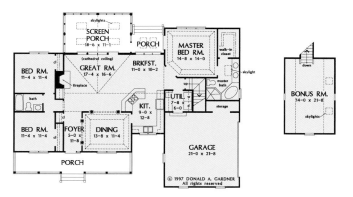

©1998 Donald A. Gardner, Inc.

GABLE TREATMENTS ALONG WITH STONE AND HORIZONTAL SIDING give a definite country flavor to this two-story home. Inside, the foyer opens to a great room that boasts a fireplace, built-ins, and a magnificent view of the backyard beyond an inviting rear porch. The kitchen is designed for high style with a column-defined cooktop island and serving-bar access to the dining area. The master suite finishes this level and includes two walk-in closets and a private bath. Two bedrooms share a full bath and bonus space on the second floor.

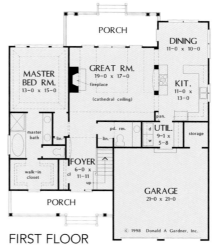

FIRST FLOOR

SECOND FLOOR

FIRST FLOOR

DECK

GREAT RM.
18-0 x 19-6
(cathedral ceiling)

BRKFST.
12-0 x 10-0

UTIL.
9-0 x 6-0

storage

master
bath

fireplace

walk-in
closet

KIT.
12-0 x 12-8

w d

balcony above

GARAGE
21-0 x 20-4

MASTER
BED RM.
12-0 x 16-8

walk-in
closet

FOYER
7-4 x
12-4
(vaulted
ceiling)

pd.
rm.

DINING
12-0 x 12-0

cl

PORCH

© 1998 Donald A. Gardner, Inc.

SECOND FLOOR

great room
below

down

railing

attic storage

attic storage

BONUS RM.
21-0 x 13-4

attic storage

balcony

down

BED RM.
12-0 x 13-0

bath

lin.

lin.

BED RM.
12-0 x 13-0

attic storage

walk-in
closet

foyer
below

walk-in
closet

attic storage

attic storage

HPK2500227

Style: Farmhouse

First Floor: 1,569 sq. ft.

Second Floor: 682 sq. ft.

Total: 2,251 sq. ft.

Bonus Space: 332 sq. ft.

Bedrooms: 3

Bathrooms: 2 ½

Width: 64' - 8"

Depth: 43' - 4"

HOME PLAN

eplans.com

THE WIDE PORCH ACROSS THE FRONT AND THE DECK OFF THE GREAT ROOM in back allow as much outdoor living as the weather permits. The foyer opens through columns from the front porch to the dining room, with a nearby powder room, and to the great room. The breakfast room is open to the great room and the adjacent kitchen. The utility room adjoins this area and accesses the garage. On the opposite side of the plan, the master suite offers a compartmented bath and two walk-in closets. A staircase leads upstairs to two family bedrooms—one at each end of a balcony that overlooks the great room. Each bedroom contains a walk-in closet, a dormer window, and access to the bath through a private vanity area.

©1998 Donald A. Gardner, Inc.

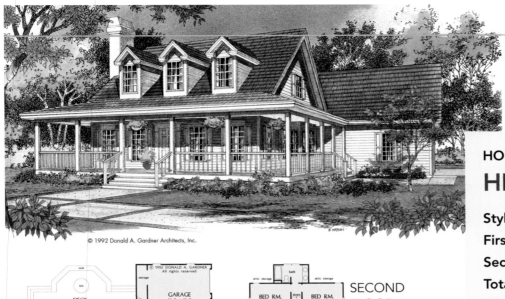

FIRST FLOOR

SECOND FLOOR

HOME PLAN
HPK2500228

Style: Farmhouse
First Floor: 1,145 sq. ft.
Second Floor: 518 sq. ft.
Total: 1,663 sq. ft.
Bonus Space: 380 sq. ft.
Bedrooms: 3
Bathrooms: 2 ½
Width: 59' - 4"
Depth: 56' - 6"

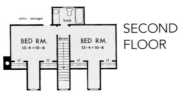

FIRST FLOOR

SECOND FLOOR

HOME PLAN
HPK2500229

Style: Tidewater
First Floor: 1,057 sq. ft.
Second Floor: 500 sq. ft.
Total: 1,557 sq. ft.
Bonus Space: 342 sq. ft.
Bedrooms: 3
Bathrooms: 2 ½
Width: 59' - 4"
Depth: 50' - 0"

COTTAGE COUNTRY

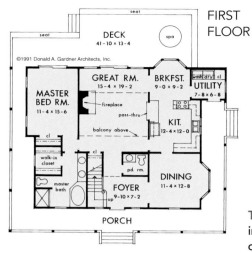

FIRST FLOOR

DECK
41–10 × 13–4

spa

©1991 Donald A. Gardner Architects, Inc.

seat

seat

GREAT RM.
15–4 × 19–2

BRKFST.
9–0 × 9–2

wash dry cl

UTILITY
7–8 × 6–8

MASTER BED RM.
11–4 × 15–6

fireplace

pass-thru

balcony above

cl

KIT.
12–4 × 12–0

walk-in closet

cl

cl

pd. rm.

DINING
11–4 × 12–8

master bath

up

FOYER
9–10 × 7–2

PORCH

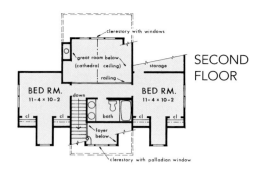

SECOND FLOOR

clerestory with windows

great room below
(cathedral ceiling)

storage

railing

BED RM.
11–4 × 10–2

BED RM.
11–4 × 10–2

cl

cl

down

bath

cl

cl

foyer below

clerestory with palladian window

HOME PLAN

HPK2500230

Style: Tidewater

First Floor: 1,325 sq. ft.

Second Floor: 453 sq. ft.

Total: 1,778 sq. ft.

Bedrooms: 3

Bathrooms: 2 ½

Width: 48' - 4"

Depth: 51' - 10"

eplans.com

THIS COMPACT DESIGN HAS ALL THE AMENITIES AVAILABLE in larger plans with little wasted space. In addition, a wraparound covered porch, a front Palladian window, dormers, and rear arched windows provide exciting visual elements to the exterior. The spacious great room has a fireplace, a cathedral ceiling, and clerestory windows. A second-level balcony overlooks this gathering area. The kitchen is centrally located for maximum flexibility in layout and features a pass-through to the great room. Besides the generous master suite with a pampering bath, two family bedrooms located on the second level share a full bath.

REAR EXTERIOR

©1991 Donald A. Gardner, Inc.

HOME PLAN
HPK2500231

Style: Farmhouse

First Floor: 1,526 sq. ft.

Second Floor: 635 sq. ft.

Total: 2,161 sq. ft.

Bonus Space: 355 sq. ft.

Bedrooms: 3

Bathrooms: 2 ½

Width: 76' - 4"

Depth: 74' - 2"

FIRST FLOOR

SECOND FLOOR

BONUS RM.
27-0 x 12-0

© 1991 Donald A. Gardner Architects, Inc.

HOME PLAN
HPK2500232

Style: Tidewater

First Floor: 1,756 sq. ft.

Second Floor: 565 sq. ft.

Total: 2,321 sq. ft.

Bedrooms: 4

Bathrooms: 3

Width: 56' - 8"

Depth: 42' - 4"

FIRST FLOOR

SECOND FLOOR

COTTAGE COUNTRY

A PROMINENT CENTER GABLE WITH AN ARCHED WINDOW ACCENTS THE FACADE of this custom cottage home, which features an exterior of cedar shakes, siding, and stone. An open floor plan with generously proportioned rooms contributes to the spacious and relaxed atmosphere. The vaulted great room boasts a rear wall of windows, a fireplace bordered by built-in cabinets, and convenient access to the kitchen. A second-floor loft overlooks the great room for added drama. The master suite is completely secluded and enjoys a cathedral ceiling, back-porch access, a large walk-in closet, and a luxurious bath. The home includes three additional bedrooms and baths, as well as a vaulted loft/study and a bonus room.

FIRST FLOOR

SECOND FLOOR

HOME PLAN

(#) HPK2500233

Style: Craftsman

First Floor: 2,477 sq. ft.

Second Floor: 742 sq. ft.

Total: 3,219 sq. ft.

Bonus Space: 419 sq. ft.

Bedrooms: 4

Bathrooms: 4

Width: 100' - 0"

Depth: 66' - 2"

eplans.com

SIDING, STONE, AND A TRIO OF FRONT-FACING GABLES ADD CHARACTER TO THE FACADE OF THIS CAPTIVATING COTTAGE with a courtyard garage. A second-floor balcony looks over the two-story foyer and the great room with its cathedral ceiling. An open and undefined central hall on the first floor is bordered on either end by built-in art niches. Bay windows extend both the breakfast area and master bedroom. The master suite features dual walk-in closets and a private bath with His and Her vanities, a separate tub and shower, and a compartmented toilet. Divided by the upstairs balcony are two family bedrooms. Accessed from the first floor, a bonus room offers options for future expansion.

HOME PLAN

HPK2500234

Style: Bungalow
First Floor: 1,734 sq. ft.
Second Floor: 547 sq. ft.
Total: 2,281 sq. ft.
Bonus Space: 381 sq. ft.
Bedrooms: 3
Bathrooms: 2 ½
Width: 60' - 8"
Depth: 65' - 6"

eplans.com

FIRST FLOOR

SECOND FLOOR

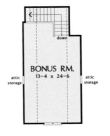

COTTAGE COUNTRY

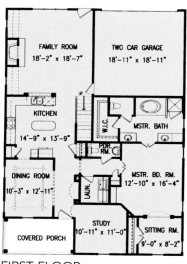

FAMILY ROOM
18'-2" x 18'-7"

TWO CAR GARAGE
18'-11" x 18'-11"

KITCHEN
14'-9" x 13'-9"

W.I.C.

MSTR. BATH

UP

PDR. RM.

DINING ROOM
10'-3" x 12'-11"

LAUN.

MSTR. BD. RM.
12'-10" x 16'-4"

STUDY
10'-11" x 11'-0"

SITTING RM.
9'-0" x 8'-2"

COVERED PORCH

FIRST FLOOR

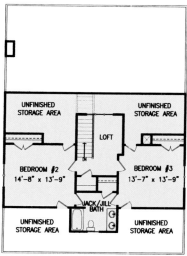

UNFINISHED STORAGE AREA

UNFINISHED STORAGE AREA

LOFT

DN

BEDROOM #2
14'-8" x 13'-9"

BEDROOM #3
13'-7" x 13'-9"

JACK/JILL BATH

UNFINISHED STORAGE AREA

UNFINISHED STORAGE AREA

SECOND FLOOR

WITH A NARROW PROFILE AND FOOTPRINT, THIS HOME WILL FIT ON THE MOST compact lot without compromising space or amenities. The covered porch is set off by an open, detailed gable, making this a neighborhood-friendly facade. A formal dining room and study flank the foyer and provide ample space for entertaining. The kitchen sports a work-top island and is just a few steps from the spacious family room. The short master suite hall opens to a comfortable and private space with an adjoining sitting room and private bath. The second floor is complete with two bedrooms, loft, full bath, and plenty of storage space.

HPK2500236

Style: Country

First Floor: 1,260 sq. ft.

Second Floor: 1,057 sq. ft.

Total: 2,317 sq. ft.

Bedrooms: 5

Bathrooms: 2 ½

Width: 35' - 0"

Depth: 56' - 0"

Foundation: Slab

eplans.com

AT HOME IN THE CITY, THIS NARROW-LOT DESIGN TAKES ADVANTAGE OF STREET views. A rear-loading, two-car garage is accessed via a rear porch and breakfast room. The adjoining C-shaped kitchen is only steps from the formal dining room. A warming fireplace can be enjoyed in the great room (and even from the dining room). A first-floor master suite provides convenience and comfort. Two walk-in closets, dual-sink vanity, soaking tub, and enclosed shower pamper and dissolve stress. The second floor is home to four bedrooms—or three bedrooms and a loft. A roomy laundry area is located on the second floor.

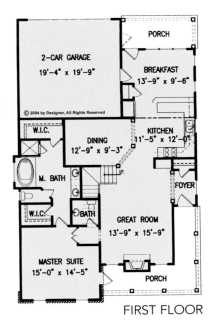

FIRST FLOOR

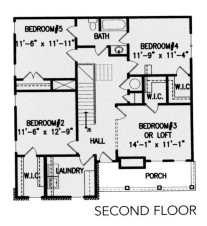

SECOND FLOOR

HOME PLAN

HPK2500237

Style: Farmhouse

First Floor: 1,649 sq. ft.

Second Floor: 1,604 sq. ft.

Total: 3,253 sq. ft.

Bedrooms: 4

Bathrooms: 3 ½

Width: 54' - 0"

Depth: 45' - 8"

Foundation: Slab, Unfinished Walkout Basement, Basement/Slab

eplans.com

COASTAL LIVING AT ITS FINEST, THIS HOME WEARS CEDAR SHINGLES AND SIDING with perfection. Front and rear porches extend living space for the family that loves the outdoors. Entertain on the weekend with well-designed formal spaces that flank the foyer. An open gallery hall transitions to the relaxed grand room featuring a fireplace and a wall of windows. Stairs to the second floor are to the rear. A spacious breakfast room offers an opportunity for guests to keep the cook company in the fantastic island kitchen. Upstairs, large bedrooms give the family plenty of elbow room. A study loft is a great place for homework and an Internet connection. Framed by double doors, the master suite has everything. A private bath features a dual-sink vanity, a separate tub and shower, a compartmented toilet, and an oversized walk-in closet.

FIRST FLOOR

SECOND FLOOR

HOME PLAN

HPK2500238

Style: Country

First Floor: 1,649 sq. ft.

Second Floor: 1,604 sq. ft.

Total: 3,253 sq. ft.

Bedrooms: 4

Bathrooms: 3 ½

Width: 69' - 6"

Depth: 45' - 8"

Foundation: Slab, Unfinished Walkout Basement

eplans.com

THE FACADE ON THIS DESIGN EVOKES TRADITIONAL AMERICAN CULTURE, and the interior hosts the best of modern-day living. A columned front porch and window shutters ensconced in stone masonry lend country charm outside. Inside presents first a grand foyer with archways to the adjoining study and dining room. A distinguished gallery and discreet powder room lie before the grand salon, with fireplace and views toward the back porch. A rear foyer provides access to the porch and to the second level of the home. The laundry and pantry are conveniently located off of the kitchen. Bedrooms for the family are found upstairs, including a master suite with a soothing private sitting room and coffered ceiling. Three family bedrooms, a loft, and a balcony looking down below round out this delightful package.

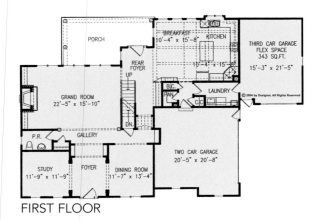

FIRST FLOOR

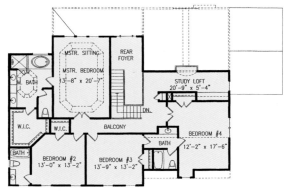

SECOND FLOOR

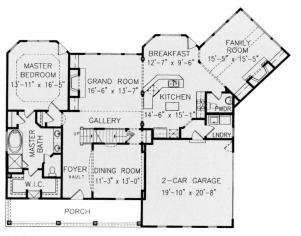

FIRST FLOOR

MASTER BEDROOM
13'-11" x 16'-5"

GRAND ROOM
16'-6" x 13'-7"

BREAKFAST
12'-7" x 9'-6"

FAMILY ROOM
15'-5" x 15'-5"

KITCHEN
14'-6" x 15'-1"

PWDR

GALLERY

MASTER BATH

W.I.C.

FOYER VAULT

DINING ROOM
11'-3" x 13'-0"

LNDRY

2-CAR GARAGE
19'-10" x 20'-8"

PORCH

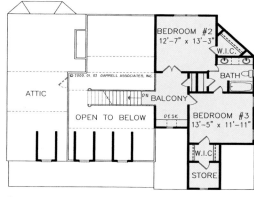

SECOND FLOOR

ATTIC

© 2000, 01, 02 GARRELL ASSOCIATES, INC

OPEN TO BELOW

BALCONY

DESK

BEDROOM #2
12'-7" x 13'-3"

W.I.C.

BATH

BEDROOM #3
13'-5" x 11'-11"

W.I.C.

STORE

PERFECT NEIGHBORHOOD CLASSIC, this design takes the good days and adds open space, functionality, popular amenities, and enough room for everyone. The family room, located at the rear, features a fireplace and built-ins. The kitchen and adjoining nook are open to both the family and grand rooms. Spacious closets, a compartmented toilet, a garden tub, and a sitting area combine to offer comfort in the master suite. A second floor expands family space with two bedrooms, a balcony with desk, and a shared bath.

HOME PLAN

HPK2500239

Style: Country

First Floor: 1,822 sq. ft.

Second Floor: 649 sq. ft.

Total: 2,471 sq. ft.

Bedrooms: 3

Bathrooms: 2 ½

Width: 64' - 9"

Depth: 52' - 7"

Foundation: Unfinished Walkout Basement

eplans.com

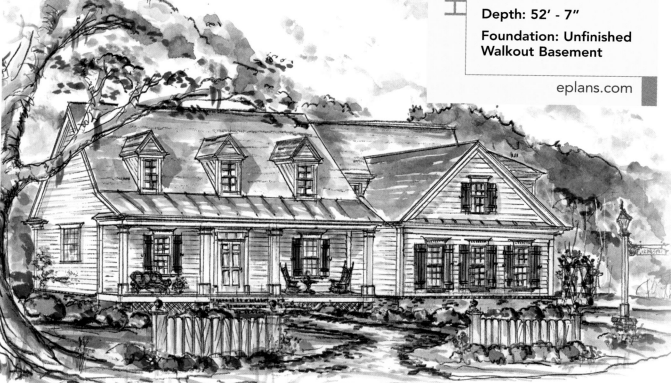

HOME PLAN

FIRST FLOOR

SECOND FLOOR

HPK2500240

Style: Country
First Floor: 1,417 sq. ft.
Second Floor: 1,169 sq. ft.
Total: 2,586 sq. ft.
Bonus Space: 119 sq. ft.
Bedrooms: 4
Bathrooms: 2 ½
Width: 52' - 0"
Depth: 43' - 6"
Foundation: Slab, Unfinished Basement, Unfinished Walkout Basement

eplans.com

A WRAPAROUND COVERED PORCH WELCOMES YOU TO THIS EFFICIENT TWO-STORY HOME. Inside, the formal rooms open directly off the foyer, and the two-story grand room is toward the rear. A private study is available for home office space. The U-shaped kitchen features a work island and an adjacent breakfast area. Upstairs, three family bedrooms share a full bath and an overlook to the grand room. The deluxe master suite offers a large private bath, huge walk-in closet, and an optional sitting area.

COTTAGE COUNTRY

(#) HPK2500241

Style: Cracker
Square Footage: 1,456
Bedrooms: 3
Bathrooms: 2
Width: 54' - 0"
Depth: 45' - 6"
Foundation: Crawlspace

eplans.com

FOR THE FAMILY THAT LIKES TO SPEND TIME OUTDOORS, this home is sure to please. Expansive rear and front porches extend living space outward, and the master suite enjoys private access to a deck. A cozy fireplace is tucked into the corner of the main living room, which is separated from the front dining room by classy columns. The center island in the kitchen eases meal preparation. The sleeping arrangements are separated from each other; the deluxe master suite, with a walk-in closet and a private bath, is on the left, and two more bedrooms are on the right side of the home. A laundry room is close by.

WELCOME HOME TO A PETITE COTTAGE THAT IS ECO-NOMICAL to build and has plenty to offer. Enter from the covered porch to a family room with great views and a warming fireplace. The sunny dining area is adjacent and can be as formal or casual as you wish. The kitchen is planned for efficiency and hosts a serving bar and rear-porch access, perfect for outdoor dining. Three family bedrooms include a master suite with a private bath and two additional bedrooms that share a full bath.

HOME PLAN

HPK2500242

Style: Cottage
Square Footage: 1,195
Bedrooms: 3
Bathrooms: 2
Width: 40' - 0"
Depth: 48' - 8"

eplans.com

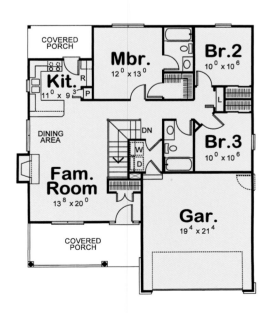

COTTAGE COUNTRY

FIRST FLOOR

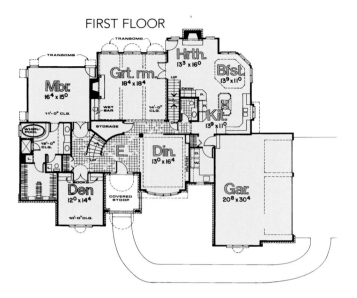

SECOND FLOOR

A CURVING STAIRCASE GRACES THE ENTRY TO THIS BEAUTIFUL HOME. Besides an oversized great room with a fireplace and arched windows, there's a cozy hearth room with its own fireplace. The gourmet kitchen has a work island and breakfast area. A secluded den contains bookcases and an arched transom above double doors. The master suite is on the first floor, thoughtfully separated from three family bedrooms upstairs. Bedrooms 2 and 4 share a full bath; Bedroom 3 has its own private bath. Note the informal second stair to the second floor originating in the hearth room.

HPK2500243

HOME PLAN

Style: New American
First Floor: 2,252 sq. ft.
Second Floor: 920 sq. ft.
Total: 3,172 sq. ft.
Bedrooms: 4
Bathrooms: 3 ½
Width: 73' - 4"
Depth: 57' - 4"

eplans.com

HOME PLAN

(#) HPK2500244

Style: Cottage
Square Footage: 1,806
Bedrooms: 3
Bathrooms: 2
Width: 55' - 4"
Depth: 56' - 0"

eplans.com

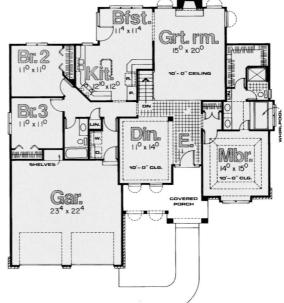

BEAUTIFUL COLUMNS AND ARCHED TRANSOMS ARE THE FOCAL POINTS of this contemporary ranch home. The 10-foot entry opens to the formal dining room and the great room, which features a brick fireplace and arched windows. The large island kitchen offers an angled range, a multitude of cabinets, and a sunny breakfast area with an atrium door to the backyard. Separate bedroom wings provide optimum privacy. The master wing to the right includes a whirlpool bath with a sloped ceiling, a plant shelf above dual lavatories, and a large walk-in closet. The family bedrooms are at the opposite end of the house and share a full bath. The laundry room serves as a mudroom entry from the garage.

COTTAGE COUNTRY

FIRST FLOOR

SECOND FLOOR

THIS HOME'S FRENCH COUNTRY CHARM EXUDES WARMTH AND COMFORT from the wrapping porch to the arching columned entrance. A gallery connects the kitchen and morning bay—a great casual hangout. The living and dining rooms share an open layout and can enjoy the fireplace from any point in the area. Bedroom 2 is easily converted into a guest room. The master suite enjoys a sitting bay with rear-deck access. Two family bedrooms feature walk-in closets and share a compartmented bath and sitting area on the second floor.

HOME PLAN

HPK2500245

Style: Farmhouse

First Floor: 2,000 sq. ft.

Second Floor: 660 sq. ft.

Total: 2,660 sq. ft.

Bedrooms: 4

Bathrooms: 3

Width: 68' - 8"

Depth: 75' - 0"

Foundation: Crawlspace, Slab, Unfinished Basement

eplans.com

THIS ALLURING CRAFTSMAN HOME INCLUDES DECORATIVE STONE DETAILING, noble pillars, and enchanting windows. The covered porch leads into the gallery and just through the pillars is the great room, where the focal point falls on the fireplace. The kitchen features an island and a snack bar with a breakfast nook nearby. Easy access to the covered rear patio is made through the nook. A guest bedroom is located away from the family sleeping quarters for privacy. Two family bedrooms and a master suite comprise the left side of the plan.

(#) HPK2500246

Style: Craftsman

Square Footage: 2,541

Bedrooms: 4

Bathrooms: 3

Width: 81' - 0"

Depth: 54' - 0"

Foundation: Crawlspace, Slab, Unfinished Basement

eplans.com

COTTAGE COUNTRY

MASTER SUITE
15⁶ X 15²

COVERED PATIO

BRKFST
12⁰ X 11⁰

GUEST BEDRM.
11⁰ X 15²

MSTR. BATH

WIC

GREAT ROOM
21⁸ X 20⁰

KITCHEN
12⁹ X 14⁵

BATH 3

TOOLS

ISLAND

BATH 2

LIN.

UTILITY

2-CAR GARAGE
20⁰ X 21⁴

BEDRM 3
12⁰ X 11⁸

GALLERY

PANTRY

BEDRM 2
11⁵ X 12⁰

COVERED PORCH

DINING
13⁴ X 11⁶

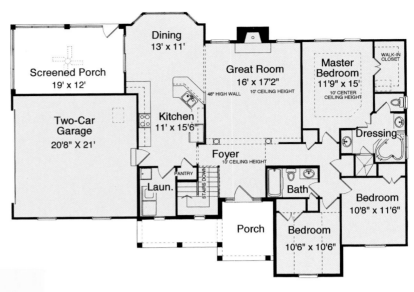

Dining
13' x 11'

Screened Porch
19' x 12'

Great Room
16' x 17'2"
48" HIGH WALL   10' CEILING HEIGHT

Master Bedroom
11'9" x 15'
10' CENTER CEILING HEIGHT

WALK-IN CLOSET

Two-Car Garage
20'8" X 21'

Kitchen
11' x 15'6"

Dressing

Foyer
10' CEILING HEIGHT

PANTRY

STAIRS DOWN

Laun.

Bath

Bedroom
10'8" x 11'6"

Porch

Bedroom
10'6" x 10'6"

HPK2500247

Style: Country

Square Footage: 1,611

Bedrooms: 3

Bathrooms: 2

Width: 66' - 4"

Depth: 43' - 10"

Foundation: Unfinished Basement

HOME PLAN

eplans.com

A STONE-AND-SIDING EXTERIOR EASILY COMBINES WITH THE FRONT COVERED PORCH on this three-bedroom ranch home. Inside, columns define the great room, which holds a warming fireplace framed by windows. The bay window in the dining room pours light into the nearby kitchen. Access the screened porch via the dining room to expand the possible living space. The master suite enjoys a walk-in closet and a luxurious bath, which includes a separate shower and whirlpool tub. Two family bedrooms share a full bath and views of the front yard. Note the two-car, side-access garage—perfect for a corner lot.

HOME PLAN
HPK2500248

Style: Colonial Revival
Square Footage: 1,627
Bedrooms: 3
Bathrooms: 2
Width: 46' - 0"
Depth: 70' - 0"
Foundation: Slab

FIRST FLOOR

SECOND FLOOR

HOME PLAN
HPK2500249

Style: Colonial Revival
First Floor: 1,788 sq. ft.
Second Floor: 720 sq. ft.
Total: 2,508 sq. ft.
Bonus Space: 384 sq. ft.
Bedrooms: 3
Bathrooms: 2 ½
Width: 78' - 8"
Depth: 77' - 10"
Foundation: Slab

COTTAGE COUNTRY

THE FANCIFUL VICTORIAN DETAILS, LATTICE WORK, ORNATE COLUMNS AND RAILING, and a cupola perched atop a standing seam metal roof set the character of this charming coastal home. Entering the double front doors into the large columned foyer, one soon realizes the excitement of this floor plan. The family room features a full wall fireplace and entertainment center. The kitchen nook and dining areas offer many opportunities for entertaining with wonderful views to the exterior. The master bedroom, with spacious bath and closet area, provides for a private retreat, with windows overlooking the backyard.

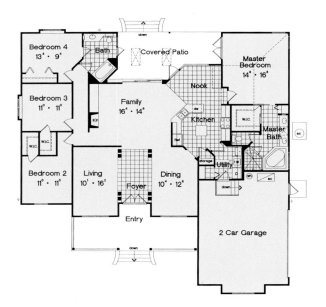

HOME PLAN

(#) HPK2500250

Style: Cracker

Square Footage: 2,151

Bedrooms: 4

Bathrooms: 2

Width: 60' - 4"

Depth: 62' - 0"

Foundation: Slab

eplans.com

THIS UNIQUE ROOFING STYLE CAPTURES YOUR ATTENTION AND THE VARYING ROOFLINES hold your interest. The foyer is open to the dining room on the left and the living room on the right. A large family room is straight ahead, featuring a built-in bookshelf and fireplace. The efficient kitchen offers plenty of counter space in a relatively small area. A wall of windows in the eating room allows light to billow into this home. The master suite includes a bath and walk-in closets. Large front and rear porches provide extensive opportunity for outdoor entertaining.

HPK2500251

HOME PLAN

Style: Cracker
First Floor: 1,320 sq. ft.
Second Floor: 552 sq. ft.
Total: 1,872 sq. ft.
Bedrooms: 3
Bathrooms: 4
Width: 56' - 0"
Depth: 61' - 0"
Foundation: Crawlspace, Slab, Unfinished Basement

eplans.com

COTTAGE COUNTRY

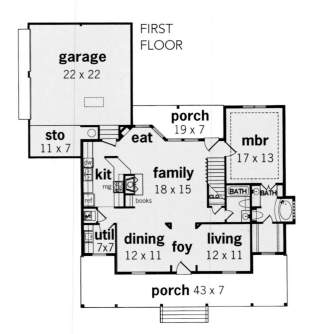

FIRST FLOOR

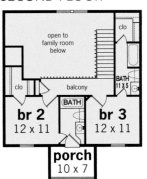

SECOND FLOOR

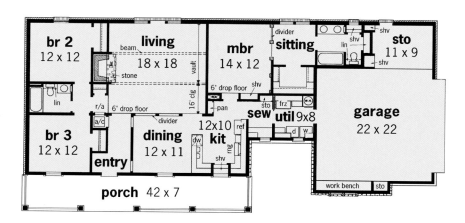

HOME PLAN

HPK2500252

Style: Farmhouse

Square Footage: 1,600

Bedrooms: 3

Bathrooms: 2

Width: 75' - 0"

Depth: 37' - 0"

Foundation: Crawlspace, Slab, Unfinished Basement

eplans.com

SOUTHERN CHARM ABOUNDS IN THIS ONE-STORY HOME WITH ITS COVERED PORCH, double dormers, and combination of stone and siding. Inside, the entry opens to the living room with its stone fireplace and beam-accented, vaulted ceiling. The U-shaped kitchen adjoins the formal dining room where dividers offer privacy between the dining and living rooms. The master suite boasts a sitting room, walk-in closet, and a private bath. On the left, two family bedrooms share a full bath.

(#) HPK2500253

Style: Tidewater

Square Footage: 1,800

Bedrooms: 3

Bathrooms: 2

Width: 66' - 0"

Depth: 60' - 0"

Foundation: Crawlspace, Slab, Unfinished Basement

eplans.com

THE ROMANCE OF A COLONIAL PLANTATION IS RESURRECTED IN THIS CHARMING DESIGN. Steps lead onto a covered porch and to an elegant double-door entry. The central living room, which opens to the rear porch, balances rooms on either side. Two family bedrooms share a full hall bath between them, to the right of the living room. To the left, the kitchen rests between the bayed eating area and the formal dining room. A hall at the rear of the plan leads to the master suite, which is secluded for privacy. A two-car garage, storage space, and a utility room complete this plan.

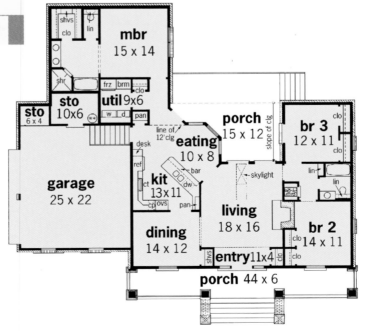

COTTAGE COUNTRY

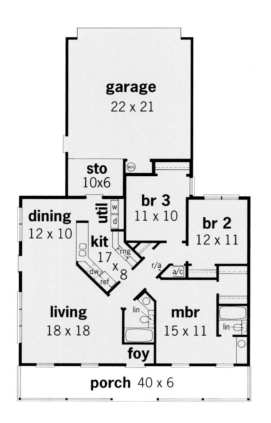

ELEGANT COLUMNS ADORN THE FRONT PORCH OF THIS PLAN AND GIVE IT CHARACTER. Though small in square footage, this home is designed for gracious living. The living and dining rooms are open and surround a galley-style kitchen with access to the two-car garage and its storage space. Bedrooms are on the right side of the plan and include a master suite and two family bedrooms. The master suite has a private bath with a compartmented tub and toilet. It also features a walk-in closet. Family bedrooms share a full hall bath.

HPK2500254

HOME PLAN

Style: Farmhouse

Square Footage: 1,266

Bedrooms: 3

Bathrooms: 2

Width: 40' - 0"

Depth: 64' - 0"

Foundation: Crawlspace, Slab

eplans.com

A COVERED FRONT PORCH GIVES THIS HOME COUNTRY CHARM and makes family and guests feel welcome. Graced by a sloped ceiling and warmed by a stone fireplace, the living room provides the perfect gathering spot. The well-equipped kitchen easily serves the dining room and adjoins a utility room that opens to the patio. The master suite offers an adjoining bath with a separate dressing area and double-sink vanity. Two family bedrooms share a full bath. The two-car garage includes a large storage area.

COTTAGE COUNTRY

THREE DORMERS, TWO CHIMNEYS, AND A COVERED FRONT PORCH combine to make this home attractive in any neighborhood. Inside, a great room greets both family and friends with a cathedral ceiling and a warming fireplace. An L-shaped kitchen features a cooktop island. The nearby dining area offers rear-porch access. Upstairs, two secondary bedrooms share a hall bath and access to a bonus room—perfect for a study or computer room.

HOME PLAN

⊕ HPK2500256

Style: Country

First Floor: 1,152 sq. ft.

Second Floor: 452 sq. ft.

Total: 1,604 sq. ft.

Bonus Space: 115 sq. ft.

Bedrooms: 3

Bathrooms: 2 ½

Width: 36' - 0"

Depth: 40' - 0"

Foundation: Crawlspace, Unfinished Basement

eplans.com

FIRST FLOOR

Deck
36'-0" x 12'-0"

Kitchen
18'-0" x 14'-5"

Utility

Pantry

Great Room
18'-0" x 16'-4"
(cathedral clg.)

Master Bedroom
13'-5" x 16'-3"

Porch
36'-0" x 8'-0"

SECOND FLOOR

Bedroom
12'-2" x 11'-10"

Bedroom
10'-0" x 11'-10"

Balcony

open to Great Room below

Bonus Rm.
13'-5" x 7'-2"

HOME PLAN

HPK2500257

Style: Farmhouse

Square Footage: 1,654

Bedrooms: 3

Bathrooms: 1 ½

Width: 51' - 5"

Depth: 66' - 7"

Foundation: Crawlspace, Slab

HOME PLAN

HPK2500258

Style: French Country

Square Footage: 2,194

Bedrooms: 2

Bathrooms: 2

Width: 73' - 0"

Depth: 61' - 8"

Foundation: Finished Walkout Basement

HOME PLAN

HPK2500259

Style: **Contemporary**

Square Footage: **2,001**

Bedrooms: **3**

Bathrooms: **2**

Width: **70' - 10"**

Depth: **48' - 8"**

Foundation: **Crawlspace**

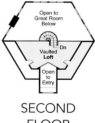

HOME PLAN

HPK2500260

Style: **Craftsman**

First Floor: **2,565 sq. ft.**

Second Floor: **263 sq. ft.**

Total: **2,828 sq. ft.**

Bedrooms: **3**

Bathrooms: **2 ½**

Width: **90' - 0"**

Depth: **85' - 0"**

Foundation: **Unfinished Basement**

HOME PLAN

HPK2500261

Style: Country
Square Footage: 1,890
Bedrooms: 3
Bathrooms: 2
Width: 66' - 0"
Depth: 52' - 0"
Foundation: Crawlspace, Unfinished Basement

OPTIONAL LAYOUT

HOME PLAN

HPK2500262

Style: Craftsman
First Floor: 2,067 sq. ft.
Second Floor: 608 sq. ft.
Total: 2,675 sq. ft.
Bonus Space: 486 sq. ft.
Bedrooms: 4
Bathrooms: 3 ½
Width: 83' - 0"
Depth: 60' - 0"
Foundation: Crawlspace

FIRST FLOOR

SECOND FLOOR

HOME PLAN #

HPK2500263

Style: Craftsman
First Floor: 1,136 sq. ft.
Second Floor: 983 sq. ft.
Total: 2,119 sq. ft.
Bedrooms: 3
Bathrooms: 2 ½
Width: 41' - 0"
Depth: 62' - 0"
Foundation: Crawlspace

FIRST FLOOR

SECOND FLOOR

HOME PLAN #

HPK2500264

Style: Country
First Floor: 1,179 sq. ft.
Second Floor: 346 sq. ft.
Total: 1,525 sq. ft.
Bedrooms: 3
Bathrooms: 2
Width: 38' - 0"
Depth: 46' - 0"
Foundation: Crawlspace, Slab

FIRST FLOOR

SECOND FLOOR

THIS CHARMING CRAFTSMAN DESIGN OFFERS A SECOND-STORY MASTER BEDROOM with four windows under the gabled dormer. The covered front porch displays column and pier supports. The hearth-warmed gathering room opens to the dining room on the right, where the adjoining kitchen offers enough space for an optional breakfast booth. A home office/guest suite is found in the rear. The second floor holds the lavish master suite and a second bedroom suite with its own private bath.

HOME PLAN

HPK2500265

Style: Craftsman
First Floor: 1,060 sq. ft.
Second Floor: 950 sq. ft.
Total: 2,010 sq. ft.
Bedrooms: 3
Bathrooms: 3
Width: 32' - 0"
Depth: 35' - 0"
Foundation: Crawlspace

eplans.com

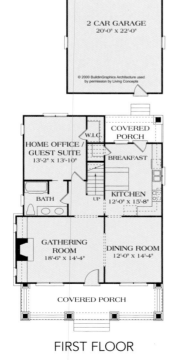

FIRST FLOOR

SECOND FLOOR

COTTAGE COUNTRY

Lap of Luxury

The plans in Villas and Estates are designed to suit the love of luxury in all of us, regardless of location. Spanning such styles as Italianate and Spanish Revival to Neoclassical, these designs are meant for larger coastal, mountain, or countryside property.

Entertainment becomes a main focus in these homes. Not only do they include dining rooms and living rooms for formal occasions as well as breakfast nooks and family rooms for casual events, there is also room for much higher-end amenities. Whether it's call a hearth room, family room, or great room, such a space in these homes becomes a central hub for family and friends and is bound to include a built-in entertainment center and a warming fireplace for amusement and comfort. The kitchen gets pampered as well, with walk-in pantries, working islands, butler's pantries, and wet bars for cocktails.

If this plan is meant to be a vacation home, the whole family is sure to enjoy it. In fact, you may find a play room for the kids, or maybe one for the adults that's large enough for a pool table, big-screen TV, or bar. A sitting or reading loft may serve more quiet forms of entertainment on rainy days spent indoors. Guests and family members will also appreciate the accommodating bedrooms, each equipped with its own private bath and walk-in closet. Outdoor spaces will surely get special attention, with balconies and upper decks accessible from the common rooms or even the bedroom suites.

MASTER SUITES (below) take center stage in larger plans. Note the private access to the lanai.

MEDITERRANEAN DESIGNS (right) are a favorite among seekers of luxury vacation homes.

e Sater Design Collection, Inc.

AN ENCLOSED LAGOON, complete with kitchen and bar, brings the vacation *inside* the home.

When it comes to luxury, the master bedroom gets a V.I.P. treatment. A sitting room may overlook the backyard and a poolside terrace—perhaps with an outdoor fireplace or summer kitchen. A large bedroom area will suit a wide bed with furniture and surrounding space, all below a decorative ceiling. Nearby, one or two walk-in closets could be the size of small rooms. The master bath will be a resort in itself, with twin vanities, a modern open shower, and a window-side tub overlooking a private garden.

Beyond all of the little extras and lavish amenities, the homes in this section provide the same quality of design, layout, and appearance as all of our homes, but with luxurious taste and a desire to meet your every need. In short, these homes are the very best our designers have to offer.

AN OPEN FLOOR PLAN reveals wide interior vistas throughout the home.

FIRST FLOOR

SECOND FLOOR

REAR EXTERIOR

THIS AWARD-WINNING TWO-STORY HOME EMBRACES MANY UNIQUE FEATURES. Entering through the stylish front steps and double entry doors provides a magnificent view of the pool area beyond the living room. A fireplace and built-in shelves grace one wall of the living room. The oversized family room features a built-in entertainment center and a second fireplace. The spacious master suite includes a large sitting area. The luxurious master bath features an oversized tub and a large dual-head shower area. Two huge walk-in closets and His and Hers water closets complete this bathroom design. The study with built-in bookshelves, large guest bedroom suite, powder room, pool bath, utility room, and two separate two-car garages complete the first floor. Large pocket sliders open to the covered lanai and outdoor kitchen area.

HPK2500266

HOME PLAN

Style: Italianate
First Floor: 5,060 sq. ft.
Second Floor: 1,720 sq. ft.
Total: 6,780 sq. ft.
Bedrooms: 5
Bathrooms: 5 ½
Width: 103' - 0"
Depth: 126' - 2"
Foundation: Slab

eplans.com

HOME PLAN

HPK2500267

Style: Italianate

Square Footage: 4,000

Bonus Space: 630 sq. ft.

Bedrooms: 3

Bathrooms: 4

Width: 74' - 6"

Depth: 104' - 10"

Foundation: Slab

eplans.com

THIS STUNNING HOME WON THE PARADE OF HOMES AWARD FOR BEST ARCHITECTURAL DESIGN. It features a unique balance of coziness and elegance. The floor plan flows flawlessly without compromising privacy or style. Natural views and outdoor living spaces enhance the open, spacious feeling inside this home. The overall layout and flow of the house maximize daylight while reflecting grandeur and richness. A pass-through wet bar may also be used as a butler's pantry. The loft above the garage is a fun and logical use of space for a second-floor game room or media room. The gourmet kitchen is superior in design and convenience. The dropped coffered ceiling in the kitchen provides intimate recessed lighting and a wonderful place to display art and kitchen decor.

VILLAS AND ESTATES

FIRST FLOOR

SECOND FLOOR

HPK2500268

HOME PLAN

Style: Italianate

First Floor: 3,633 sq. ft.

Second Floor: 695 sq. ft.

Total: 4,328 sq. ft.

Bedrooms: 5

Bathrooms: 5 ½

Width: 115' - 7"

Depth: 109' - 8"

Foundation: Slab

eplans.com

ARCHED WINDOWS AND A DRAMATIC PORTICO WITH SCROLLED COLUMNS are gracefully featured in this Mediterranean design. The foyer is just as expressive, with more scrolled columns and soft curves to match the arched doorway. Mosaic tiles on the floor and steps bring touches of color and polish to earth-toned surfaces. The master suite and bath with patio are to the right of the plan; the guest rooms are to the left, near the family room and kitchen. A spacious lanai, here enclosed by a greenhouse, features a pool and spa lined with trees and other botanicals. Notice the wet bar, ready with cool drinks for visitors to this unexpected sanctuary.

REAR EXTERIOR

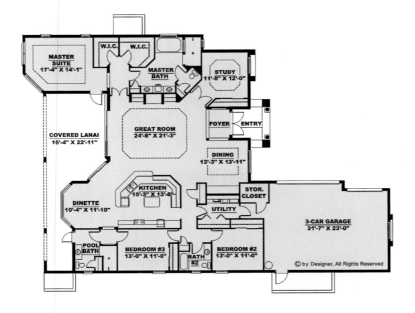

HOME PLAN

HPK2500269

Style: Mediterranean

Square Footage: 2,832

Bedrooms: 3

Bathrooms: 3

Width: 68'-10"

Depth: 94'-8"

Foundation: Slab

eplans.com

A COVERED PATIO ALONG THE BACK OF THE FLOOR PLAN is the main attraction here. Providing rear perspective to the great room from the foyer, this feature is widely accessible. Step directly from the pool bath or from the master suite; or simply enjoy the view over breakfast, or dinner for two. Escape to the study for private meetings or serious reflection. Dine formally beneath a vaulted ceiling. The kids have their own bath, and you can keep an eye on them while you do laundry or rummage through boxes. The garage can house an extra vehicle for the teenager.

VILLAS AND ESTATES

FIRST FLOOR

SECOND FLOOR

A MEDITERRANEAN DREAM—AMENITIES ABOUND THROUGHOUT THIS THREE-BEDROOM HOME. With large rooms and spacious outdoor living areas, this home is great for entertaining. A summer kitchen on the covered lanai and a full pool bath invite the possibility of warm weather fun. The lavish master suite sits to the right of the first floor, equipped with a sitting area, His and Her walk-in closets, and a dual-sink vanity. Upstairs houses two additional family bedrooms—both with full baths—a loft area, and a large study. A three-car garage completes this plan.

HOME PLAN

HPK2500270

Style: Italianate

First Floor: 2,114 sq. ft.

Second Floor: 924 sq. ft.

Total: 3,038 sq. ft.

Bedrooms: 3

Bathrooms: 4

Width: 60' - 0"

Depth: 62' - 8"

Foundation: Slab

eplans.com

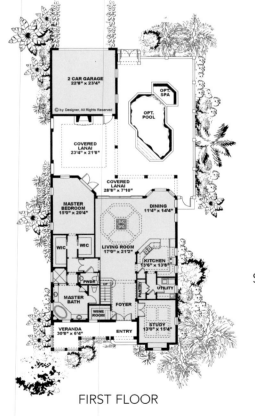

FIRST FLOOR

SECOND FLOOR

HPK2500271

Style: Cottage

First Floor: 2,289 sq. ft.

Second Floor: 1,090 sq. ft.

Total: 3,379 sq. ft.

Bedrooms: 3

Bathrooms: 3 ½

Width: 45' - 0"

Depth: 109' - 4"

Foundation: Crawlspace

eplans.com

A COZY, COUNTRY-STYLE EXTERIOR OPENS UP TO EXPOSE AN INTERIOR OF SUBLIME LUXURY. A wine room right off the foyer immediately reveals that the homeowners have a knack for tasteful entertainment. Space for both formal and informal gatherings is provided by an expansive living room, an open dining room adjoining a gourmet kitchen, and a sprawling lanai. An outdoor fireplace supplies warmth on chilly nights, while tiled floors within keep the home feeling comfortably cool through summer in the subtropics.

HOME PLAN

HPK2500272

Style: Italianate

Square Footage: 3,448

Bedrooms: 4

Bathrooms: 4

Width: 74' - 4"

Depth: 93' - 0"

Foundation: Slab

HOME PLAN

HPK2500273

Style: Mediterranean

Square Footage: 3,462

Bedrooms: 3

Bathrooms: 3

Width: 79' - 8"

Depth: 101' - 4"

Foundation: Slab

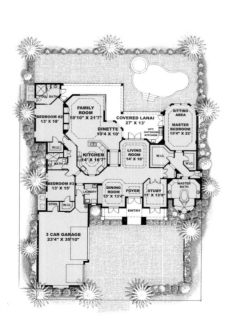

HOME PLAN
HPK2500274

Style: Mediterranean
First Floor: 2,951 sq. ft.
Second Floor: 299 sq. ft.
Total: 3,250 sq. ft.
Bedrooms: 3
Bathrooms: 3
Width: 69' - 8"
Depth: 96' - 8"
Foundation: Slab

FIRST FLOOR

SECOND FLOOR

FIRST FLOOR

HOME PLAN
HPK2500275

Style: Mediterranean
First Floor: 2,856 sq. ft.
Second Floor: 1,158 sq. ft.
Total: 4,014 sq. ft.
Bedrooms: 4
Bathrooms: 4
Width: 77' - 0"
Depth: 64' - 4"
Foundation: Crawlspace

SECOND FLOOR

VILLAS AND ESTATES

SECOND FLOOR

FIRST FLOOR

HOME PLAN

HPK2500276

Style: Mediterranean

First Floor: 2,834 sq. ft.

Second Floor: 1,364 sq. ft.

Total: 4,198 sq. ft.

Bedrooms: 5

Bathrooms: 4 ½ + ½

Width: 64' - 8"

Depth: 64' - 8"

Foundation: Slab

eplans.com

PERFECTLY SEMI-CIRCULAR ARCHES RESTING ATOP SMOOTH TUSCAN COLUMNS EVOKE THE RUSTIC ELEGANCE of an Italian villa. The impression strengthens inside, where a grand staircase spirals from cool tiled floors to a lofty coffered ceiling. Naturally, no Italian villa would be complete without a spectacular kitchen, and this one delivers. Its efficiently-angled design is reflected by the octagonal stepped ceiling, lending it aesthetic value as well as practicality.

HPK2500277

Style: Mission
First Floor: 4,747 sq. ft.
Second Floor: 1,737 sq. ft.
Total: 6,484 sq. ft.
Bonus Space: 196 sq. ft.
Bedrooms: 5
Bathrooms: 4 ½ + ½
Width: 161' - 9"
Depth: 60' - 7"
Foundation: Crawlspace

eplans.com

REAR EXTERIOR

THE FACADE IS A MIX OF CALIFORNIA MISSION STYLE AND ITALIANATE with stone siding, stucco accents, and a tile roof. The thoroughly modern interior is nearly mansion-sized and designed for luxury living. Some of the many elements you'll love about this design include four family bedrooms (two with private baths), a master suite with His and Hers walk-in closets and dressing areas, two laundry areas, a home theater room, a vaulted playroom, and a unique tower room with attached deck. Choose formal or casual dining spaces—they flank the island kitchen, which also boasts a pizza oven and walk-in pantry. A butler's pantry and a wet bar add convenience to entertaining. Enjoy the outdoor spaces with three trellised porches at the rear of the plan. A three-car garage accesses the main part of the house via a handy mudroom.

VILLAS AND ESTATES

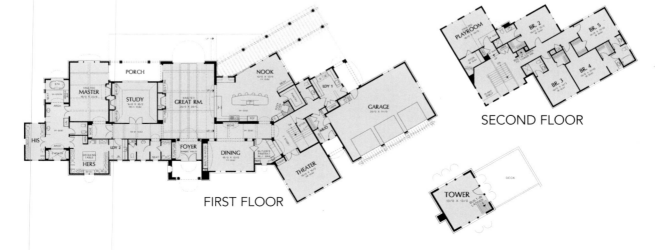

FIRST FLOOR

SECOND FLOOR

TOWER

FIRST FLOOR

Master Suite
14'8" x 15'4"

Living
15'2" x 17'10"

Screened Porch
14' x 9'6"

Dining
14'2" x 10'10"

Entry

Kitchen

Pool

Family
13'10" x 13'10"

Nook
7'10" x 9'6"

Up

Utility

Guest Suite
10'4" x 12'8"

Gated Entry

Garage
21'8" x 22'10"

SECOND FLOOR

Bedroom
11'2" x 12'10"

Open to Family Below

Dn

Bedroom
12' x 14'2"

IT'S JUST A FEW STEPS TO THE POOL FROM ALMOST ANYWHERE IN THIS HOME! The family room, owners' bath, and guest suite all open to the courtyard. The balcony upstairs overlooks the family room and pool area, and the staircase leads right down to a set of sliding glass doors that also open to the pool. Upstairs bedrooms share a bathroom that is compartmented by a pocket door. A laundry chute in the large linen closet deposits items right by the washing machine downstairs. In the kitchen, a U-shaped counter nestles into its own bay. Sliding glass doors in the dining room open onto a screened porch for outdoor dining. The spacious living room serves as a buffer between the active family gathering areas and the secluded owners' suite. The highlight here is a corner spa tub brightened by glass blocks.

HOME PLAN

HPK2500278

Style: Spanish Revival

First Floor: 1,748 sq. ft.

Second Floor: 581 sq. ft.

Total: 2,329 sq. ft.

Bonus Space: 238 sq. ft.

Bedrooms: 4

Bathrooms: 3 ½

Width: 48' - 0"

Depth: 73' - 0"

Foundation: Slab, Unfinished Basement

eplans.com

Patio

Great Room

Dining **Living**

Patio **Patio**

Kitchen **Up**

Bedroom
12'4" x 12'10"

Entry

Master Suite
21' x 19'

Bedroom
11'2" x 12'

Utility

Entry Courtyard

Garage
23' x 27'6"

FIRST FLOOR

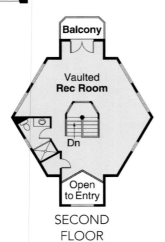

Balcony

**Vaulted
Rec Room**

Dn

**Open
to Entry**

SECOND
FLOOR

HPK2500279

Style: Mediterranean

First Floor: 2,375 sq. ft.

Second Floor: 604 sq. ft.

Total: 2,979 sq. ft.

Bedrooms: 3

Bathrooms: 3

Width: 77' - 1"

Depth: 85' - 8"

Foundation: Crawlspace

eplans.com

AN INGENIOUS PLAN IS HIDDEN WITHIN A MEDITERRANEAN-STYLE EXTERIOR, complete with a tile roof and colonnaded courtyard. The welcoming entrance leads into a hexagonal space which houses the kitchen, dining room, and gathering areas. Two wings extend from the central space, giving maximum privacy to the master suite, to the right, and two family bedrooms to the left. A stairway rises through the center of the gathering space to a vaulted rec room, where a full bath enables the space to serve as a guest room in a pinch. A patio wraps around the entire back of the home for ultimate outdoor living.

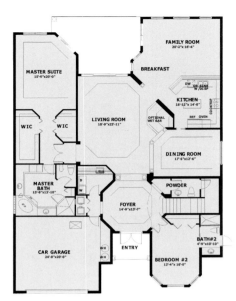

FIRST FLOOR

SECOND FLOOR

A WIDE BAY CREATES THE EFFECT OF A TURRET AND HOUSES BEDROOMS UPSTAIRS AND DOWN. Tucked behind the turret is an arched entry opening to an octagonal foyer with a spectacular vaulted ceiling. Through a columned doorway lies the spacious living room. An optional wet bar facilitates special events. A formal dining room is open to the living room, and a passage leads to the breakfast room, kitchen, and family room. On the opposite side of the plan lies the master suite, complete with dual walk-in closets and a sumptuous bath made for sharing. Upstairs, two additional bedrooms suites share a balcony overlooking the foyer.

HOME PLAN

(#) HPK2500280

Style: Mediterranean

First Floor: 2,993 sq. ft.

Second Floor: 729 sq. ft.

Total: 3,722 sq. ft.

Bedrooms: 4

Bathrooms: 4 ½

Width: 54' - 9"

Depth: 74' - 9"

Foundation: Slab

eplans.com

THIS EXPANSIVE PLAN CREATES THREE SEPARATE LIVING AREAS, offering ultimate privacy to family and visitors. Vaulted living areas divide the lower floor's bedroom suite from the kitchen and family room. Upstairs, a bridge spans the vaulted spaces, serving as the only link between the master suite and two family bedrooms. Bay windows increase the space and light in both of these rooms and add interest to the exterior. Beyond the pool, a cabana features all the amenities of a small apartment, making it a perfect place to house guests.

HOME PLAN

HPK2500281

Style: Mediterranean
First Floor: 2,819 sq. ft.
Second Floor: 1,800 sq. ft.
Total: 4,619 sq. ft.
Bedrooms: 5
Bathrooms: 6 ½
Width: 83' - 8"
Depth: 83' - 10"
Foundation: Slab

eplans.com

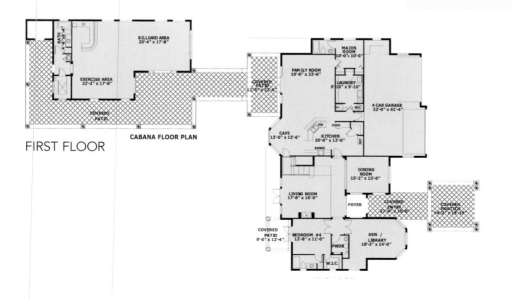

FIRST FLOOR

SECOND FLOOR

VILLAS AND ESTATES

FIRST FLOOR

SECOND FLOOR

HPK2500282

Style: Norman

First Floor: 2,280 sq. ft.

Second Floor: 329 sq. ft.

Total: 2,609 sq. ft.

Bedrooms: 4

Bathrooms: 3

Width: 68' - 8"

Depth: 78' - 6"

Foundation: Crawlspace, Slab

HOME PLAN #

eplans.com

BRING THE OUTDOORS IN! A glass-enclosed atrium sits at the center of this fantastic plan, giving all the major rooms double exposure to light and nature. A rustic stone tower draws visitors through the courtyard to the entry, which opens to a vaulted foyer highlighted by a large planter whose backdrop is the atrium. To the right, two family bedrooms share a dual-sink bath. The master suite lies alongside the atrium and opens to a screened porch at the rear of the home. On the other side of the atrium is the breakfast nook; here, a glass block wall acts as a decorative screen for the wet bar that serves the great room. The hearth-warmed great room offers access to the atrium and two porches, making it the hub of indoor and outdoor gatherings.

HOME PLAN

HPK2500283

Style: Mediterranean

Main Level: 2,347 sq. ft.

Second Level: 1,800 sq. ft.

Third Level: 1,182 sq. ft.

Lower Level: 1,688 sq. ft.

Total: 7,017 sq. ft.

Bedrooms: 4

Bathrooms: 5 ½

Width: 75' - 5"

Depth: 76' - 4"

Foundation: Finished Walkout Basement

eplans.com

A LEVEL FOR EVERYONE! ON THE FIRST FLOOR, there's a study with a full bath, a formal dining room, a grand room with a fireplace, and a fabulous kitchen with an adjacent morning room. The second floor contains three suites—each with a walk-in closet—two full baths, a loft, and a reading nook. A lavish master suite on the third floor is full of amenities, including His and Hers walk-in closets, a huge private bath, and a balcony. In the basement, casual entertaining takes off with a large gathering room, a home theater, and a spacious game room.

MAIN LEVEL

SECOND LEVEL

THIRD LEVEL

LOWER LEVEL

VILLAS AND ESTATES

THE DRAMATIC ENTRANCE OF THIS GRAND SUN COUNTRY HOME gives way to interesting angles and optimum livability inside. Columns frame the formal living room, which provides views of the rear grounds from the foyer. The private master bedroom is contained on the left portion of the plan. Here, a relaxing master bath provides an abundance of amenities that include a walk-in closet, a bumped-out whirlpool tub, a separate shower, and a double-bowl vanity. A clutter room and powder room complete this wing. Centrally located for efficiency, the kitchen easily serves the living room—via a pass-through—as well as the formal dining room, family room, and flex room. Three secondary bedrooms share two full baths.

HOME PLAN

HPK2500284

Style: Spanish Revival
Square Footage: 2,966
Bedrooms: 4
Bathrooms: 3 ½
Width: 114' - 10"
Depth: 79' - 2"
Foundation: Slab

eplans.com

HPK2500285

Style: Mediterranean

Square Footage: 2,678

Bedrooms: 5

Bathrooms: 4

Width: 76' - 6"

Depth: 77' - 4"

Foundation: Slab

eplans.com

HOME PLAN

THE HOME YOU'VE BEEN LOOKING FOR—A STATELY STUCCO ONE-STORY HOME with a spellbinding entrance. With five bedrooms it's sized just right. For added flexibility, the guest room located to the front of the plan can be used as a home office. The great room will accommodate any size gathering and will do so with the charm of a fireplace, built-ins, and extensive rear patio access. The dining room sits in a bay that looks out to the side yard and is easily served by the spacious, hardworking kitchen. Another bedroom, just off the laundry room, provides more space for guests or even a second office space.

VILLAS AND ESTATES

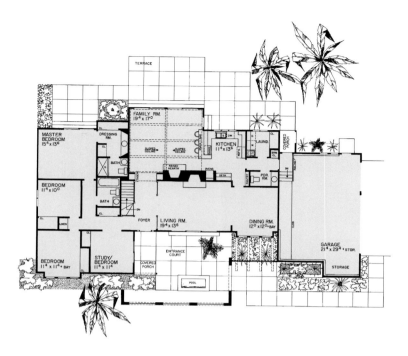

HPK2500286

HOME PLAN

Style: Spanish Revival

Square Footage: 2,261

Bedrooms: 4

Bathrooms: 2 ½

Width: 85' - 8"

Depth: 46' - 0"

Foundation: Unfinished Basement

eplans.com

A PRIVACY WALL AROUND THE COURTYARD WITH A POOL AND TRELLISED PLANTER area is a gracious way by which to enter this one-story design. The Spanish flavor is accented by the grillwork and the tiled roof. The front living room has sliding glass doors that open to the entrance court. The adjacent dining room features a bay window. Informal activities will be enjoyed in the rear family room with a sloped, beamed ceiling; a raised-hearth fireplace; sliding glass doors to the terrace; and a snack bar. The sleeping wing can remain quiet away from the plan's activity centers. Notice the three-car garage with extra storage space.

REAR EXTERIOR

HOME PLAN

HPK2500287

Style: Prairie
First Floor: 3,201 sq. ft.
Second Floor: 950 sq. ft.
Total: 4,051 sq. ft.
Bedrooms: 5
Bathrooms: 4
Width: 154' - 0"
Depth: 94' - 8"
Foundation: Slab

eplans.com

A LONG, LOW-PITCHED ROOF DISTINGUISHES THIS SOUTHWESTERN-STYLE FARMHOUSE DESIGN. The tiled entrance leads to a grand dining room and opens to a formal parlor secluded by half-walls. A country kitchen with a cooktop island overlooks the two-story gathering room with its full wall of glass, fireplace, and built-in media shelves. The master suite satisfies the most discerning tastes with a raised hearth, an adjacent study or exercise room, access to the wraparound porch, and a bath with a corner whirlpool tub. Rooms upstairs can serve as secondary bedrooms for family members, be converted to home office space, or used as guest bedrooms.

FIRST FLOOR

SECOND FLOOR

VILLAS AND ESTATES

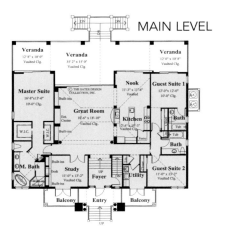

MAIN LEVEL

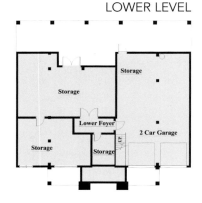

LOWER LEVEL

THIS ENTICING EUROPEAN VILLA BOASTS AN ITALIAN CHARM AND A DISTINCT MEDITERRANEAN FEEL. The foyer steps lead up to the formal living areas. To the left, a study is expanded by a vaulted ceiling and double doors that open to the front balcony. The island kitchen is conveniently open to a breakfast nook. The guest quarters reside on the right side of the plan—one suite boasts a private bath; the other uses a full hall bath. The secluded master suite features two walk-in closets and a pampering whirlpool master bath. The home is completed by a basement-level garage.

HOME PLAN

HPK2500288

Style: Mediterranean
Main Level: 2,385 sq. ft.
Lower Level: 109 sq. ft.
Total: 2,494 sq. ft.
Bedrooms: 3
Bathrooms: 3
Width: 60' - 0"
Depth: 52' - 0"
Foundation: Slab

eplans.com

REAR EXTERIOR

© Sater Design Collection, Inc.

HOME PLAN

HPK2500289

Style: Mediterranean

Square Footage: 2,794

Bedrooms: 3

Bathrooms: 3

Width: 70' - 0"

Depth: 98' - 0"

Foundation: Slab

eplans.com

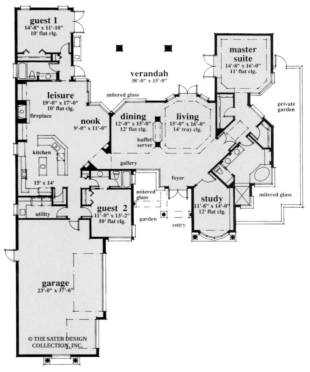

CLASSIC COLUMNS, CIRCLE-HEAD WINDOWS, AND A BAY-WINDOWED STUDY give this stucco home a wonderful street presence. The foyer leads to the formal living and dining areas. An arched buffet server separates these rooms and contributes to an open feeling. The kitchen, nook, and leisure room are grouped for informal living. A desk/message center in the island kitchen, art niches in the nook, and a fireplace with an entertainment center and shelves add custom touches. Two secondary suites have guest baths and offer full privacy from the master wing. The master suite hosts a private garden area; the bath features a walk-in shower that overlooks the garden and a water closet. Large His and Hers walk-in closets complete these private quarters.

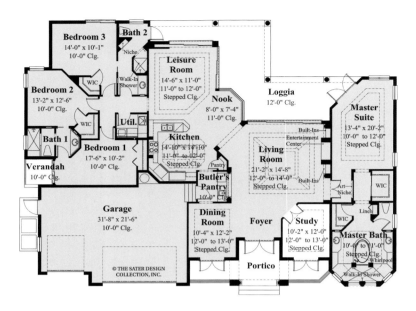

Floor plan labels:

Bedroom 3
14'-0" x 10'-1"
10'-0" Clg.

Bath 2

Niche

Leisure Room
14'-6" x 11'-0"
11'-0" to 12'-0"
Stepped Clg.

Loggia
12'-0" Clg.

Bedroom 2
13'-2" x 12'-6"
10'-0" Clg.

WIC

Walk-In Shower

Nook
8'-0" x 7'-4"
11'-0" Clg.

Master Suite
13'-4" x 20'-2"
10'-0" to 12'-0"
Stepped Clg.

WIC

Util.

Kitchen
14'-10" x 14'-10"
11'-0" to 12'-0"
Stepped Clg.

Built-Ins
Entertainment Center

Living Room
21'-2" x 14'-8"
12'-0" to 14'-0"
Stepped Clg.

Bath 1

Bedroom 1
17'-6" x 10'-2"
10'-0" Clg.

Pantry

Built-Ins

Art Niche

WIC

Verandah
10'-0" Clg.

Butler's Pantry
10'-0"

Linen

Garage
31'-8" x 21'-6"
10'-0" Clg.

Dining Room
10'-4" x 12'-2"
12'-0" to 13'-0"
Stepped Clg.

Foyer

Study
10'-2" x 12'-0"
12'-0" to 13'-0"
Stepped Clg.

Master Bath
10'-0" to 11'-0"
Stepped Clg.

WIC

Whirlpool

Walk-In Shower

Portico

© THE SATER DESIGN COLLECTION, INC.

HPK2500290

Style: Italianate

Square Footage: 2,808

Bedrooms: 4

Bathrooms: 3

Width: 80' - 10"

Depth: 59' - 10"

Foundation: Slab

eplans.com

THE NOBLE FAMILIES OF ROME, LIKE CITY-DWELLERS TODAY, understood the need for a country home—a place where they could commune with nature and rejuvenate their spirits in an informal setting. This Italianate villa is a classic example of a country home, rustic and expansive, with all the amenities of city life contained inside. Bedroom suites are imagined as spa-like retreats; the gourmet kitchen is shaped by the concept of cooking as a recreational activity. Gathering areas and dining areas are casual and open, and of course, there is plenty of room for outdoor relaxation.

HOME PLAN

#️⃣ HPK2500291

Style: Italianate

Square Footage: 2,907

Bedrooms: 3

Bathrooms: 2 ½

Width: 65' - 0"

Depth: 84' - 0"

Foundation: Slab

eplans.com

REAR EXTERIOR

THE FINE SYMMETRY OF AN ITALIANATE FACADE WILL MAKE A LASTING IMPRESSION ON VISITORS to this grand manor. Beyond the portico, the living room and dining room demonstrate the designer's emphasis on high, stepped ceilings and dramatically angled interior walls. To the left, an extraordinary master bath—with dual vanities and a corner tub overlooking a private garden—and a huge walk-in closet make up the master suite. At the rear, the leisure room and breakfast nook provide casual spaces for family gatherings around the kitchen and benefit from natural light entering by way of the lanai. To the right, two bedrooms share a full bath. The utility room located near the garage is a handy space for laundry and other housework. Sculpture niches adorn the walls throughout the house.

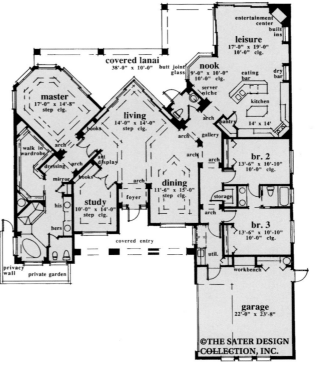

©THE SATER DESIGN COLLECTION, INC.

VILLAS AND ESTATES

FIRST FLOOR

SECOND FLOOR

A UNIQUE COURTYARD PROVIDES A HAPPY MEDIUM FOR INDOOR/OUTDOOR LIVING IN THIS DESIGN. Inside, the foyer opens to a grand salon with a wall of glass, providing unobstructed views of the backyard. Informal areas include a leisure room with an entertainment center and glass doors that open to a covered poolside lanai. An outdoor fireplace enhances casual gatherings. The master suite is filled with amenities that include a bayed sitting area, access to the rear lanai, His and Hers closets, and a soaking tub. Upstairs, two family bedrooms—both with private decks—share a full bath. A detached guest house has a cabana bath and an outdoor grill area.

HPK2500292

Style: Mediterranean

First Floor: 3,134 sq. ft.

Second Floor: 610 sq. ft.

Total: 3,744 sq. ft.

Bedrooms: 4

Bathrooms: 3 ½

Width: 80' - 0"

Depth: 96' - 0"

Foundation: Slab

eplans.com

REAR EXTERIOR

©The Sater Design Collection, Inc.

HOME PLAN

HPK2500293

Style: Mediterranean
First Floor: 3,328 sq. ft.
Second Floor: 497 sq. ft.
Total: 3,825 sq. ft.
Bedrooms: 3
Bathrooms: 4
Width: 89' - 9"
Depth: 104' - 0"
Foundation: Slab

eplans.com

FIRST FLOOR

Lanai 12'-0" Ceiling
Guest Bath 10'-0" Ceiling
Leisure Room 17'-4" x 22'-11" Vaulted Ceiling
Nook 12'-0" Ceiling
Guest Suite 17'-5" x 17'-8" 10'-0" - 11'-6" Stepped Ceiling
Lanai 12'-0" Ceiling
Master Suite 16'-2" x 21'-10" 10'-0" - 12'-0" Stepped Ceiling
Living Room 18'-8" x 19'-1" 12'-0" - 14'-0" Stepped Ceiling
Kitchen 16'-0" x 14'-6" 11'-0"-12'-0" Stepped Ceiling
Atrium
WIC
WIC
Study 13'-0" x 13'-0" 13'-0"-13'-0" Stepped Ceiling
Foyer
Dining Rm. 13'-0" x 13'-0" 12'-0" - 13'-0" Stepped Ceiling
Bath 2
Bedroom 2 16'-6" x 11'-6" 10'-0" Ceiling
Master Bath 10'-0" Ceiling
Entry
Utility 8'-2" x 7'-8"
Up
© THE SATER DESIGN COLLECTION, INC.
Garage 22'-8" x 32'-10" 9'-0" Ceiling

SECOND FLOOR

Bonus Room 23'-3" x 19'-10" Vaulted Ceiling
WIC
Storage

THIS COASTAL DREAM HOME IS DESIGNED FOR WARM WEATHER, luxurious living, and effortless entertaining. A grand entry opens to a palatial living room with a stepped ceiling and panoramic views. The study and dining room are nearby, each with a bayed window wall to let natural light pour in. Everyday living takes place in the uniquely shaped leisure room, which enjoys easy access to the spacious rear lanai. A centrally located island kitchen prepares gourmet meals and snacks on the go. A family bedroom features a semiprivate bath and views of the atrium. The master suite reigns over the left wing, opulent with a soothing bedroom, spectacular bath, and plenty of walk-in closet space. Completing the plan is a magnificent guest suite with a bathroom that can double as a pool bath.

REAR EXTERIOR

PERFECT FOR THE CALIFORNIA COAST, THIS STUCCO DESIGN is an alluring masterpiece. The luxurious interior is introduced by a set of double doors that open into the spacious foyer. The foyer is flanked on either side by the study and exquisite dining room shaped by elegant columns. Straight ahead, the formal living room opens through two sets of double doors onto a rear terrace. The gourmet island kitchen overlooks the tiled nook and leisure room. An outdoor kitchen conveniently serves the pool area, which features a cozy spa and cascading spillover. The master suite indulges with enchanting style. Walk past two walk-in closets to the spacious master bath with whirlpool tub luxury. A door from the master bath accesses a private side garden. Two guest suites on the opposite side of the home share a full bath off the utility room. A three-car garage completes this plan.

HOME PLAN

HPK2500294

Style: Mediterranean

Square Footage: 3,688

Bedrooms: 3

Bathrooms: 3 ½

Width: 129' - 0"

Depth: 102' - 0"

Foundation: Slab

eplans.com

REAR EXTERIOR

© The Sater Design Collection, Inc.

HOME PLAN

HPK2500295

Style: Italianate

First Floor: 3,933 sq. ft.

Second Floor: 719 sq. ft.

Total: 4,652 sq. ft.

Bedrooms: 4

Bathrooms: 4 ½

Width: 91' - 4"

Depth: 109' - 0"

Foundation: Slab

eplans.com

BEAUTIFUL AND SPACIOUS, THE ARTFUL DISPOSITION OF THIS LUXURIOUS VILLA has a distinctly Mediterranean flavor. Dramatic and inspiring, the vaulted entry is set off by a dashing arch framed by columns, a barrel ceiling, and double doors that open to an expansive interior. The octagonal living room provides a fireplace and opens through two sets of lovely doors to the rear lanai. The master wing is a sumptuous retreat with double doors that open from a private vaulted foyer. One of the spacious guest suites can easily convert to personal quarters for a live-in relative. Another guest suite boasts a full bath, a bay window, and a walk-in closet. An upper-level loft leads to a third guest suite.

FIRST FLOOR

SECOND FLOOR

VILLAS AND ESTATES

FIRST FLOOR

SECOND FLOOR

HPK2500296

HOME PLAN

Style: Italianate

First Floor: 4,137 sq. ft.

Second Floor: 876 sq. ft.

Total: 5,013 sq. ft.

Bedrooms: 4

Bathrooms: 5

Width: 81' - 10"

Depth: 113' - 0"

Foundation: Slab

eplans.com

DECORATIVE COLUMNS GRACE THE ENTRANCE OF THIS MAJESTIC ESTATE, adding elegance and allure to an already impressive facade. Inside, the open layout lends itself to entertaining with the living and dining rooms centrally located, adjacent to a wet bar. The master suite dominates the right side of the plan, complete with a sitting room and privacy garden and replete with upgraded amenities, including a morning kitchen. The spacious study is conveniently located nearby. Boasting a built-in entertainment center, the leisure room at the rear of the home will be a family favorite. An outdoor kitchen on the veranda makes alfresco meals an option. The second floor houses a bedroom, full bath, and loft—perfect for guests.

REAR EXTERIOR

HOME PLAN

HPK2500297

Style: Mediterranean

First Floor: 4,385 sq. ft.

Second Floor: 1,431 sq. ft.

Total: 5,816 sq. ft.

Bedrooms: 5

Bathrooms: 6

Width: 88' - 0"

Depth: 110' - 1"

Foundation: Slab

eplans.com

REAR EXTERIOR

FIRST FLOOR

SECOND FLOOR

LOW ROOFLINES AND GRAND ARCHES LEND A MEDITERRANEAN FLAVOR to this contemporary estate. Lovely glass-paneled doors lead to an open interior defined by decorative columns, stone arches, and solid coffered ceilings. A formal living room boasts a fireplace, access to the veranda, and over-sized windows for amazing views. Leisure space near the kitchen invites casual gatherings and allows the family to relax in front of a built-in entertainment center. A favorite feature, the outdoor kitchen encourages dining alfresco. A secluded master suite—with a sitting area, splendid bath, and access to the veranda—stretches across the left wing, which includes a quiet study with a vintage high-beamed ceiling. Among the four additional bedroom suites, one boasts a morning kitchen, and two others have access to a private deck or veranda.

VILLAS AND ESTATES

FIRST FLOOR

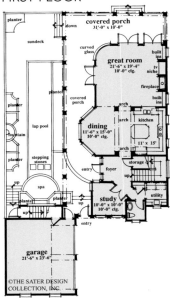

- covered porch 31'-0" x 10'-0"
- planter
- sundeck
- curved glass
- great room 21'-6" x 19'-4" 10'-0" clg.
- built ins
- tv niche
- fireplace
- covered porch
- built ins
- planter
- arch
- dining 11'-6" x 15'-0" 10'-0" clg.
- kitchen
- lap pool
- 11' x 15'
- fountain
- planter
- arch
- stepping stones
- foyer
- storage
- up
- up
- entry
- spa
- study 10'-0" x 10'-0" 10'-0" clg.
- utility
- up
- planter
- entry
- garage 21'-6" x 23'-6"
- ©THE SATER DESIGN COLLECTION, INC.

SECOND FLOOR

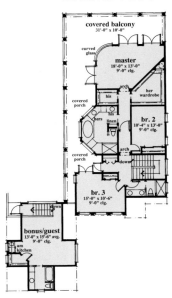

- covered balcony 31'-0" x 10'-0"
- curved glass
- master 18'-0" x 13'-0" 9'-0" clg.
- arch
- his
- her wardrobe
- covered porch
- hers
- linen
- br. 2 10'-4" x 13'-0" 9'-0" clg.
- covered porch
- arch
- down
- br. 3 15'-0" x 10'-6" 9'-0" clg.
- down
- bonus/guest 13'-0" x 15'-6" avg. 9'-0" clg.
- am kitchen

REAR EXTERIOR

LOUVERED SHUTTERS, CIRCLE-HEAD WINDOWS, and a courtyard are images from the Charleston Row past brought up-to-date in a floor plan for today's lifestyles. From the great room, three sets of French doors open to the covered porch and sundeck. The U-shaped kitchen includes a central island and adjoins the dining bay. The second floor includes two family bedrooms, a master suite, and a bonus room with a private bath, walk-in closet, and morning kitchen. A covered balcony is accessible from the master suite and Bedroom 3.

HOME PLAN

HPK2500298

Style: Italianate
First Floor: 1,293 sq. ft.
Second Floor: 1,580 sq. ft.
Total: 2,873 sq. ft.
Bonus Space: 426 sq. ft.
Bedrooms: 3
Bathrooms: 2 ½
Width: 50' - 0"
Depth: 90' - 0"
Foundation: Slab

eplans.com

© The Sater Design Collection, Inc.

FIRST FLOOR

SECOND FLOOR

HPK2500299

HOME PLAN

Style: Italianate

First Floor: 2,083 sq. ft.

Second Floor: 1,013 sq. ft.

Total: 3,096 sq. ft.

Bedrooms: 4

Bathrooms: 3 ½

Width: 74' - 0"

Depth: 88' - 0"

Foundation: Slab

eplans.com

THIS COUNTRY VILLA DESIGN IS ACCENTED BY A GAZEBO-STYLE FRONT PORCH and an abundance of arched windows. Most of the rooms in this house are graced with tray, stepped, or vaulted ceilings, enhancing the entire plan. The first-floor master suite boasts multiple amenities, including a private lanai, His and Hers walk-in closets, and a bayed whirlpool tub. Other highlights on this floor include a study with a window seat and built-in cabinetry, a bayed breakfast nook, a butler's pantry in the island kitchen, a utility room, and an outdoor kitchen on the lanai. Three secondary bedrooms reside upstairs, along with two full baths.

THIS MODERN TAKE ON THE ITALIAN VILLA BOASTS PLENTY OF INDOOR/OUT-DOOR FLOW. Four sets of double doors wrap around the great room and dining area and open to the stunning veranda. The great room is enhanced by a coffered ceiling and built-in cabinetry, and the entire first floor is bathed in sunlight from a wall of glass doors overlooking the veranda. The dining room connects to a gourmet island kitchen. Upstairs, a beautiful deck wraps gracefully around the family bedrooms. The master suite is a skylit haven enhanced by a sitting bay, which features a vaulted octagonal ceiling and a cozy two-sided fireplace. Private double doors access the sundeck from the master suite, the secondary bedrooms, and the study.

HOME PLAN

HPK2500300

Style: Italianate

First Floor: 1,266 sq. ft.

Second Floor: 1,324 sq. ft.

Total: 2,590 sq. ft.

Bedrooms: 3

Bathrooms: 2 ½

Width: 34' - 0"

Depth: 63' - 2"

Foundation: Slab

eplans.com

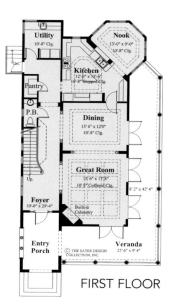

FIRST FLOOR

SECOND FLOOR

© The Sater Design Collection, Inc.

©The Sater Design Collection, Inc.

HOME PLAN

(#) HPK2500301

Style: New American

First Floor: 1,266 sq. ft.

Second Floor: 1,324 sq. ft.

Total: 2,590 sq. ft.

Bedrooms: 3

Bathrooms: 2 ½

Width: 34' - 0"

Depth: 63' - 2"

Foundation: Crawlspace

eplans.com

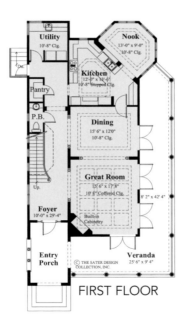

FIRST FLOOR

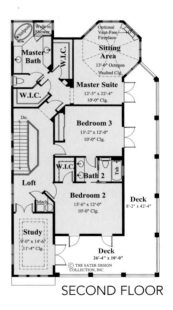

SECOND FLOOR

THIS FLORIDIAN-STYLE HOME BOASTS AN IMPRESSIVE BALCONY THAT IS SURE TO CATCH THE EYE. A large veranda borders two sides of the home. The entry leads into a long foyer, which runs from the entrance to the rear of the design. The coffered great room enjoys a fireplace, built-in cabinetry, and French doors to the veranda; the dining room also accesses the veranda. The island kitchen leads into a bayed nook, perfect for Sunday morning breakfasting. The second floor is home to two family bedrooms—both with access to the deck—a study, and a luxurious master suite. A vaulted sitting area, full bath, and deck access are just some of the highlights of the master suite.

VILLAS AND ESTATES

FIRST FLOOR

ARCHED IRON GATES IN THE PORTICO OFFER REGAL ENTRY TO A FABULOUS secluded courtyard. Rooms surround a pool and fountain with lots of glass for seamless indoor-outdoor living. A second floor features two guest suites and a loft, plus a balcony and deck that offer views of the courtyard from two different perspectives. The master suite has an elegant foyer and a private garden.

SECOND FLOOR

HOME PLAN

HPK2500302

Style: Mediterranean

First Floor: 2,254 sq. ft.

Second Floor: 777 sq. ft.

Total: 3,031 sq. ft.

Bedrooms: 4

Bathrooms: 5

Width: 52' - 0"

Depth: 95' - 8"

Foundation: Slab

eplans.com

© Sater Design Collection, Inc.

© The Sater Design Collection

HPK2500303

Style: Mediterranean

First Floor: 2,920 sq. ft.

Second Floor: 1,478 sq. ft.

Total: 4,398 sq. ft.

Bedrooms: 6

Bathrooms: 4 ½

Width: 69' - 4"

Depth: 95' - 4"

Foundation: Slab

eplans.com

FIRST FLOOR

SECOND FLOOR

A STONE TURRET HOUSES AN AMAZING MASTER BATH IN THIS ELEGANT TUSCAN RETREAT. A whirlpool tub occupies the center of the octagonal room, separating His space from Hers. There are even discrete water closets! The walk-in shower occupies the alcove behind the tub and may be entered from either side of the bath. Windows are placed high in the walls, providing light without compromising privacy. The adjoining suite has access to the rear veranda, which can serve as an extension of the living and dining areas by throwing open the four sets of French doors that line these rooms. Across the columned gallery are three sets of French doors that open to the front portico, creating comfortable breezes within.

VILLAS AND ESTATES

PERFECT FOR A CORNER LOT, THIS MEDITERRANEAN VILLA IS A BEAUTIFUL ADDITION TO ANY NEIGHBORHOOD. Low and unassuming on the outside, this plan brings modern amenities and classic stylings together for a great family home. The study and two-story dining room border the foyer; an elongated gallery introduces the great room. Here, a rustic beamed ceiling, fireplace, and art niche are thoughtful touches. The step-saving U-shaped kitchen flows into a sunny bayed breakfast nook. To the far right, two bedrooms share a full bath. The master suite is separated for privacy, situated to the far left. French-door access to the veranda and a sumptuous bath make this a pleasurable retreat.

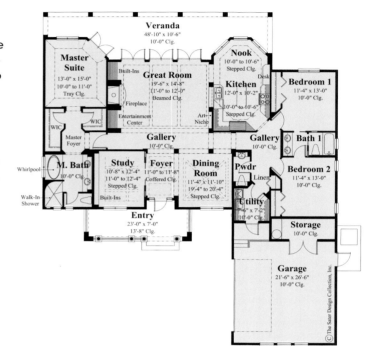

HOME PLAN

HPK2500304

Style: Mediterranean

Square Footage: 2,191

Bedrooms: 3

Bathrooms: 2 ½

Width: 62' - 10"

Depth: 73' - 6"

Foundation: Slab

eplans.com

(#) HPK2500305

Style: Mediterranean
Square Footage: 2,387
Bedrooms: 3
Bathrooms: 3
Width: 53' - 6"
Depth: 94' - 6"
Foundation: Slab

eplans.com

©The Sater Design Collection, Inc.

THIS SUNNY DESIGN OPENS THROUGH DOUBLE DOORS INTO THE GREAT ROOM. A rounded dining area contributes a sense of the dramatic and is easily served by the roomy kitchen. A relaxing study also provides outdoor access. Two secondary bedrooms enjoy ample closet space and share a bath that includes dual vanities. In the master suite, a tiered ceiling and lots of windows gain attention. A luxury bath, with a compartmented toilet, a garden tub, dual vanities, and a separate shower, also offers a walk-in closet. A bath with a stall shower serves the outdoor living areas.

VILLAS AND ESTATES

WITH CALIFORNIA STYLE AND MEDITERRANEAN GOOD LOOKS, this striking stucco manor is sure to delight. The portico and foyer open to reveal a smart plan with convenience and flexibility in mind. The columned living room has a warming fireplace and access to the rear property. In the gourmet kitchen, an open design with an island and walk-in pantry will please any chef. From here, the elegant dining room and sunny nook are easily served. The leisure room is separated from the game room by a built-in entertainment center. The game area can also be finished off as a bedroom. To the rear, a guest room is perfect for frequent visitors or as an in-law suite. The master suite features a bright sitting area, oversized walk-in closets, and a pampering bath with a whirlpool tub. Extra features not to be missed include the outdoor grill, game-room storage, and gallery window seat.

© The Sater Design Collection, Inc.

(#) HPK2500306

Style: Italianate

Square Footage: 3,743

Bedrooms: 4

Bathrooms: 3 ½

Width: 80' - 0"

Depth: 103' - 8"

Foundation: Slab

eplans.com

©The Sater Design Collection, Inc.

THE UNUSUAL LOCATION OF THE GUEST SUITE AT THE FRONT OF THE PLAN and central placement of the courtyard speak of Mediterranean influences in this grand design. Featuring a full bath, walk-in closet, and easy access to the pool, the guest suite will appropriately pamper overnight visitors. At the right of the plan are the shared spaces of the home. A tremendous leisure room, nook, dining room, and great room provide adequate space for even the largest gatherings. The master suite and bath are tucked away at the rear and left of the plan, and offer private access to the rear loggia. Upstairs, three more bedrooms share two baths and separate balconies.

HOME PLAN

HPK2500307

Style: Italianate
First Floor: 2,852 sq. ft.
Second Floor: 969 sq. ft.
Total: 4,151 sq. ft.
Bonus Space: 330 sq. ft.
Bedrooms: 5
Bathrooms: 4 ½
Width: 80' - 0"
Depth: 96' - 0"
Foundation: Slab

eplans.com

FIRST FLOOR

SECOND FLOOR

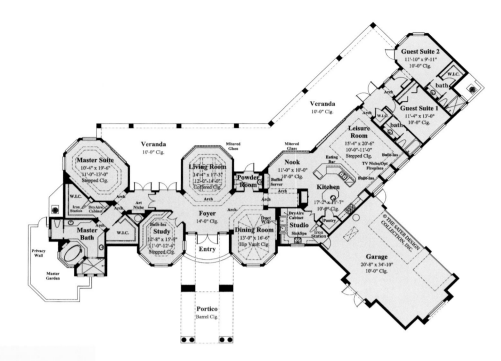

#HOME PLAN

HPK2500308

Style: Mediterranean

Square Footage: 3,398

Bedrooms: 3

Bathrooms: 3 ½

Width: 121' - 5"

Depth: 96' - 2"

Foundation: Slab

eplans.com

BRINGING THE OUTDOORS IN THROUGH A MULTI-TUDE OF BAY WINDOWS is what this design is all about. The grand foyer opens to the living room with a magnificent view to the covered lanai. The study and dining room flank the foyer. The master suite is found on the left with an opulent private bath and views of the private garden. To the right, the kitchen adjoins the nook that boasts a mitered-glass bay window overlooking the lanai. Beyond the leisure room are two guest rooms, each with a private bath.

© The Sater Design Collection, Inc.

A CAREFUL BLEND OF HORIZONTAL SIDING AND STUCCO ACCENTS lends a continental appeal to this voguish home. Cutting-edge style continues with an interior plan designed to accommodate traditional events as well as casual living. A grand foyer opens to two octagonal formal rooms and a gallery hall that leads to the master suite and a guest and living wing. The master suite features a dressing area with a three-way mirror, art niche, and walk-in closet designed for two. Three guest suites share two baths and a private hall with a laundry.

HOME PLAN

HPK2500309

Style: Neoclassical

Square Footage: 3,215

Bedrooms: 4

Bathrooms: 3

Width: 104' - 4"

Depth: 74' - 6"

Foundation: Slab

eplans.com

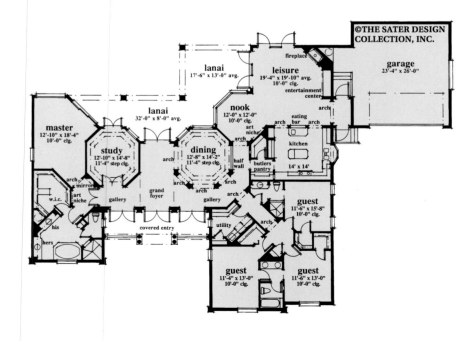

©THE SATER DESIGN COLLECTION, INC.

VILLAS AND ESTATES

FIRST FLOOR

veranda
40'-0" x 9'-0"

leisure
19'-4" x 17'-4"
10' high clg.

optional entertainment center

master suite
15'-0" x 18'-2"
11' step clg.

fireplace

pantry

living
20'-2" x 15'-8"
2 story clg.

desk

kitchen
12' x 12'

nook
9'-0" x 11'-0"

up

utility

study
13'-4" x 12'-0"
12'-6" high clg.

foyer

dining
13'-6" x 14'-0"
vault. clg.

entry

garage
22'-4" x 42'-8"

©THE Sater DESIGN COLLECTION, INC.

SECOND FLOOR

deck

loft
19'-8" x 14'-4"

wetbar

down

open to living below

br. 3
16'-10" x 11'-4"
9'-4" clg.

br. 2
11'-4" x 14'-10"
9'-4" clg.

THIS BEAUTIFUL HOME HAS MANY APPEALING ATTRIBUTES, including a bowed dining room and a living room with a fireplace and outdoor access. For family gatherings, the kitchen remains open to the living areas. A study off the foyer will be much appreciated. A full bath leads to the outdoors—perfect for poolside. The master suite enjoys its own personal luxury bath with a whirlpool tub, dual lavatories, a compartmented toilet and bidet, and a separate shower. Dual walk-in closets provide ample storage space. Upstairs, two bedrooms share a full bath. A loft with a wet bar accommodates playtime. A wraparound deck is an added feature.

HOME PLAN

HPK2500310

Style: New American

First Floor: 2,551 sq. ft.

Second Floor: 1,037 sq. ft.

Total: 3,588 sq. ft.

Bedrooms: 3

Bathrooms: 3 ½

Width: 76' - 0"

Depth: 90' - 0"

Foundation: Slab

eplans.com

HOLZHALER INK 94

© The Sater Design Collection, Inc.

HPK2500311

Style: Mediterranean

Square Footage: 2,089

Bedrooms: 4

Bathrooms: 3

Width: 61' - 8"

Depth: 50' - 4"

Foundation: Slab

eplans.com

THIS FOUR-BEDROOM, THREE-BATH HOME OFFERS THE FINEST IN MODERN AMENITIES. The already spacious family room opens up to the terrace via 12-foot pocket sliding doors, or stay inside to enjoy the fireplace and built-in media center. At left, two family bedrooms share a full bath, and one bedroom suite provides for overnight guests. The master suite, located just off the kitchen and nook, is private yet easily accessible. Note the enviable walk-in closet, step-down shower, and private toilet. The exterior features a robust columned entry and full-height windows.

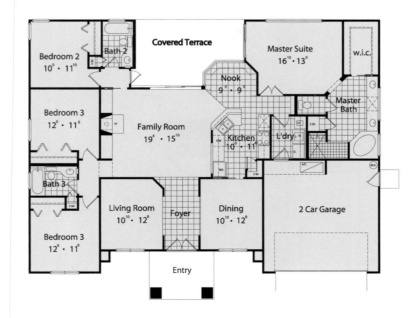

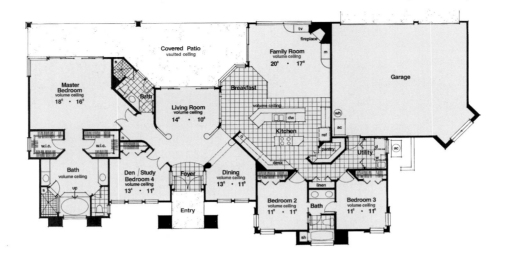

LONG SIGHTLINES AND ACUTE ANGLES CREATE DYNAMIC INTERNAL VISTAS AND ENABLE EASY FLOW-THROUGH of foot traffic. The effects are most noticeable from the foyer, which creates a point of focus for the living room, dining room, and den. To the right, an island kitchen serves the breakfast nook and spacious family room. The den may also convert to a fourth bedroom, if desired. A large pantry provides ample space for food storage. At the other end of the home, a resplendent master suite provides a luxury retreat for homeowners. Majestic columns of brick add warmth to a striking exterior.

HOME PLAN # HPK2500312

Style: Mediterranean

Square Footage: 2,597

Bedrooms: 4

Bathrooms: 3

Width: 96' - 6"

Depth: 50' - 0"

Foundation: Slab

eplans.com

A BEAUTIFUL CURVED PORTICO PROVIDES A MAJESTIC ENTRANCE to this one-story home. To the left of the foyer is a den/bedroom with a private bath, ideal for use as a guest suite. The exquisite master suite features a see-through fireplace and an exercise area with a wet bar. The family wing is geared for casual living with a powder room/patio bath, a huge island kitchen with a walk-in pantry, a glass-walled breakfast nook, and a grand family room with a fireplace and media wall. Two family bedrooms share a private bath.

HOME PLAN

HPK2500313

Style: Mediterranean

Square Footage: 3,556

Bedrooms: 4

Bathrooms: 3 ½

Width: 85' - 0"

Depth: 85' - 0"

Foundation: Slab

eplans.com

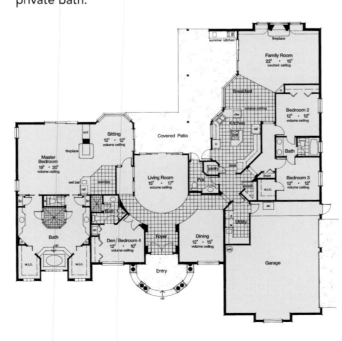

THIS HOME BOASTS GREAT CURB APPEAL WITH ITS MEDITERRANEAN INFLUENCES—glass block and muntin windows, decorative oval window, impressive pillars, and a stucco facade. The family side of this home abounds with thoughtful design features, like the island in the kitchen, the media/fireplace wall in the family room, and the mitered glass breakfast nook. A dramatic arched entry into the master suite leads to a gently curving wall of glass block, a double vanity, extra large shower, compartmented toilet, and large walk-in closet. Also special is the design of the three secondary bedrooms, which share private bath facilities.

HOME PLAN

HPK2500314

Style: Mediterranean

Square Footage: 2,348

Bedrooms: 4

Bathrooms: 3

Width: 61' - 4"

Depth: 65' - 0"

Foundation: Slab

eplans.com

INDOOR AND OUTDOOR LIVING ARE ENHANCED BY THE BEAUTIFUL COURTYARD that decorates the center of this home. A gallery leads to a kitchen featuring a center work island and adjacent breakfast room. To the left, the gallery leads to the formal living room and master suite. The secluded master bedroom features a tray ceiling and double doors that lead to a covered patio. The second floor contains a full bath shared by two family bedrooms and a loft that provides flexible space.

HPK2500315

Style: Mediterranean
First Floor: 2,264 sq. ft.
Second Floor: 820 sq. ft.
Total: 3,084 sq. ft.
Bedrooms: 4
Bathrooms: 3
Width: 66' - 0"
Depth: 78' - 10"
Foundation: Slab

eplans.com

FIRST FLOOR

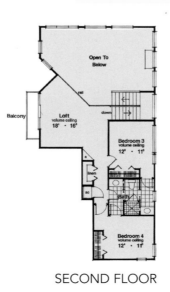

SECOND FLOOR

OPTIONAL LAYOUT

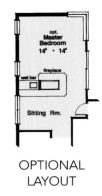

OPTIONAL
LAYOUT

A LUXURIOUS MASTER SUITE IS JUST ONE OF THE HIGHLIGHTS offered with this stunning plan—an alternate plan for this suite features a sitting room, wet bar, and fireplace. Two family bedrooms to the right share a full bath with a dual-sink vanity and a gallery hall that leads directly to the covered patio. Tile adds interest to the living area and surrounds the spacious great room, which offers a fireplace and access to the rear patio. A formal dining room and a secluded den or study flank the foyer.

 # HPK2500316

HOME PLAN

Style: Mediterranean

Square Footage: 2,125

Bedrooms: 3

Bathrooms: 2

Width: 65' - 0"

Depth: 56' - 8"

Foundation: Slab

eplans.com

HOME PLAN

HPK2500317

Style: Mediterranean

Square Footage: 3,743

Bedrooms: 4

Bathrooms: 3 ½

Width: 86' - 8"

Depth: 95' - 0"

Foundation: Slab

eplans.com

A CENTRAL FOYER GIVES WAY TO AN EXPANSIVE DESIGN. Straight ahead, the living room features French doors set in a bay area. To the left, columns and a coffered ceiling offset the exquisite formal dining room. A fireplace warms the large family room, which adjoins the breakfast nook. Traffic flows easily through the ample kitchen with cooktop island and pass-through to the patio. The master bedroom features a tray ceiling, walk-in closet, and sumptuous bath with shower and step-up tub overlooking a private garden. Two bedrooms are joined by an optional media room and optional study, which could bring the count up to five bedrooms if necessary.

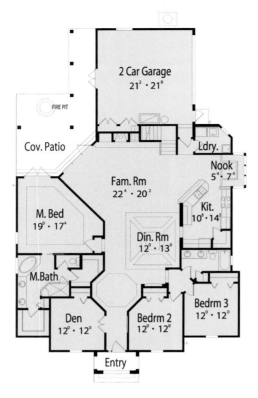

MULTIPLE ROOFLINES, SHUTTERS, AND A CHARMING VAULTED ENTRY lend interest and depth to the exterior of this well-designed three-bedroom home. Inside, double doors to the left open to a cozy den. The dining room, open to the family room and foyer, features a stunning ceiling design. A fireplace and patio access and view adorn the family room. Two family bedrooms share a double-sink bathroom to the right, and the master bedroom resides to the left. Note the private patio access, two walk-in closets, and luxurious bath that ensure a restful retreat for the homeowner.

HOME PLAN

HPK2500318

Style: Cottage

Square Footage: 2,293

Bonus Space: 509 sq. ft.

Bedrooms: 3

Bathrooms: 2

Width: 51' - 0"

Depth: 79' - 4"

Foundation: Slab

eplans.com

REAR EXTERIOR

HPK2500319

HOME PLAN

Style: New American

Square Footage: 3,723

Bonus Space: 390 sq. ft.

Bedrooms: 5

Bathrooms: 4

Width: 82' - 4"

Depth: 89' - 0"

Foundation: Slab

eplans.com

THE WARMTH OF A BRICK FACADE, INTRICATE MOLDING, AND PALLADIAN WINDOWS set this home apart from the rest. The wood detailing continues inside this magnificent home. The floor plan is a play on octagonal shapes, which create angular vistas throughout the home. Columns and pediments greet you in the formal living and dining rooms, bathed in natural light. The master suite enjoys all the latest amenities, including a sitting room, a tray ceiling, His and Hers bath appointments, doorless shower, and huge closets. The family side of this home has tile-lined traffic areas, large bedrooms, an island kitchen, and a bonus room with balcony. Details like a window in the laundry room and direct access to the three-car garage make this the perfect house.

VILLAS AND ESTATES

FIRST FLOOR

SECOND FLOOR

DENTILS ACCENT THE HIPPED ROOF AND WHITE DOUBLE COLUMNS OUTLINE THE ENTRY of this lovely three-bedroom home. Formal entertaining will be enjoyed at the front of the plan, in either the dining room or study. Tucked out of sight from the living room, yet close to the dining area, the island kitchen features acres of counter space and a convenient utility room. The breakfast nook sits open to the family room, sharing the spacious views and warming fireplace of this relaxing informal zone. A wonderful master suite fills the right side of the plan with luxury elements, such as a sitting room, large walk-in closet, and soaking tub. Two family bedrooms to the left of the plan share a full bath.

HOME PLAN

HPK2500320

Style: Mediterranean
First Floor: 3,097 sq. ft.
Second Floor: 873 sq. ft.
Total: 3,970 sq. ft.
Bedrooms: 3
Bathrooms: 4
Width: 78' - 0"
Depth: 75' - 4"
Foundation: Slab

eplans.com

HOME PLAN

HPK2500321

Style: Mediterranean

Square Footage: 2,660

Bedrooms: 4

Bathrooms: 3

Width: 66' - 4"

Depth: 74' - 4"

Foundation: Slab

eplans.com

CIRCLE-TOP WINDOWS ARE BEAUTIFULLY SHOWCASED IN THIS MAGNIFICENT HOME. The double-door entry leads into the foyer and welcomes guests into a formal living and dining room area with wonderful views. As you approach the entrance to the master suite, you pass the den/study, which can easily become a guest or bedroom suite. A gently bowed soffit and stepped ceiling treatments add excitement to the master bedroom, with floor-length windows framing the bed. The bay-window sitting area further enhances the opulence of the suite. The master bath comes complete with a double vanity, a make-up area, and a soaking tub balanced by the large shower and private toilet chamber. The walk-in closet caps off this well-appointed space with ample hanging and built-in areas.

(#) HPK2500322

Style: Italianate

Square Footage: 3,424

Bonus Space: 507 sq. ft.

Bedrooms: 5

Bathrooms: 4

Width: 82' - 4"

Depth: 83' - 8"

Foundation: Slab

eplans.com

THIS LOVELY FIVE-BEDROOM HOME EXUDES THE BEAUTY AND WARMTH OF A MEDITERRANEAN VILLA. The foyer views explode in all directions with the dominant use of octagonal shapes throughout. Double doors lead to the master wing, which abounds with niches. The sitting area of the master bedroom has a commanding view of the rear gardens. A bedroom just off the master suite is perfect for a guest room or office. The formal living and dining rooms share expansive glass walls and marble or tile pathways. The mitered glass wall of the breakfast nook can be viewed from the huge island kitchen. Two secondary bedrooms share the convenience of a Pullman-style bath. An additional rear bedroom completes this design.

THIS ESTATE EMBRACES THE STYLE OF SOUTHERN FRANCE. Double doors open to a formal columned foyer and give views of the octagonal living room beyond. To the left is the formal dining room that connects to the kitchen via a butler's pantry. To the right is an unusual den with octagonal reading space. The master wing is immense, featuring a wet bar, a private garden, and an exercise area. Two secondary bedrooms have private baths; Bedroom 2 has a private terrace. An additional bedroom with a private bath resides on the second floor, making it a perfect student's retreat. Also on the second floor are a game loft and a storage area.

HOME PLAN

(#) HPK2500323

Style: Mediterranean
First Floor: 3,739 sq. ft.
Second Floor: 778 sq. ft.
Total: 4,517 sq. ft.
Bedrooms: 4
Bathrooms: 5 ½ + ½
Width: 105' - 0"
Depth: 84' - 0"
Foundation: Slab

eplans.com

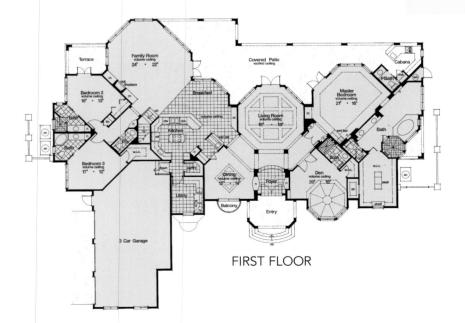

FIRST FLOOR

SECOND FLOOR

VILLAS AND ESTATES

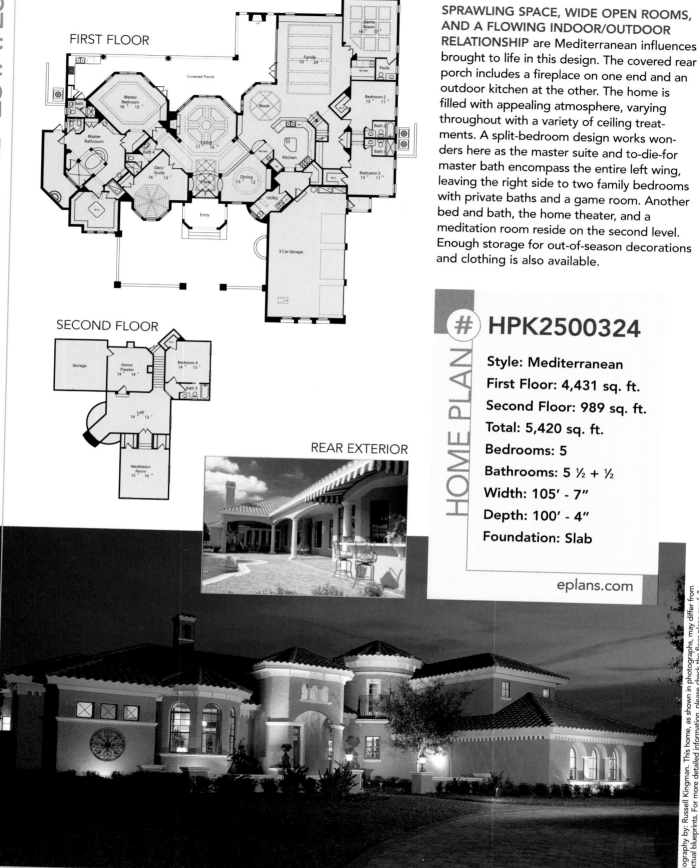

FIRST FLOOR

Covered Porch

Master Bedroom
16' x 15'

Master Bathroom

Bath

Bath 4

Den/Study
16' x 12'

Living
17' x 16'

Foyer

Dining
13' x 12'

Entry

Nook

Kitchen

Utility

Family
19' x 24'

Game Room

Pwdr.

Bedroom 2
13' x 11'

Bath 2

Bath

Bedroom 3
13' x 11'

3 Car Garage

SECOND FLOOR

Storage

Home Theater
14' x 14'

Bedroom 4
14' x 13'

Bath 5

Loft
19' x 13'

Meditation Room
15' x 16'

REAR EXTERIOR

SPRAWLING SPACE, WIDE OPEN ROOMS, AND A FLOWING INDOOR/OUTDOOR RELATIONSHIP are Mediterranean influences brought to life in this design. The covered rear porch includes a fireplace on one end and an outdoor kitchen at the other. The home is filled with appealing atmosphere, varying throughout with a variety of ceiling treatments. A split-bedroom design works wonders here as the master suite and to-die-for master bath encompass the entire left wing, leaving the right side to two family bedrooms with private baths and a game room. Another bed and bath, the home theater, and a meditation room reside on the second level. Enough storage for out-of-season decorations and clothing is also available.

HPK2500324

HOME PLAN

Style: Mediterranean
First Floor: 4,431 sq. ft.
Second Floor: 989 sq. ft.
Total: 5,420 sq. ft.
Bedrooms: 5
Bathrooms: 5 ½ + ½
Width: 105' - 7"
Depth: 100' - 4"
Foundation: Slab

eplans.com

HOME PLAN

(#) HPK2500325

Style: Italianate

Main Level: 2,895 sq. ft.

Second Level: 905 sq. ft.

Lower Level: 2,563 sq. ft.

Total: 6,363 sq. ft.

Bedrooms: 5

Bathrooms: 6 ½

Width: 73' - 4"

Depth: 89' - 0"

Foundation: Finished Basement

eplans.com

REAR EXTERIOR

TO THE LEFT OF THE FACADE, PAIRED WINDOWS ON A WHITE WALL EFFECT A SUBTLE BUT CERTAIN MEDITERRANEAN STYLE to this grand design. The same appreciation for naturalistic forms can be seen in the rounded hallway from the main dining room to the nook and kitchen. A luxurious master suite occupies the left side of the plan, with private access to the covered patio. Guests will enjoy similar comforts in interestingly shaped rooms and full baths.

LOWER LEVEL

MAIN LEVEL

SECOND LEVEL

VILLAS AND ESTATES

HOME PLAN
HPK2500326

Style: Mediterranean

Square Footage: 2,258

Bonus Space: 426 sq. ft.

Bedrooms: 4

Bathrooms: 3

Width: 62' - 4"

Depth: 57' - 0"

Foundation: Slab

HOME PLAN
HPK2500327

Style: Mediterranean

Square Footage: 3,060

Bedrooms: 4

Bathrooms: 3

Width: 64' - 8"

Depth: 74' - 8"

Foundation: Slab

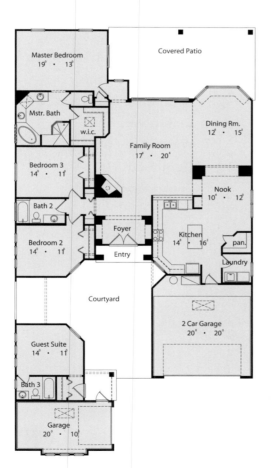

Master Bedroom
19⁸ · 13⁸

Covered Patio

Mstr. Bath

w.i.c.

Dining Rm.
12⁷ · 15⁵

Family Room
17⁷ · 20⁴

Bedroom 3
14⁰ · 11⁰

Nook
10⁴ · 12²

Bath 2

Foyer

Kitchen
14⁴ · 16²

pan.

Bedroom 2
14⁰ · 11⁰

Entry

Laundry

Courtyard

2 Car Garage
20⁰ · 20⁰

Guest Suite
14⁰ · 11⁰

Bath 3

Garage
20⁰ · 10⁰

HPK2500328

Style: Spanish Revival
Square Footage: 2,447
Bedrooms: 4
Bathrooms: 3
Width: 93' - 0"
Depth: 50' - 0"
Foundation: Slab

eplans.com

THIS SUN COUNTRY DESIGN PAMPERS VISITORS
with its own guest house—including a bath and garage—separated from the main house by a courtyard. Three bedrooms, including the master suite, and two bathrooms comprise the left wing of this one-story masterpiece. The family room is centrally located to be the hub of all activity within, and a covered patio serves the outdoors well. The C-shaped kitchen enjoys a walk-in pantry, an island, access to both the garage and laundry facilities, and proximity to the breakfast nook. The dining room is nearby as well, for more formal occasions.

FIRST FLOOR

SECOND FLOOR

THE EXTERIOR OF THIS DAZZLING HOME IS REFLECTIVE OF 1930S-STYLE RESIDENTIAL ARCHITECTURE. Upon entering the foyer, a view of the outdoor herb gardens and stone fountain appears. The formal living room, with its traditional bay-windowed wall and French doors to the patio, is timeless. The formal dining room boasts columns and traditional window treatments, all authentic 1930s-period design. This home welcomes family living with the trilogy of family room, nook, and kitchen all sharing one space. The three bedrooms on the second level make maximum use of space and vistas. The master suite offers a deck, a bay window, a walk-in closet, and a spacious bath with a see-through fireplace at the tub.

HPK2500329

Style: Mediterranean

First Floor: 1,624 sq. ft.

Second Floor: 1,167 sq. ft.

Total: 2,791 sq. ft.

Bedrooms: 4

Bathrooms: 3

Width: 55' - 0"

Depth: 68' - 0"

Foundation: Slab

HOME PLAN

eplans.com

HPK2500330

HOME PLAN

Style: Mediterranean
Square Footage: 1,894
Bonus Space: 283 sq. ft.
Bedrooms: 4
Bathrooms: 3
Width: 44' - 0"
Depth: 71' - 4"
Foundation: Slab

eplans.com

THIS DESIGN DOES A MASTERFUL JOB OF ARRANGING FOUR BEDROOMS AND GENEROUS LIVING SPACE on a single level. A narrow footprint enhances its versatility. The angled entrance opens to a vista of the entire home. A bay-shaped dining area is carved out of the spacious gathering area, which opens at the rear to a covered patio. The kitchen is artfully placed to serve both the dining area and the breakfast nook. The master suite is located in a private corner of the plan. Two additional bedrooms and a shared bath are accessed from an alcove under the stairs. A fourth bedroom suite is located off the foyer. The upstairs area may be finished as desired for extra space. An extra-large garage may be used as a workshop or for storage.

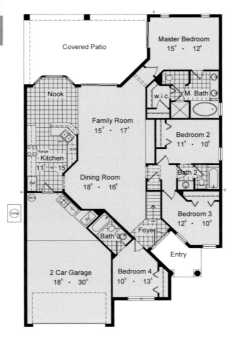

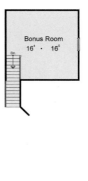

THIS MEDITERRANEAN BEAUTY HAS IT ALL, INCLUDING TWO MASTER SUITES! The first floor is designed for entertaining with a large formal dining room. Two sets of elegant French doors open to the front veranda. A large gathering room features a fireplace, patio access, and a breakfast nook at one end. At the other end is a parlor that could accomodate a pool table or home theater system. A large island kitchen is open to the gathering room, thereby integrating most of the lower level.

FIRST FLOOR

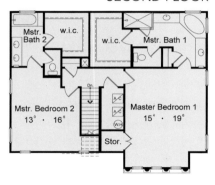

HPK2500331

Style: Mediterranean

First Floor: 1,490 sq. ft.

Second Floor: 1,061 sq. ft.

Total: 2,551 sq. ft.

Bedrooms: 2

Bathrooms: 2 ½

Width: 44' - 8"

Depth: 51' - 0"

Foundation: Slab

HOME PLAN

eplans.com

SECOND FLOOR

INTRODUCING THE DOUBLE MASTER SUITE, AN INCREDIBLY VERSATILE ARRANGEMENT that expands the boundaries of luxury living. This Mediterranean-flavored plan provides private space for two couples, enabling its use as a vacation home or full-time home for an extended family. Or, the homeowners may choose to spread out over two private levels. Imagine having one's own private bath, closet, and dressing area! Both levels have access to decks, and the lower master suite shares a through-fireplace with the gathering room. Two additional bedrooms upstairs share a split bath; one has a private deck.

HOME PLAN

HPK2500332

Style: Mediterranean
First Floor: 1,596 sq. ft.
Second Floor: 1,491 sq. ft.
Total: 3,087 sq. ft.
Bedrooms: 4
Bathrooms: 3 ½
Width: 42' - 0"
Depth: 52' - 0"
Foundation: Slab

eplans.com

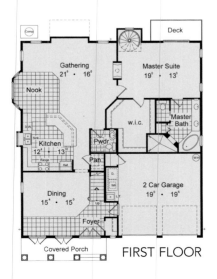

FIRST FLOOR

SECOND FLOOR

VILLAS AND ESTATES

FIRST FLOOR

2 Car Gar.

Pwdr.

Covered Patio

Nook

Kit
12' · 13'

M Bed
18' · 16'

Fam Rm
16' · 22'

Parl.

Laundry

Din Rm
16' · 12'

M Bath

clo.

clo.

Den
12' · 12'

Foyer

Liv Rm
11' · 11'

Entry

SECOND FLOOR

Unfinished Bonus Rm
13' · 18'¹⁰

Bedrm 4
12' · 12'

Bath 3

Bedrm 2
12' · 12'

Bath 2

Bedrm 3
12' · 11'¹⁰

FOR SERENE BEAUTY, BOTH INSIDE AND OUT, this two-story European-style home can't be beat. The elegant front entry and the covered rear patio call out for the right combination of flowers and shrubs to enhance the home's graceful exterior features. Downstairs, the master suite gloriously offers twin walk-in closets and vanities, a gigantic tub, and a separate shower; upstairs, three bedrooms share two baths and a computer room. The living areas on the first level are designed for full comfort and ease for a busy family and for formal get-togethers. A good-sized laundry room and a two-car garage with the option of building a room above it complete this plan.

HOME PLAN # HPK2500333

Style: **Italianate**

First Floor: **2,567 sq. ft.**

Second Floor: **844 sq. ft.**

Total: **3,411 sq. ft.**

Bonus Space: **297 sq. ft.**

Bedrooms: **4**

Bathrooms: **3 ½ + ½**

Width: **56' - 8"**

Depth: **85' - 4"**

Foundation: **Slab**

eplans.com

(#) HOME PLAN

HPK2500334

Style: Italianate

First Floor: 3,745 sq. ft.

Second Floor: 1,250 sq. ft.

Total: 4,995 sq. ft.

Bedrooms: 4

Bathrooms: 4 ½

Width: 95' - 4"

Depth: 89' - 10"

Foundation: Slab

eplans.com

GIVING THE IMPRESSION OF A LUXURIOUS VILLA RESORT, this Italian Country home is a study in fine living. Arched windows mark the grand entry, where a formal foyer reveals an elegant dining room on the right and a light-filled great room just ahead. Three family suites are located on the left, graced by a curved-window hallway. The master suite enjoys solitude on the upper level and hosts a private sitting room and lavish bath with a separate vanity and Roman tub. Other extras not to be missed: a cabana bath, eight pairs of French doors to the rear lanai, and ample garage storage.

SECOND FLOOR

FIRST FLOOR

FIRST FLOOR

SECOND FLOOR

(#) HPK2500335

Style: **Mediterranean**

First Floor: **3,130 sq. ft.**

Second Floor: **465 sq. ft.**

Total: **3,595 sq. ft.**

Bedrooms: **3**

Bathrooms: **4**

Width: **76' - 0"**

Depth: **96' - 11"**

Foundation: **Slab**

HOME PLAN

eplans.com

EXPANSION IS THE NAME OF THE GAME WITH THIS BEAUTIFUL HOME. Entering from the magnificent portico to the open foyer, one gets a sense of how big this home is. To the right is the dining room, framed by decorative columns. To the left is the den with a pocket door to the master suite. The master suite has His and Her walk-in closets, and a luxurious bath complete with a columned garden tub, His and Her vanities, a walk-in shower, and a private toilet chamber. The secondary bedrooms are a few steps down from the main floor. The oversized island kitchen and nook are ideal for a growing family. They are open to the family room which has stair access to the second floor game room. Also upstairs are a series of unfinished spaces that can be used for a varity of applications.

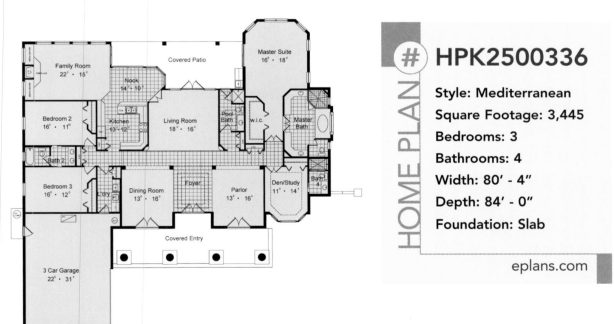

HOME PLAN

THIS BEAUTIFUL FLORIDA-STYLE HOME BOASTS AN IMPRESSIVE, COLUMNED ENTRY. French doors open into the formal dining room to the left of the foyer and a parlor to the right. A spacious living room provides even more space for entertaining. Everyday family activities will revolve around the open kitchen, breakfast nook, and family room, where a fireplace, built-in cabinetry, and a wall of windows collaborate to make this the coziest room in the house. Two family bedrooms share a compartmented bath on this side of the plan. The master suite occupies the opposite wing. A bay-windowed den or study is easily accessible from the master suite; the adjoining full bath enables it to convert to a private guest suite.

VILLAS AND ESTATES

FIRST FLOOR

SECOND FLOOR

THE UNIQUE FLOOR PLAN OF THIS HOME CREATES GRACEFUL OPEN SPACES that combine with its expansive windows for an elegant look that is hard to surpass. Upon entry into the foyer, one is impressed by the long vistas through the rooms. Straight ahead is the living room, which opens to the covered patio beyond. To the left is a bay-windowed bedroom that could also be used as a study. Through double doors one enters the lavish master suite, complete with sitting area, His and Her walk-in closets, and a spacious master bath. To the right of the foyer are the formal dining room and the family gathering areas. The kitchen has dual islands and a walk-in pantry. It easily serves both the dining room and the nook, whose mitered glass wall overlooks the covered patio. The octagonal family room has a fireplace and entertainment media areas. There are also three family bedrooms here, two baths, and stairs to the bonus space above.

HOME PLAN

HPK2500337

Style: Mediterranean

First Floor: 3,464 sq. ft.

Second Floor: 660 sq. ft.

Total: 4,124 sq. ft.

Bedrooms: 6

Bathrooms: 5

Width: 82' - 4"

Depth: 84' - 8"

Foundation: Slab

eplans.com

HOME PLAN

HPK2500338

Style: Mediterranean

First Floor: 3,476 sq. ft.

Second Floor: 1,633 sq. ft.

Total: 5,109 sq. ft.

Bonus Space: 352 sq. ft.

Bedrooms: 4

Bathrooms: 4 ½

Width: 80' - 0"

Depth: 98' - 0"

Foundation: Slab

eplans.com

FIRST FLOOR

SECOND FLOOR

ALLURING ARCHES CAPTIVATE IN THE CURB APPEAL OF THIS HOME. Graceful arches appear again upon entering the foyer, which leads directly into the living room that opens to the covered patio beyond. On one side of this home is the master wing; pass the den/study and enter the large master suite with sitting area and access to the covered patio. The master bath features large His and Her walk-in closets, a corner tub, large walk-in shower, and separate vanities. The core of this home is the columned and arched formal dining room and living room. A turreted stairwell is flanked by a bedroom and spacious family room, kitchen, and breakfast nook. Note the game room beyond, ideal for a pool table. The second floor has two additional bedrooms with private baths, a loft area, and a large bonus room. Note the deep balcony that each of the bedrooms and loft have access to.

FIRST
FLOOR

SECOND
FLOOR

ITALIAN GRANDURE IS EVIDENT IN THIS OLD WORLD HOME.
A turretted, two-story foyer greets visitors, and opens into the voluminous two-story great room central to this plan. Entry to the master suite and private one-car garage is also accessible from the foyer. The master suite has it all with a wet-sink opposite the entry to an oversized master bath with garden tub, walk-in shower, private toilet chamber and His and Her vanities. On the other side of the great room are arched entries to the dining hall with coffered ceiling and island kitchen. The large kitchen has a break-fast nook with corner-less sliding glass doors leading to the cov-ered patio area, providing a wonderful sense of space. Also off of the great room is a secondary bedroom and bath, laundry room, and two-car garage. Stairs lead to two additional bedrooms that share a Jack-and-Jill bath, loft area, and media room. A balcony overlooks the spacious great room below.

HPK2500339

HOME PLAN

Style: Italianate

First Floor: 2,522 sq. ft.

Second Floor: 1,067 sq. ft.

Total: 3,589 sq. ft.

Bedrooms: 4

Bathrooms: 3 ½

Width: 60' - 0"

Depth: 80' - 4"

Foundation: Slab

eplans.com

THIS MAGNIFICENT MEDITERRANEAN-STYLE HOME IS FULL OF THE CHARMS that make entertaining gracious and family life comfortable. From the elegant covered entry, pass into the foyer or through separate French doors into the den on the right and the formal dining room on the left. A superb kitchen, sunlit breakfast nook, and family room flow together, creating a relaxed unit. Splendor awaits in the master suite with its gracefully curved bedchamber, huge walk-in wardrobes, and a luxuriant bath. On the opposite side of the house, a guest bedroom enjoys a full bath. Two more bedrooms share a bath on the second level, and additional space is available for another bedroom and bath. The rear covered patio can be entered from the living room, the master suite, or the breakfast nook. Three vehicles will easily fit into the side-loading garage.

HOME PLAN # HPK2500340

Style: Italianate

First Floor: 2,926 sq. ft.

Second Floor: 1,268 sq. ft.

Total: 4,194 sq. ft.

Bonus Space: 353 sq. ft.

Bedrooms: 4

Bathrooms: 3 ½

Width: 75' - 0"

Depth: 85' - 4"

Foundation: Slab

eplans.com

FIRST FLOOR

SECOND FLOOR

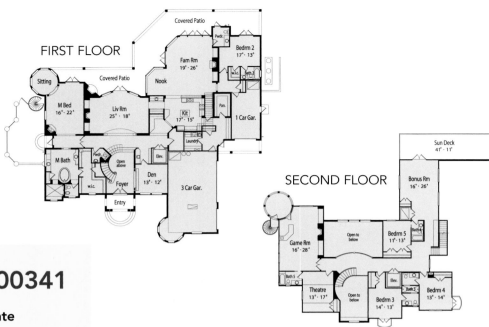

FIRST FLOOR

Covered Patio

Sitting

M Bed
16' · 22'

Covered Patio

Liv Rm
25' · 18'

Nook

Fam Rm
19' · 26'

Bedrm 2
17' · 13'

Bath 2

w.i.c.

Pan.

Kit
17' · 15'

1 Car Gar.

M Bath

Pwdr.

Open
above

Elev.

Laundry

w.i.c.

Foyer

Den
13' · 12'

3 Car Gar.

Entry

SECOND FLOOR

Sun Deck
41' · 11'

Bonus Rm
16' · 26'

Game Rm
16' · 28'

Open to
below

Bedrm 5
11' · 13'

Bath 4

Bath 5

Theatre
13' · 17'

Open to
below

Bedrm 3
14' · 13'

Elev.

Bath 3

Bedrm 4
13' · 14'

HOME PLAN

HPK2500341

Style: Italianate

First Floor: 4,323 sq. ft.

Second Floor: 2,226 sq. ft.

Total: 6,549 sq. ft.

Bonus Space: 453 sq. ft.

Bedrooms: 5

Bathrooms: 5 ½ + ½

Width: 98' - 8"

Depth: 102' - 8"

Foundation: Slab

eplans.com

THIS ITALIAN RENAISSANCE MARVEL HAS IT ALL—five bedrooms, a game room, a theater, and expansive areas for formal parties and relaxed barbecues. A covered patio winds around the entire rear of the home, and a sundeck is located on the second level. A wet bar and circular balcony, with an outside spiral stairway, make the upstairs game room a great party site. The lavish master suite features a circular sitting area with windows drawing in natural light from many directions. A spiral stairway winds gracefully upstairs from the impressive main-floor entry, or, if you prefer, take the elevator. A semicircular turret on the corner of the three-car garage is not only flashy, it is a handy storage area.

HOME PLAN

HPK2500342

Style: Mediterranean

First Floor: 5,251 sq. ft.

Second Floor: 1,154 sq. ft.

Total: 6,405 sq. ft.

Bedrooms: 5

Bathrooms: 5 ½ +
2 Half-Baths

Width: 104' - 6"

Depth: 113' - 0"

Foundation: Slab

eplans.com

AN ABUNDANCE OF ARCHED WINDOWS, TILED ROOF, AND TASTEFUL TURRETS signal high-style Italianate. Enter directly into a large living room with cornerless sliding glass doors that give the room a sense of great expansion into the covered patio area. Pass the study on the way to the master suite that features an exercise room, island tub, large corner shower, private toilet chamber, and a walk-in closet. The dining room has an interconnecting butler's pantry that leads to a prep area adjacent to the large dual-island kitchen. The kitchen leads directy into a spacious breakfast nook and family room. The secondary bedrooms upstairs and down each have a private bath. Additional features include a game room with large wet bar and powder room off the family room, a media room on the second floor, and a spacious four-car garage.

FIRST FLOOR

SECOND FLOOR

VILLAS AND ESTATES

FIRST FLOOR

SECOND FLOOR

A STUNNING EUROPEAN-STYLE HOME WITH NUMEROUS SUN-CATCHING MULTIPANED WINDOWS and an impressive entryway beckons you. Four (or five) bedrooms and five full baths house a large family or overnight guests luxuriously. Special ceiling treatments in the first-floor master suite, grand foyer, dining room, and welcoming family room add to the flair of this plan. Sliding glass doors in the living room and rounded windows in the nook provide access and views to the covered rear patio, ideal for outdoor entertaining and relaxing. A quiet study off the foyer adds wonderful work-at-home space or a room for the family computer. The loft and media room upstairs bring the family together.

HPK2500343

HOME PLAN #

Style: Italianate

First Floor: 2,699 sq. ft.

Second Floor: 1,006 sq. ft.

Total: 3,705 sq. ft.

Bedrooms: 4

Bathrooms: 5

Width: 65' - 0"

Depth: 95' - 0"

Foundation: Slab

eplans.com

HPK2500344

Style: Mediterranean
First Floor: 2,058 sq. ft.
Second Floor: 712 sq. ft.
Total: 2,770 sq. ft.
Bedrooms: 3
Bathrooms: 2 ½
Width: 57' - 3"
Depth: 81' - 3"
Foundation: Crawlspace

eplans.com

IF YOU'VE ALWAYS DREAMED OF OWNING A VILLA, we invite you to experience this European lifestyle—on a perfectly manageable scale. This home offers the best of traditional formality and casual elegance. The foyer leads to the great room, with a bold but stylish fireplace and three French doors to the rear terrace—sure to be left open during fair weather. The large kitchen opens gracefully to a private dining room that has access to a covered outdoor patio. The master suite combines great views and a sumptuous bath to complete this winning design. Upstairs, a balcony hall overlooking the great room leads to two family bedrooms that share a full hall bath.

REAR EXTERIOR

FIRST FLOOR

SECOND FLOOR

THIS EXPANSIVE VACATION HOME IS IN HARMONY WITH ITS SURROUNDINGS and in tune with the demands of today's free-flowing lifestyles. Stonework and shingles echo wilderness textures and colors, yet the balanced roofline conveys a sense of tranquility. A wraparound porch is highly inviting. Just as the porch opens onto the great outdoors, the foyer inside opens to the spaciousness of a great room soaring two stories high to an elegant ceiling. A warming hearth links the great room and the dining room. There's plenty of opportunity for privacy in the master suite and upstairs bedrooms.

FIRST FLOOR

HOME PLAN

(#) HPK2500345

Style: Country

First Floor: 1,606 sq. ft.

Second Floor: 902 sq. ft.

Total: 2,508 sq. ft.

Bonus Space: 376 sq. ft.

Bedrooms: 3

Bathrooms: 3 ½

Width: 107' - 0"

Depth: 43' - 0"

Foundation: Unfinished Walkout Basement

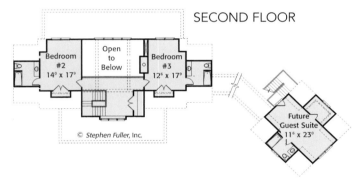

SECOND FLOOR

eplans.com

© Stephen Fuller, Inc.

THIS GRAND TWO-STORY HOME IS DEFINED BY TWO GARAGES, each with two stalls, connected by a gracefully arched portico. Throughout the home, you will be impressed with the attention paid to the ceiling design, including step ceilings in the dining room, den, and master suite. As you enter the home, you will find the den to your left and a formal dinging room to your right. Straight ahead lies the great room with fourteen-foot ceilings, an expansive wall of windows, and a fireplace flanked by built-in cabinetry. To the right, the kitchen features a breakfast bar that overlooks an octagonal nook with a unique tray ceiling and a spacious hearth room, complete with cathedral ceiling and warming fireplace. The master suite occupies the left side of the home and features a spacious walk-in closet with a central island. Upstairs you'll find three additional bedrooms; two share a compartmented bath and the third enjoys a private bath.

HOME PLAN

HPK2500346

Style: Country

First Floor: 2,980 sq. ft.

Second Floor: 1,328 sq. ft.

Total: 4,308 sq. ft.

Bedrooms: 4

Bathrooms: 3 ½

Width: 136' - 0"

Depth: 70' - 0"

Foundation: Unfinished Basement

eplans.com

FIRST FLOOR

SECOND FLOOR

FIRST FLOOR

SECOND FLOOR

AT JUST OVER 5,200 SQUARE FEET, the immensity of this estate is scarcely realized from the exterior alone. Step inside and the clever layout intrigues and impresses. No detail is overlooked. The kitchen is arranged for convenient interaction with the adjacent nook and family room. A nearby covered porch invites alfresco meals. Upstairs, the master suite befits the owner of this exquisite home. Three additional family bedrooms share two full baths. A large bonus room offers a wealth of possibilities.

HOME PLAN

(#) HPK2500347

Style: Craftsman

First Floor: 2,750 sq. ft.

Second Floor: 2,500 sq. ft.

Total: 5,250 sq. ft.

Bedrooms: 5

Bathrooms: 4 ½

Width: 98' - 0"

Depth: 74' - 0"

Foundation: Crawlspace

eplans.com

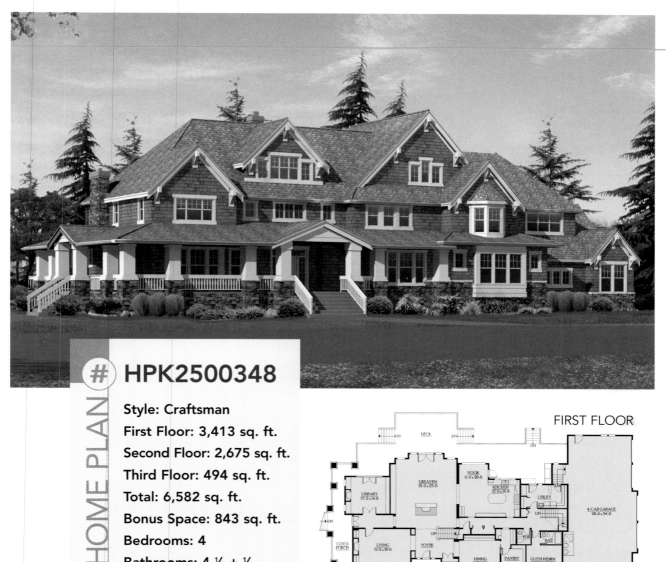

(#) HPK2500348

Style: Craftsman

First Floor: 3,413 sq. ft.

Second Floor: 2,675 sq. ft.

Third Floor: 494 sq. ft.

Total: 6,582 sq. ft.

Bonus Space: 843 sq. ft.

Bedrooms: 4

Bathrooms: 4 ½ + ½

Width: 118' - 0"

Depth: 61' - 6"

Foundation: Crawlspace

eplans.com

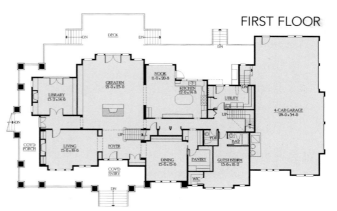

FIRST FLOOR

SECOND FLOOR

THIRD FLOOR

DELIGHT IN ALL THAT THIS LAVISH CRAFTSMAN HOME HAS TO OFFER. The attractive wraparound porch adds instant curb appeal to the front and side of the home. A generous rear deck highlights the back of the home. Entertainment possibilities are endless. Inside, the appeal is equally undeniable. A fireplace in the library proffers a cozy sanctuary to read or work at home. On the second floor, the master suite enjoys a private deck facing the rear of the home. Unique room shapes add space & interest to the remaining family bedrooms. Each accesses a private, full bath. The third floor houses an office or additional storage space.

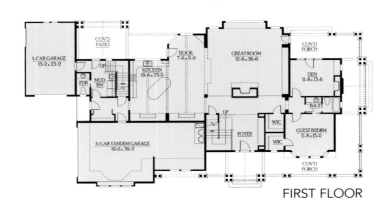

FIRST FLOOR

SECOND FLOOR

(#) HPK2500349

Style: Craftsman

First Floor: 2,360 sq. ft.

Second Floor: 1,940 sq. ft.

Total: 4,300 sq. ft.

Bedrooms: 4

Bathrooms: 3 ½

Width: 105' - 4"

Depth: 53' - 0"

Foundation: Crawlspace

eplans.com

AN ABUNDANCE OF WINDOWS PROVIDES A WEALTH OF NATURAL LIGHT and exceptional views throughout this luxurious Craftsman home. The open floor plan adds spaciousness and invites the possibility for entertaining. A guest suite accesses a full, private bath ideal for an elderly visitor. Upstairs, the master suite enjoys a private deck that overlooks the backyard. A bridge separates the master suite from the remaining bedrooms creating a private retreat. The large playroom is great for kids and adults alike.

REAR EXTERIOR

REAR EXTERIOR

HOME PLAN

HPK2500350

Style: Craftsman
First Floor: 2,010 sq. ft.
Second Floor: 2,090 sq. ft.
Total: 4,100 sq. ft.
Bedrooms: 4
Bathrooms: 3 ½
Width: 90' - 0"
Depth: 66' - 6"
Foundation: Crawlspace

eplans.com

A CRAFTSMAN MASTERPIECE, THIS HOME IS PERFECT FOR A FOREST OR FAIRWAY LOT. Its wraparound porch adds warmth to the facade and is a great place to watch the world go by. A side-entry garage and decorative shop bay further enhance its curb appeal. The popular family living layout features vaulted formal living and dining rooms off the volume foyer, complemented by a spacious informal living area with a covered patio that is ideal for outdoor dining. The angled front stair leads directly to the luxury master suite with its private sitting room and grand bath. A second stair provides quiet access to the children's bedrooms with connecting bath, guest suite with private bath, and large vaulted bonus room.

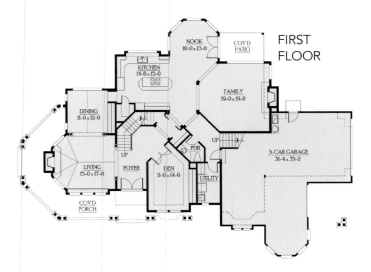

FIRST FLOOR

SECOND FLOOR

VILLAS AND ESTATES

FIRST FLOOR

SECOND FLOOR

HOME PLAN #

HPK2500351

Style: Craftsman

First Floor: 1,425 sq. ft.

Second Floor: 1,380 sq. ft.

Total: 2,805 sq. ft.

Bedrooms: 3

Bathrooms: 2 ½

Width: 48' - 0"

Depth: 60' - 0"

Foundation: Crawlspace

HOME PLAN #

HPK2500352

Style: Craftsman

First Floor: 2,010 sq. ft.

Second Floor: 2,020 sq. ft.

Total: 4,030 sq. ft.

Bedrooms: 4

Bathrooms: 3 ½

Width: 85' - 0"

Depth: 58' - 0"

Foundation: Crawlspace

FIRST FLOOR

SECOND FLOOR

REAR EXTERIOR

HOME PLAN

HPK2500353

Style: Craftsman

First Floor: 3,970 sq. ft.

Second Floor: 3,430 sq. ft.

Total: 7,400 sq. ft.

Bedrooms: 5

Bathrooms: 5 ½

Width: 136' - 2"

Depth: 125' - 6"

Foundation: Crawlspace

eplans.com

A SHINGLE-STYLE MANSION ON A GRAND SCALE, this American classic displays charm on the outside and luxury within. Its sweeping elevations are highlighted by sculptural columned porches, gazebos, porches, bays, turrets, and dormers. Carefully designed alignments and interior volumes create dramatic spatial sequences, the impact of which are not diminsihed by their practicality. Packed with elegant detail and thoughtful features, this design is a perfect place to escape from the routine of everyday life.

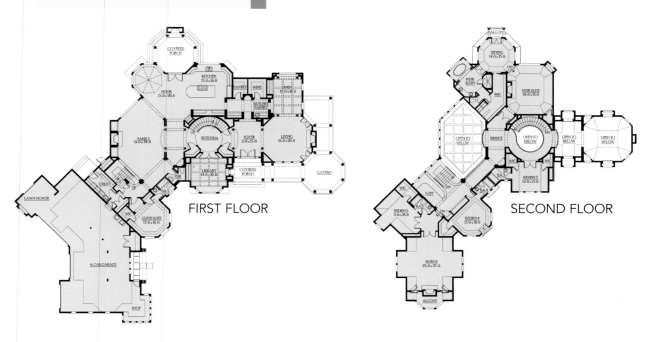

FIRST FLOOR

SECOND FLOOR

Completing the Picture

A truly gratifying landscape design takes cues from the architecture of the home, your sense of style, and the natural properties of the land. You will also need to make a decision about the kind of landscape you desire. For instance, perennials and bulbs used throughout a design will establish a garden theme and provide cutting flowers for indoor bouquets. But remember that a garden will need a lot of care and attention, which may not be ideal for a seasonal home. Similarly, edible gardens are very appropriate in a country-inspired design, but need to be protected from the elements. More shaded parts of the landscape call for sitting areas or outdoor structures, such as storage sheds or small barns.

The right landscaping design will effectively frame your home from the rest of the neighborhood. If your lot will not allow the placement of a tall fence or natural barrier between the home and the next-door neighbor, place "retreat" areas away from property lines. That is, resist the natural urge to place quiet areas in only the corners of the yard. With the right design, owners can create a relaxing getaway right in the middle of the plan.

The virtue of a predrawn landscape and project plan is that you can enjoy the benefits of a professional design without paying for custom landscaping.

THE FULL BEAUTY of a landscape plan stems from how it can mature and grow naturally around the home. No two garden plans will be identical.

A GOOD LANDSCAPE DESIGN lets nature take its course. Only then will dwelling areas feel welcoming and special.

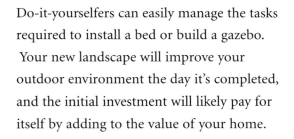

Do-it-yourselfers can easily manage the tasks required to install a bed or build a gazebo. Your new landscape will improve your outdoor environment the day it's completed, and the initial investment will likely pay for itself by adding to the value of your home.

HPK2500380

Square Footage: 1,031
Width: 18' - 0"
Depth: 32' - 0"

HPK2500381

Square Footage: 1,050
Width: 20' - 0"
Depth: 30' - 0"

HPK2500382

Square Footage: 336
Width: 14' - 0"
Depth: 24' - 0"

HPK2500383

Square Footage: 384
Width: 16' - 0"
Depth: 24' - 0"

HPK2500384

Square Footage: 704
Width: 16' - 0"
Depth: 24' - 0"

HPK2500385

Square Footage: 576
Width: 24' - 0"
Depth: 24' - 0"

HPK2500386

Square Footage: 656
Width: 16' - 0"
Depth: 24' - 0"

HPK2500387

Square Footage: 336
Width: 14' - 0"
Depth: 24' - 0"

HPK2500388

Square Footage: 910
Width: 24' - 0"
Depth: 24' - 0"

HPK2500389

Square Footage: 998
Width: 24' - 0"
Depth: 26' - 0"

HPK2500390

Square Footage: 1,400
Width: 28' - 0"
Depth: 30' - 0"

HPK2500391

Square Footage: 662
Width: 28' - 0"
Depth: 26' - 0"

HPK2500392

Square Footage: 741
Width: 24' - 8"
Depth: 32' - 0"

HPK2500393

Square Footage: 1,071
Width: 34' - 0"
Depth: 24' - 0"

HPK2500394

Square Footage: 713
Width: 28' - 0"
Depth: 26' - 0"

HPK2500395

Square Footage: 1,080
Width: 24' - 0"
Depth: 42' - 0"

HPK2500396

Square Footage: 1,456
Width: 36' - 0"
Depth: 22' - 0"

HPK2500397

Width: 17' - 0"
Depth: 11' - 8"

HPK2500398

Square Footage: 144
Width: 12' - 0"
Depth: 12' - 0"

HPK2500399

Square Footage: 192
Width: 16' - 0"
Depth: 12' - 0"

HPK2500400

Square Footage: 100
Width: 10' - 0"
Depth: 10' - 0"

HPK2500401

Square Footage: 144
Width: 12' - 0"
Depth: 16' - 0"

HPK2500402

Square Footage: 288
Width: 20' - 0"
Depth: 16' - 0"

HPK2500403

Square Footage: 432
Width: 20' - 0"
Depth: 30' - 0"

HPK2500404

Square Footage: 64
Width: 8' - 0"
Depth: 8' - 0"

HPK2500405

Square Footage: 96
Width: 8' - 0"
Depth: 12' - 0"

HPK2500406

Square Footage: 144
Width: 12' - 0"
Depth: 12' - 0"

HPK2500407

Square Footage: 144
Width: 12' - 0"
Depth: 12' - 0"

HPK2500408

Square Footage: 160
Width: 16' - 0"
Depth: 12' - 0"

HPK2500409

Width: 8' - 0"
Depth: 8' - 0"

HPK2500410

Width: 3' - 0"
Depth: 4' - 0"

HPK2500411

Width: 4' - 3"
Depth: 6' - 0"

HPK2500412

Square Footage: 96
Width: 8' - 0"
Depth: 16' - 0"

LANDSCAPE PLANS

THE LANDSCAPE AROUND THIS RUSTIC STONE-FRONTED HOUSE IS TRULY CHARMING. The designer organizes the space into separate, easily maintained units that blend into a pleasing whole. The planting pockets—in front of the large window and the two areas bisected by pavers to the right of the drive—contain well-behaved plants that require little care to maintain their good looks.

A ribbon of small and moderate-sized shrubs, underplanted with a weed-smothering groundcover and spring bulbs, surrounds the lawn. A single deciduous tree, set in a circle of bulbs and easy-care perennials that juts into the lawn, screens the entryway from street view and balances a triad of slow-growing, narrow conifers to the far left of the house. Shrubs in front of the windows were chosen for their low, unobtrusive growth habit. A dwarf conifer with pendulous branches forms the focus of the shrub grouping in front of the larger window.

Paving is a strong unifying force in this design. Although packed with interesting plants, this landscape is quite manageable for the easy-care gardener.

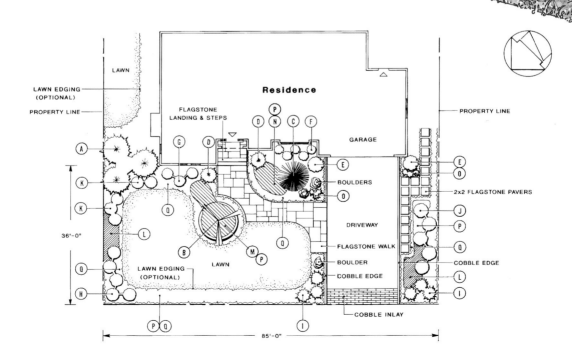

PLAN

 # HPK2500354

Season: Spring

Design by: Salvatore A. Masullo

eplans.com

PLAN

HPK2500355

Season: Summer

Design by: David Poplawski

eplans.com

SET IN A FRIENDLY AND HOMEY LANDSCAPE BRIM-
MING WITH FLOWERS FROM SPRING THROUGH FALL,
this farmhouse's country atmosphere is complete. Masses
of perennials and bulbs used throughout the property create a garden setting and provide armloads of flowers that
can be cut for indoor bouquets. The floral beauty doesn't
stop there; the designer artfully incorporates unusual
specimens of summer- and fall-blooming trees and shrubs
into the landscape design to elevate the changing floral
scene to eye-level and above.

To match the informal mood of the house, both the front
walkway and driveway cut a curved, somewhat mean-
dering path. A parking spur at the end of the driveway
provides extra parking space and a place to turn around.
Fieldstones, whose rustic character complements the
country setting, pave the front walk. The stone piers and
picket fence at the entrance to the driveway frame the
entry and match the detail and character of the house's
stone foundation and porch railing. The stone wall at the
side of the property further carries out this theme.

Large specimen trees planted in the lawn set the house
back from the road and provide a show of autumn color.
Imagine completing the country theme in this tranquil
setting by hanging a child's swing from the tree nearest
the front porch.

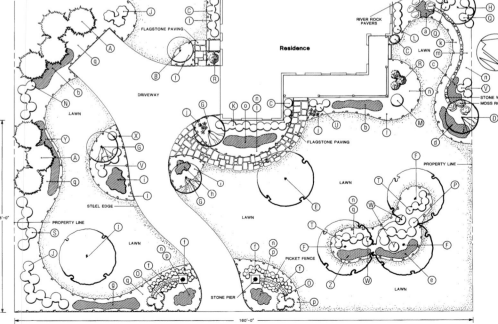

THE LOW, SPRAWLING LINES OF THIS RANCH HOUSE AND ITS RED-TILE ROOF EVOKE THE SPANISH MISSION STYLE reminiscent of the easy-living, comfortable nature of Southwestern life. The landscape designer chooses both hardscaping and softscaping to complement the house and the climate. Exposed aggregate walks, simple yet attractive, lead to both main and secondary entrances and blend well with the contemporary Southwestern architecture.

The bed bordering the walkway to the secondary entrance is bermed slightly to block the view of the walkway used by the homeowner, preventing the visitor from approaching the wrong door. The V-shaped driveway provides a convenient parking spur and the angles of the driveway create visual excitement in the design. Three flowering trees spaced out near the corners of the driveway reinforce the V-shape and provide welcome summer color.

PLAN # HPK2500356

Season: Summer
Design by: Damon Scott

eplans.com

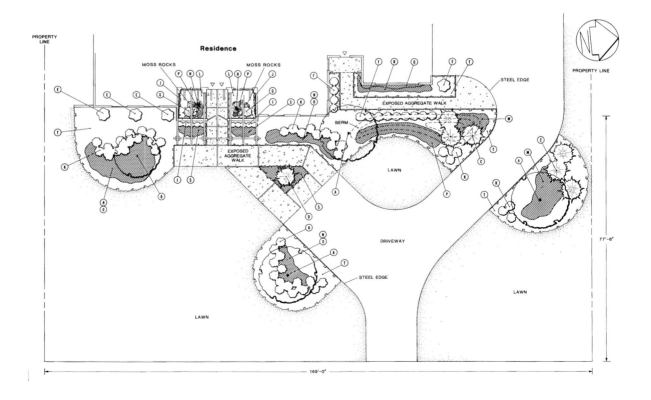

The tree on the right frames the entrance to the garage, the one on the left frames the view to the door, and the one in the center buffers the view to the secondary entrance. Together, the three balance each other, forming a pleasing triangle. The planting border running in front of the garage wing continues on the other side of the driveway, strengthening the lines of the bed and creating a transition between front and back. Without the continuation of the planting area, the landscaping would abruptly end; with it, the sight line gracefully continues. At the end of a second sight line, the small flowering tree at the left corner of the house creates a view for a visitor strolling up the walk.

An effective landscape design matches the climate here, heat-tolerant plants work together to create a perfect cooling combination for a hot climate.

THE PROBLEM FACING THE LANDSCAPE DESIGNER OF THIS ONE-STORY HOME IS TO CREATE INTIMACY AND FRIENDLINESS where a three-car garage near the front entrance necessitates a lot of pavement. The designer turns what could have been a barren driveway into a functional and attractive space by using trees and the sides of the L-shaped house as the walls of an airy entrance court. Cobble inlay marks the main garage and entrance to the home and provides an interesting change in texture. The second garage is blocked from immediate view from both sides by a peninsular bed, which clearly separates it from the primary garage.

Enclosing a more intimate courtyard, a low picket fence and bluestone walk define the front door, bringing an informal,

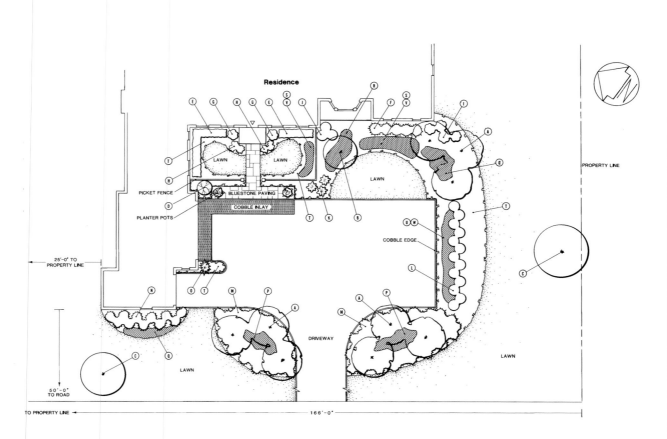

Residence

LAWN · LAWN

PICKET FENCE

BLUESTONE PAVING

COBBLE INLAY

PLANTER POTS

25'-0" TO PROPERTY LINE

LAWN

COBBLE EDGE

PROPERTY LINE

50'-0" TO ROAD

LAWN

DRIVEWAY

LAWN

TO PROPERTY LINE ← 166'-0" →

homey feeling to the setting. Small grassed areas within this doorstep garden and in the semicircular area along the rest of the house provide a green carpet that carries the perimeter lawn into the interior court. The small tree before the window of the master bedroom creates a pretty, ever-changing view through the window and blocks headlights from shining inside.

Graceful trees, masses of cheerful flowering perennials, and the flowing lines of the circular planting beds work together to create a friendly setting for this country home. It's simply pretty as a picture! Also shown here is home plan HPB921 by Home Planners. A canopy of trees draws visitors inside the courtyard here, and the doorstep garden outlined by a picket fence and carpeted in green provides a friendly greeting on an intimate scale.

 # HPK2500357

PLAN

Season: Spring
Design by: David Poplawski

eplans.com

IF YOU LOOK AT THIS LANDSCAPE DESIGN AND ASK YOURSELF, "IS THAT REALLY A SWIMMING POOL?" then the designer is to be congratulated for succeeding. Yes, it is a swimming pool, but the pool looks more like a natural pond and waterfall—one that you might discover in a clearing in the woods during a hike in the wilderness. Although the pool is not included in the blueprints for this design, the surrounding landscape lends itself to its placement. Leave the pool out for a pleasing rock garden, play area, or romantic gazebo hideaway. The designer achieves an aesthetically pleasing, natural look by employing several techniques. Large boulders form the waterfalls, one of which falls from a holding pond set among the boulders. If you do not choose to build a pool here, the boulders could empty into a pond or calming fountain. River-rock paving—the type

PLAN

HPK2500004

Season: Summer
Design by: Damon Scott

eplans.com

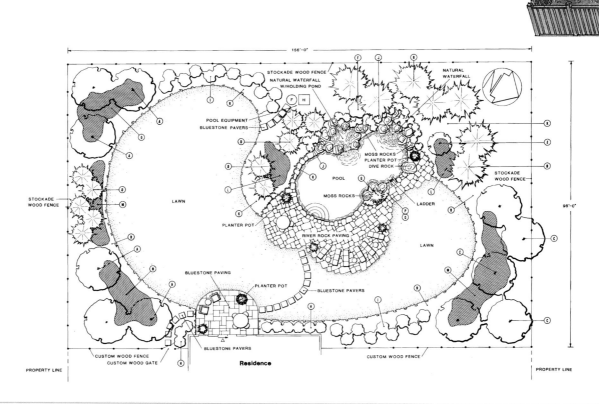

of water-worn rocks that line the cool water of a natural spring or a rushing stream—adds a touch of wilderness. The beautiful grassy areas of the landscape offer a serene setting with abundant floral and foliage interest throughout the year. For security reasons, a wooden stockade fence surrounds the entire backyard, yet the plantings camouflage it well. The irregular kidney shape of the lawn is pleasing to look at and beautifully integrates this naturalistic landscaping into its man-made setting.

Abundant floral and foliage interest year-round, river-rock paving, and border plantings bring a wonderful, natural setting to your own backyard.

#HPK2500358

Season: Summer
Design by: Damon Scott

eplans.com

THIS DESIGN PROVES THAT "DROUGHT TOL-ERANT" AND "LOW MAINTENANCE" DON'T HAVE TO MEAN BORING. This attractive back-yard looks lush, colorful, and inviting but relies entirely on plants that flourish, even if water is scarce. This means you won't spend any time tending to their watering needs once the plant-ings are established. Even the lawn is planted with a newly developed turf grass that tolerates long periods of drought. The designer specifies buffalo grass, a native grass of the American west, for the lawn. The grass has fine-textured, grayish-green leaf blades; tolerates cold; and needs far less water to remain green and healthy than most lawns. It goes completely dormant during periods of

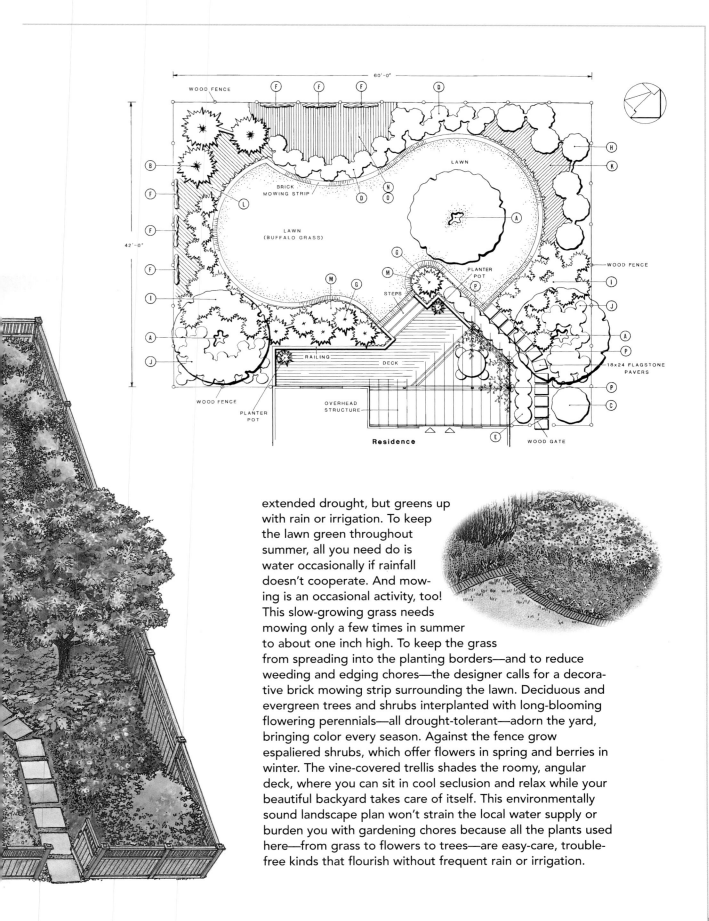

60'-0"

WOOD FENCE

F F F D

42'-0"

B

F

F

F

I

A

J

BRICK
MOWING STRIP

L

LAWN

D

N

D O

G

M M

G

STEPS

G

LAWN
(BUFFALO GRASS)

A

PLANTER
POT

P

H

K

WOOD FENCE

I

J

A

P

18x24 FLAGSTONE
PAVERS

RAILING

DECK

WOOD FENCE

PLANTER
POT

OVERHEAD
STRUCTURE

Residence

E

P

C

WOOD GATE

extended drought, but greens up with rain or irrigation. To keep the lawn green throughout summer, all you need do is water occasionally if rainfall doesn't cooperate. And mowing is an occasional activity, too! This slow-growing grass needs mowing only a few times in summer to about one inch high. To keep the grass from spreading into the planting borders—and to reduce weeding and edging chores—the designer calls for a decorative brick mowing strip surrounding the lawn. Deciduous and evergreen trees and shrubs interplanted with long-blooming flowering perennials—all drought-tolerant—adorn the yard, bringing color every season. Against the fence grow espaliered shrubs, which offer flowers in spring and berries in winter. The vine-covered trellis shades the roomy, angular deck, where you can sit in cool seclusion and relax while your beautiful backyard takes care of itself. This environmentally sound landscape plan won't strain the local water supply or burden you with gardening chores because all the plants used here—from grass to flowers to trees—are easy-care, trouble-free kinds that flourish without frequent rain or irrigation.

THIS COLORFUL BACKYARD SERVES AS A SPECIAL WEEKEND RETREAT where you and your family can spend your free time relaxing and entertaining. Enjoy a quiet afternoon reading or lounging in the hammock under the romantic arbor, or host a cook-out for your friends on the spacious patio complete with an outdoor kitchen. Both the patio and the hammock provide refuge from the hot summer sun—a vine-covered overhead trellis and leafy trees pro-tect the patio, and the hammock hideaway tucked in the corner of the yard can catch a breeze while reflecting the sun's hot rays. Just right for a lazy afternoon snooze, the hammock structure nestles within an intimate flowery set-ting that encloses and enhances the space. Flagstone pavers lead the way from the patio to the hammock, fol-lowing the gentle curve of the border, and flagstones mark the entrance from the gates at each side of the yard for easy access. Privacy-protecting evergreen trees and shrubs

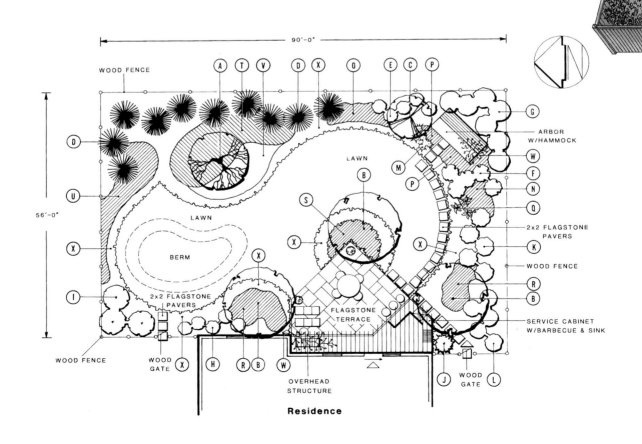

 # HPK2500359

PLAN

Season: Summer

**Design by: Michael
J. Opisso**

eplans.com

fill the rear of the property, and all are gracefully set off by a purple-foliaged weeping specimen tree located on sight lines from both the patio and the arbor. (In some regions, another type of eye-catching specimen tree is substituted for the purple-foliaged tree.) For color contrast, long-blooming, yellow-flowering perennials surround the tree. The designer includes large patches of other easy-care perennials that punctuate the rest of the landscape with splashes of color from spring through fall to create a welcoming backyard retreat. An arbor-covered hammock and a spacious patio with a kitchen provide comfortable spots for relaxing outdoors while enjoying the colorful flowering perennials.

DESIGNED PRIMARILY FOR EXERCISE, A LAP POOL IS MUCH LONGER THAN IT IS WIDE, although it does allow two people to swim comfortably side by side. It's also shallower than pools designed for high diving. This long, narrow pool fits economically into a small backyard because it takes up less space and costs less to build. Although intended for a healthy workout, the pool will certainly provide cooling relief from sultry summer days for all family members, not just the athletically minded.

The lap pool not only serves as a recreational feature, but it also organizes the space in the landscape, acting as the main point of interest. The designer situated the pool easily within the confines of a modest-sized backyard by locating it off-center and at the focal point of a line of sight leading between two oval flowering trees and ending with a small specimen tree on the other side of the pool. The brick patio offsets the visual weight of the pool, balancing the design. The designer worked to vary the pattern and direction in the

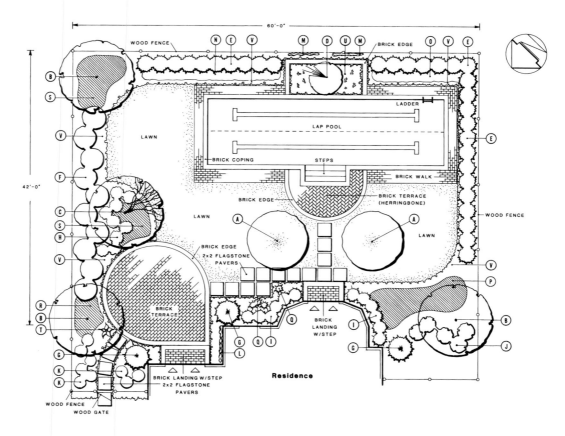

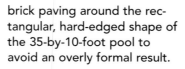

brick paving around the rectangular, hard-edged shape of the 35-by-10-foot pool to avoid an overly formal result.

A path of flagstone pavers, leading from the gate to the brick terrace and from the terrace to the pool, provides easy circulation through the landscape. Swimmers can reach the pool from two doors of the house. Although the perimeter plantings ensure privacy for the swimmer, a variety of flowering shrubs and perennials creates a spring-through-fall display of flower and leaf color for all to enjoy.

Even modest-sized backyards have room for a lap pool for the athletically minded and those seeking a refreshing dip. This elegant backyard plan incorporates a lovely patio and pool with a generous lawn, evergreens for privacy, and flowering trees and shrubs for spring beauty.

 # HPK2500360

PLAN

Season: Spring

Design by: Tom Nordloh

eplans.com

LANDSCAPE PLANS

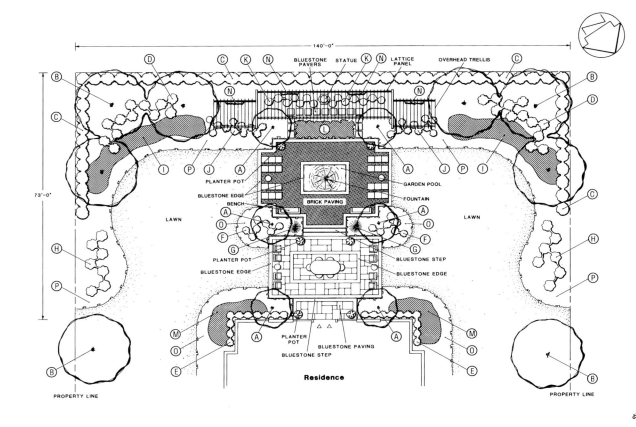

140'-0"

73'-0"

D
C K N BLUESTONE PAVERS STATUE K N LATTICE PANEL OVERHEAD TRELLIS C
B N N B
C D
I P J A A J P I
PLANTER POT A A
BLUESTONE EDGE GARDEN POOL C
BENCH FOUNTAIN H
BRICK PAVING
LAWN A A LAWN P
O O
F F
G G
PLANTER POT BLUESTONE STEP
BLUESTONE EDGE BLUESTONE EDGE
H
P
M M
A A
PLANTER POT
O BLUESTONE PAVING O
E BLUESTONE STEP E
B B

Residence

PROPERTY LINE   PROPERTY LINE

WANT TO PLAY A ROLE FROM THE GREAT GATSBY?

Then close your eyes and imagine being a guest at a large party in this magnificent garden designed for formal entertaining. Imagine standing in the house at the French doors, just at the entrance to the paved area, and looking out at this perfectly symmetrical scene. The left mirrors the right; a major sight line runs straight down the center past the fountain to the statue that serves as a focal point at the rear of the garden. Three perfectly oval flowering trees on each side of the patio frame the sight line, as well as help to delineate the pavement from the planted areas of the garden. The flagstone patio along the house rises several steps above the brick patio, giving it prominence and presenting a good view of the rest of the property. The change in paving materials provides a separate identity to each area; yet, by edging the brick with bluestone to match the upper patio the two are tied together. Pink and purple flowering shrubs and perennials provide an elegant color scheme throughout the growing season. A vine-covered lattice panel featuring royal purple flowers that bloom all summer long creates a secluded area that is accessible by paving stones at the rear of the property. What a perfect spot for a romantic rendezvous!

PLAN

**HPK2500361**

Season: Summer

Design by: Michael J. Opisso

eplans.com

THERE'S SOMETHING ENTICING AND ROMANTIC ABOUT A GARDEN GAZEBO. It creates an intimate spot to sit and talk, perhaps making the difference between having a few friends over and having a party. If you enjoy entertaining, this backyard design, featuring both a roomy deck and a lovely gazebo, may be the one for your family. The gazebo (not included in the plan) acts as the main focal point of the design, drawing the eye by its shape, size, and location and enticing visitors by the stepping-stone path leading to its cozy confines. The lush plantings surrounding the gazebo anchor it to the design, creating a flowery setting that helps keep the structure cool and inviting.

The other primary feature of this garden is a large deck. The deck features octagonal lines to echo and complement the shape of the gazebo and has

HPK2500362

Season: Summer
Design by: David Poplawski

eplans.com

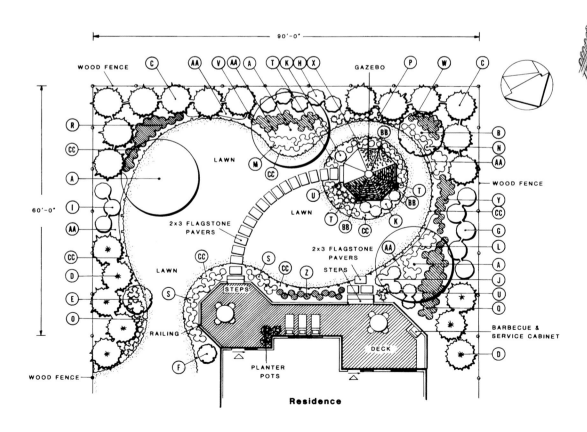

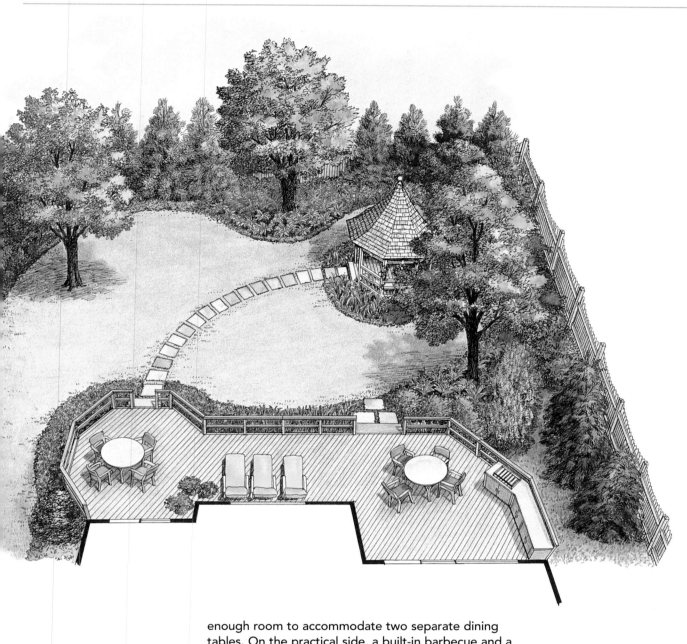

enough room to accommodate two separate dining tables. On the practical side, a built-in barbecue and a storage cabinet turn the deck into an outdoor extension of your home's living space. The informal style of the design incorporates sunny and shady areas, as well as a mix of evergreen and deciduous trees and shrubs, to create a variety of textures and patterns. Background plantings of tall evergreens assure privacy, and a wide variety of flowering shrubs and perennials add seasonal color and interest. Three deciduous shade trees frame the skyline, providing necessary summer shade and letting in warming winter sun.

A SECOND-STORY DECK CAN BE THE ANSWER TO MANY DIFFICULT LANDSCAPING ISSUES. Even a high deck can have two levels and, therefore, two separate use areas, and the designer accomplishes this with this deck. The upper area features a built-in barbecue, service cabinet, and space for dining. The lower area invites family and guests to lounge and relax in the sun. Filled with masses of annuals, the planters bring living color above ground. Without screening, the underside of the deck would be an eyesore when viewed from the yard. The designer solved this problem by enclosing the void beneath the deck with latticework and using a hedge to soften the effect. If the area beneath the deck is to be used as storage, a door can be added to the latticework.

HPK2500363

Season: Summer

Design by: Michael J. Opisso

eplans.com

Three flowering trees at the corners of the deck anchor this shape and further serve to bring color and greenery up high. Tall evergreens help to screen the deck from the neighbors. High above the rest of the garden, this second-story deck affords a beautiful view of the grounds.

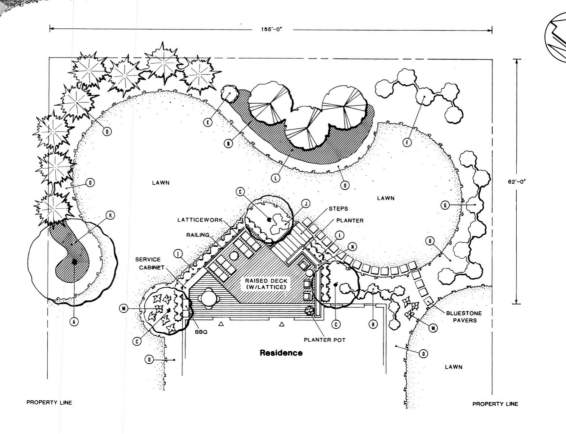

LANDSCAPE PLANS

THERE ARE FEW PLACES MORE TRANQUIL, MORE RELAXING, OR MORE COOLING on a hot summer day than a garden with a view of the water—even if the water is no more than a garden pool. In the garden pictured here, two ponds filled with water lilies are used to create a tranquil setting. The first pond is situated near the house, where it is visible from the indoors. The deck is cantilevered over the pond to enhance the closeness of the water and is covered with an overhead trellis, which ties the two areas together. The trellising also frames the view of the pond from the deck and of the deck from the garden areas. A second, smaller pond is set into the corner of the garden and has a backdrop of early-spring flowering trees, ferns, and shade-loving perennials. This intimate retreat is made complete by setting a bench and planter pots beside the pond. Throughout the property, river-rock paving enhances the natural feeling of

PLAN

HPK2500364

Season: Summer

Design by: Michael J. Opisso and Damon Scott

eplans.com

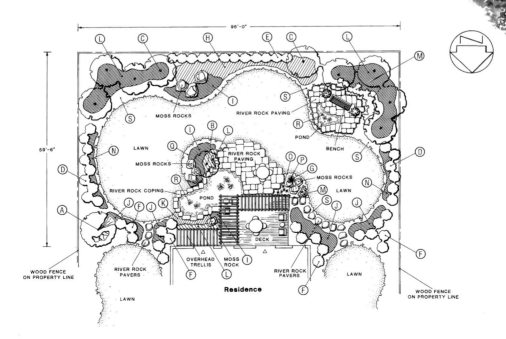

the water and provides a sitting area nearby for quiet contemplation. Moss rocks, placed in strategic places in the garden, further carry out the naturalistic theme, as do most of the landscape plants. The shrubs and perennials bordering the undulating lawn provide the needed soft-textured, informal look that makes both ponds seem natural and right at home. Although the ponds are not included in the blueprints for this design, the surrounding landscape lends itself to their placement.

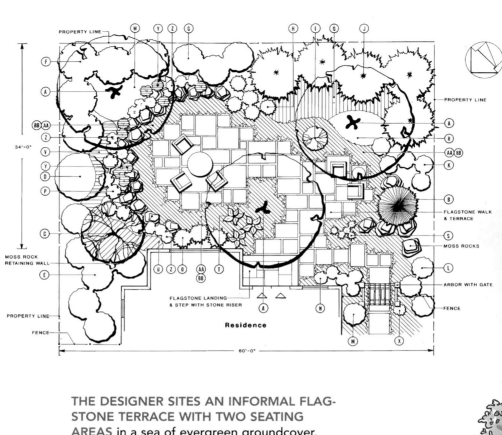

PROPERTY LINE

34'-0"

MOSS ROCK
RETAINING WALL

PROPERTY LINE

FENCE

PROPERTY LINE

FLAGSTONE LANDING
& STEP WITH STONE RISER

Residence

60'-0"

FLAGSTONE WALK
& TERRACE

MOSS ROCKS

ARBOR WITH GATE

FENCE

THE DESIGNER SITES AN INFORMAL FLAG-STONE TERRACE WITH TWO SEATING AREAS in a sea of evergreen groundcover, entirely eliminating a lawn and making the garden about as carefree as it can be. Evergreens on the property border create privacy, while airy trees create a lacy overhead canopy. The overall effect is serene.

A half-circle rock wall built of small moss-covered boulders sets off the larger of the two seating areas and gives dimension to the area. Several types of perennials spill over the top and sprout from the crevices of the wall, decorating the area with their dainty flowers and foliage and creating a soft, natural look. Flowering shrubs—many of which also display evergreen leaves—give the garden year-round structure and interest while offering easy-care floral beauty. The lack of a lawn makes this garden especially easy to care for. You'll spend many more hours just relaxing in this backyard retreat than you will taking care of it.

HPK2500365

PLAN

Season: Summer
Design by: Michael
J. Opisso

eplans.com

HPK2500366

PLAN

Season: Spring
Design by: Jim Morgan

eplans.com

WHEN SMALL TREES, FLOWERING SHRUBS, PERENNIALS, AND GROUNDCOVERS are planted together, the result is a lovely mixed border that looks great throughout the year. The trees and shrubs—both evergreen and deciduous types—provide structure and form in winter, while also offering decorative foliage and flowers in other seasons. Perennials and bulbs occupy large spaces between groups of woody plants and contribute leaf texture and floral color to the scene. Even though this border contains a lot of plants, it is easy to care for. That's part of the beauty of a mixed border—the woody plants are long-lived and need little pruning if allowed to grow naturally. By limiting the number of perennials and blanketing the ground with weed-smothering groundcovers, maintenance is kept to a minimum without sacrificing beauty. You can install this mixed border in a sunny location almost anywhere on your property, though it's intended to run along the back of an average-sized lot. If your property is larger or smaller than the one in this plan, you can alter the design by either increasing or decreasing the number of plants in each grouping. Evergreen and deciduous shrubs and small trees, mixed with drifts of bulbs and flowering perennials, create an ever-changing border that's gorgeous every month of the year.

LET THE COLORS OF OLD GLORY SHINE IN YOUR YARD with this red, white, and blue flower garden. Designed as a dramatic island bed to be planted in any open, sunny location in your yard, this versatile garden features combinations of flowering perennials and annuals carefully selected so the bed blooms from spring through fall in an ever-changing display of the colors of the American flag. The long-blooming annuals, which should be planted in the spots where bulbs flower in spring, provide a constant mass of color against which the perennials bloom in an exciting sequence.

Red can be a difficult color in the garden, since scarlet tones, with their hints of orange, clash terribly with crimson shades, with their hints of blue or purple. Likewise, blue comes in many tints, not all of which combine well with the various reds. White flowers separate and calm the strong blues and reds of this bold color scheme, giving the garden brightness and sparkle. The designer selected the flowers for their pure, bright colors, choosing ones that blossom in the red and blue tints that look great together and that will assuredly look superb when planted as the centerpiece of your backyard.

(#) HPK2500367

Season: Summer
Design by: Michael J. Opisso

eplans.com

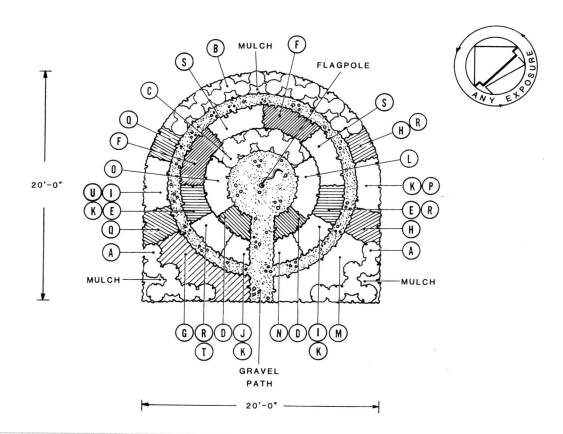

The designer planned the garden in a somewhat formal fashion, with blocks of plants laid out around a wood-chip path and central flagpole. The path affords you access to the flowers for easy planting and tending, while bringing you right into the garden where you can enjoy the flowers at close range.

The bold and dramatic color scheme of this island flower bed is further emphasized by the formal nature of the garden plan. Geometrically laid out in changing bands of flowers, the garden forms a dynamic centerpiece for any summer yard.

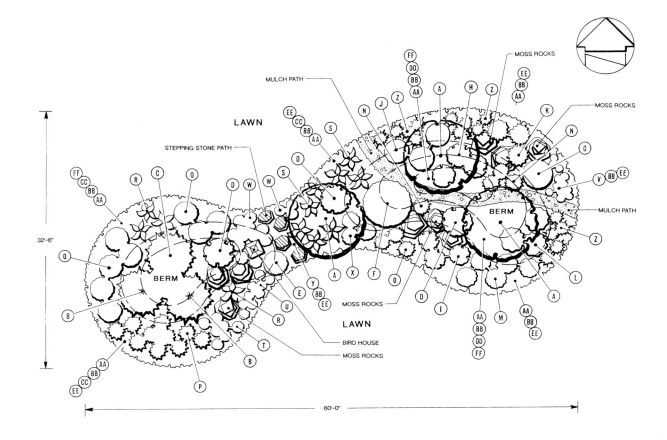

MULCH PATH

MOSS ROCKS

LAWN

STEPPING STONE PATH

MOSS ROCKS

32'-6"

BERM

BERM

MULCH PATH

MOSS ROCKS

LAWN

BIRD HOUSE

MOSS ROCKS

60'-0"

ONE OF THE GREAT JOYS OF A LOVELY LOW-MAINTE-NANCE GARDEN is having the time to really enjoy it. If you'd like a garden bed that is eye-catching as well as easy-care, this design is for you. This bow-tie-shaped bed contains a delightful variety of low-maintenance perennials, evergreens, deciduous trees and shrubs, and spring bulbs. Such a diverse blend of easy-care plants guarantees you'll have both year-round color and the time to take pleasure in every season's display. The berms at each end of the bed create a small valley that is tra-versed by a natural stone path. Trees screen the peak of the higher berm, adding a bit of mystery and encouraging visitors to explore. Two path-ways—one of mulch, the other of stepping stones—make it easy to enjoy the plantings up close and to per-form maintenance tasks, such as occa-sional deadheading

PLAN

 # HPK2500368

Season: Summer

Design by: Jeffery Diefenbach

eplans.com

and weeding. Moss rocks in three areas of the garden and a birdhouse near the stepping-stone path provide pleasing structure and interest. Locate this easy-care bed in an open area of lawn in the front- or backyard to create a pretty view that can be enjoyed from indoors and out.

A FLOWER-FILLED GARDEN CREATED IN THE ROMANTIC STYLE OF AN ENGLISH BORDER need not demand much care, as this lovely design illustrates. The designer carefully selects unfussy bulbs and perennials and a few flowering shrubs, all of which are disease- and insect-resistant, noninvasive, and don't need staking or other maintenance. A balance of spring-, summer-, and fall-blooming plants keeps the border exciting throughout the growing season. Because English gardens are famous for their gorgeous roses, the designer included several rosebushes, but chooses ones unharmed by bugs and mildew. Hedges form a backdrop for most English flower gardens; the designer planted an informal one here to reduce pruning. A

HPK2500369

Season: Summer
Design by: Maria Morrison

PLAN

eplans.com

generous mulched path runs between the flowers and the hedge, so it's easy to tend them, while the edging keeps grass from invading and creating a nuisance. Plant this border along any sunny side of your property. Imagine it along the back of the yard, where you can view it from a kitchen window or from a patio or deck; along one side of the front yard; or planted with the hedge bordering the front lawn and providing privacy from the street.

Brimming with easy-care flowers from spring through fall, this low-maintenance flower border evokes the spirit of an English garden, but doesn't require a staff to take care of it.

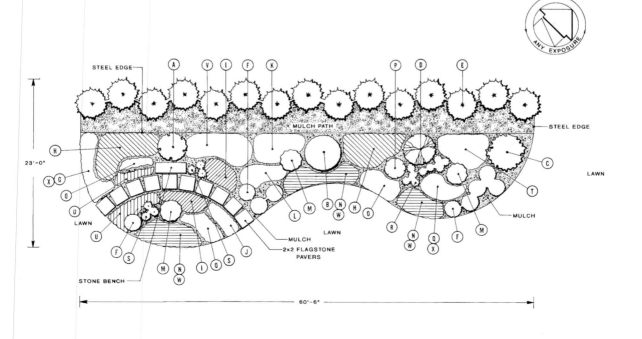

LANDSCAPE PLANS

PLAN

HPK2500370

Season: Summer
Design by: Patrick J. Duffe

eplans.com

ALTHOUGH DRY, SUNNY SITES CAN BE CHAL-LENGING, it's possible to enjoy a lush, colorful garden even in areas of your yard with fast-draining, sandy soil and full-sun exposure. Place this three-pronged bed anywhere in your landscape that gets the full force of the sun. The garden will be sure to thrive, since the designer takes special care to select water-thrifty plants.

Once these water-wise perennials become established, you'll expend very little effort keeping them watered. Keep in mind, however, that even drought-tolerant perennials need to be well watered during the first year after planting. And during periods of extreme heat or prolonged drought, you'll probably need to water a bit more than usual.

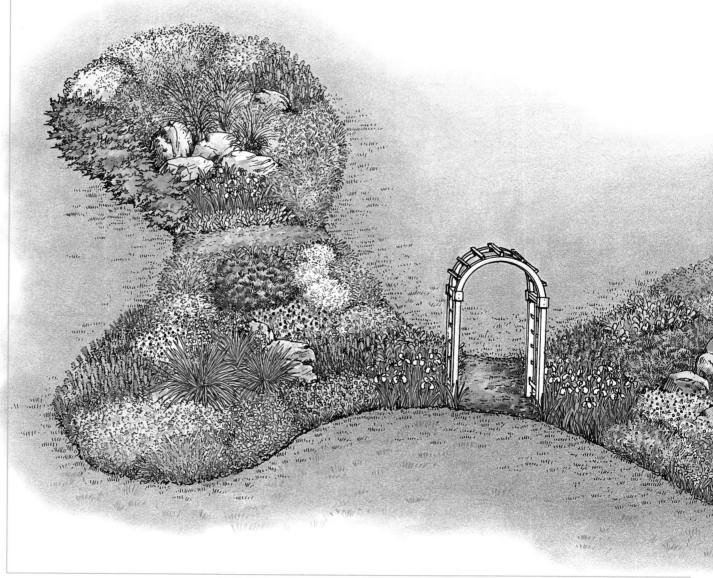

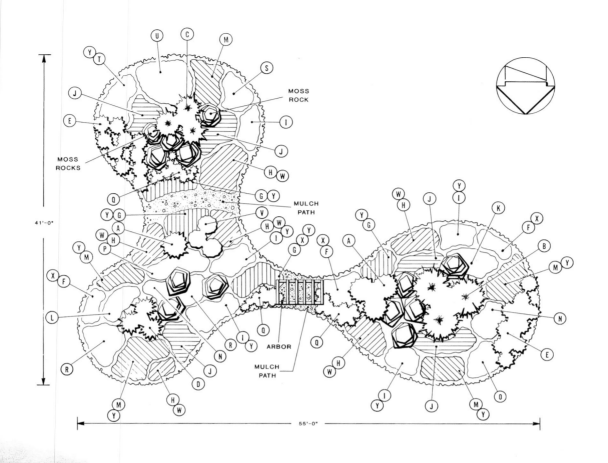

MOSS
ROCK

MOSS
ROCKS

41'-0"

MULCH
PATH

MULCH
PATH

ARBOR

55'-0"

This colorful garden is divided into three planting areas by two shredded-mulch paths. A wooden arbor over one path adds structure, provides a visual anchor, and creates interesting shadows as the sun passes overhead. Moss rocks create a second, stronger visual anchor and furnish a backdrop for the surrounding plants. The ornamental grasses and yuccas add height and a sense of balance to the composition.

NOT ALL FLOWERS NEED EVEN MOISTURE AND RICH SOIL to perform well. This design features a beautiful array of perennials that bloom prolifically in poor soil and drought conditions.

LANDSCAPE PLANS

When easy-care, disease- and insect-resistant shrubs are used to create a border and allowed to grow naturally without excessive pruning, the result is a beautiful, practically maintenance-free garden.

NOTHING BEATS FLOWERING SHRUBS AND TREES FOR AN EASY-CARE SHOW OF FLOWERS AND FOLIAGE throughout the seasons. This lovely garden includes shrubs that bloom at various times of the year—from late winter right into autumn—so that blossoms will always be decorating this garden. In autumn, the leaves of the deciduous shrubs turn flaming shades of yellow, gold, orange, and red. (These colors appear even more brilliant when juxtaposed against the deep greens of the evergreen shrubs.) During the coldest months, when the flowers and fall foliage are finally finished, many of the plants feature glossy red berries or evergreen leaves that take on deep burgundy hues.

The designer balances the border with a tall evergreen and two flowering trees, which serve as anchors at the border's widest points. Most shrubs are grouped in all-of-a-kind drifts to create the most impact—low, spreading types in the front and taller ones in the back—but several specimens appear alone as eye-catching focal points. A few large drifts of easy-care, long-blooming perennials, interplanted with spring-flowering bulbs, break up the shrubbery to give a variety of textures and forms.

Designed for the back of an average-sized lot, this easy-care border can be located in any sunny area of your property. It makes a perfect addition to any existing property with only a high-maintenance lawn and little other landscaping. The design adds year-round interest, creates privacy, and reduces maintenance.

(#) HPK2500371

PLAN

Season: Spring

Design by: Salvatore A. Masullo

eplans.com

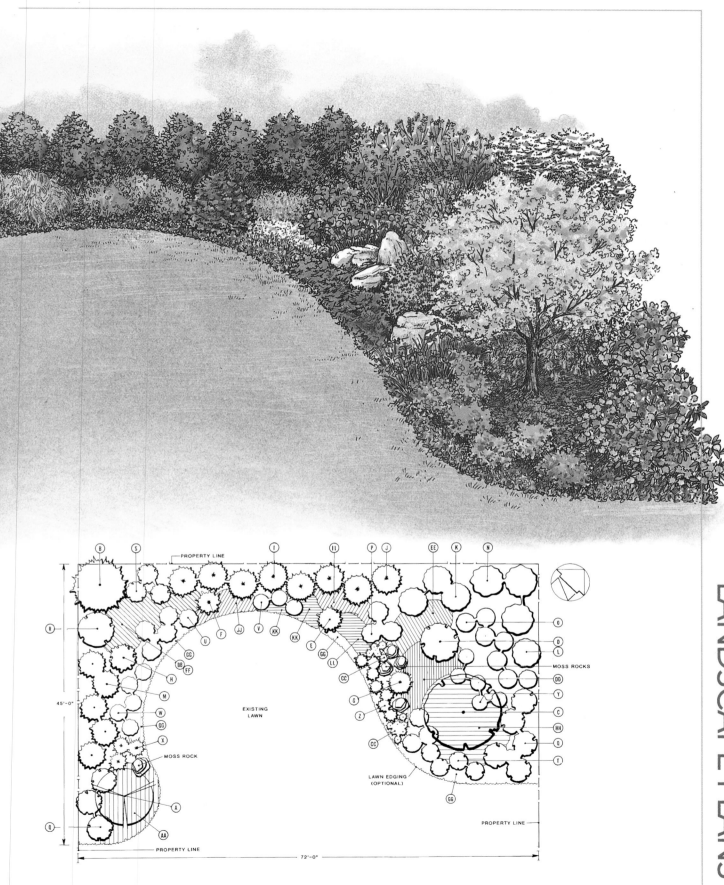

EXISTING
LAWN

PROPERTY LINE

MOSS ROCKS

MOSS ROCK

LAWN EDGING
(OPTIONAL)

PROPERTY LINE

PROPERTY LINE

45'-0"

72'-0"

BURSTING WITH EXUBERANT OLD-FASHIONED BLOSSOMS, this friendly cottage garden is designed to be enjoyed from both sides of the fence. The garden invites passersby to pause and enjoy the show from the street or sidewalk, thus creating a friendly neighborhood feeling. However, where space is very limited, you might prefer to plant only the inside of the fence and to plant the street side with a mowing strip of grass or a low-maintenance groundcover. You could even reverse the plan and install the hedge on the street side. Whether you have a sidewalk or not, leave a buffer between the edge of the border and the street so that if you live in a cold-winter

climate, there'll be room to pile snow. Flowering perennial and annual climbing vines cover the wooden arbor, creating a romantic entrance. Roses, bulbs, perennials, annuals, and a compact evergreen hedge are arranged in a classic cottage-garden style that is casual but not haphazard. The designer achieves a pleasant sense of unity by repeating plants and colors throughout the design without repeating a symmetrical planting pattern. This helps create the casual feeling essential to a cottage garden. Create a friendly neighborhood feeling by planting this flower-filled cottage garden along the front of your property.

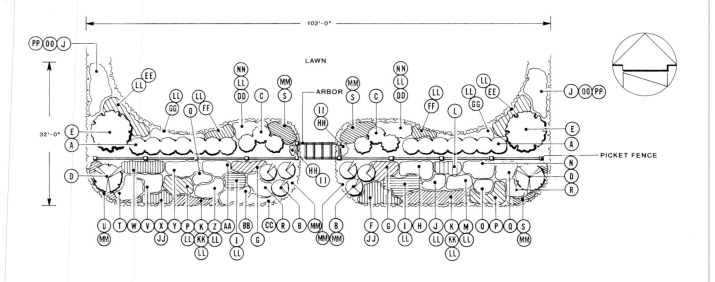

LANDSCAPE PLANS

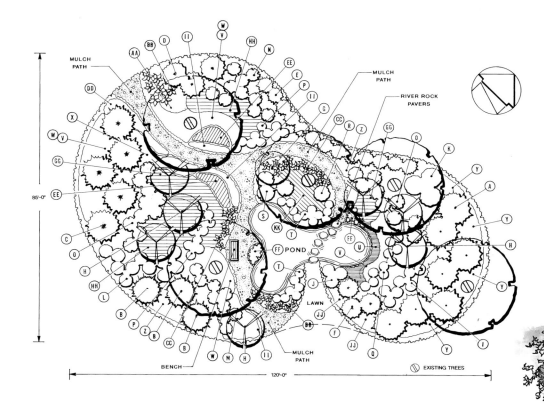

MULCH
PATH

MULCH
PATH

RIVER ROCK
PAVERS

85'-0"

POND

LAWN

BENCH

MULCH
PATH

120'-0"

⊘ EXISTING TREES

DESIGNED TO BE AN OASIS IN THE SHADE,
these garden beds surround a dramatic, yet naturalistic focal point—a small pond. The three lobes
of the centrally located pond dictate the rhythm
and design concept of the surrounding beds.

Visitors enter via one of three entrances that
divide the garden into three distinct beds: a large
semicircular bed to the northwest, a roughly S-
shaped bed to the southwest, and an island bed
in the center, nearest the pond. Stepping-stones,
set on a slightly sunken ridge, cut across the pond
and allow visitors a panoramic view of the garden
from the central tone.

Midsize evergreens ring the entire garden, giving
it a sense of privacy and seclusion. A diverse mix
of shade-loving flowering shrubs
and trees, ferns, and perennials
provide varying texture and
color throughout the year.

Site this garden under
existing, high-canopied
trees. To prevent fallen tree

leaves from clogging the pond and fouling the water, cover the pond surface with bird netting in autumn. The black netting is almost invisible and allows you to easily catch and scoop out the leaves. Although the pond is not included in the blueprints for this design, the surrounding landscape lends itself to its placement.

Plant this lovely pond garden where its shade-loving plants will flourish. You'll enjoy the beauty of this design all year long.

PLAN

HPK2500373

Season: Spring

Design by: Salvatore A. Masullo

eplans.com

LANDSCAPE PLANS

With more than 50 years of experience in the industry and millions of blueprints sold, Hanley Wood is a trusted source of high-quality, high-value pre-drawn home plans.

Using pre-drawn home plans is a **reliable, cost-effective way** to build your dream home, and our vast selection of plans is second-to-none. The nation's finest designers craft these plans that builders know they can trust. Meanwhile, our friendly, knowledgeable customer service representatives can help you every step of the way.

WHAT YOU'LL GET WITH YOUR ORDER

The contents of each designer's blueprint package is unique, but all contain detailed, high-quality working drawings. You can expect to find the following standard elements in most sets of plans:

I. FRONT PERSPECTIVE

This artist's sketch of the exterior of the house gives you an idea of how the house will look when built and landscaped.

4. HOUSE AND DETAIL CROSS-SECTIONS

Large-scale views show sections or cutaways of the foundation, interior walls, exterior walls, floors, stairways, and roof details. Additional cross-sections may show important changes in floor, ceiling, or roof heights, or the relationship of one level to another. These sections show exactly how the various parts of the house fit together and are extremely valuable during construction. Additional sheets may include enlarged wall, floor, and roof construction details.

2. FOUNDATION AND BASEMENT PLANS

This sheet shows the foundation layout including concrete walls, footings, pads, posts, beams, bearing walls, and foundation notes. If the home features a basement, the first-floor framing details may also be included on this plan. If your plan features slab construction rather than a basement, the plan shows footings and details for a monolithic slab. This page, or another in the set, may include a sample plot plan for locating your house on a building site. Additional sheets focus on foundation cross-sections and other details.

3. DETAILED FLOOR PLANS

These plans show the layout of each floor of the house. Rooms and interior spaces are carefully dimensioned, doors and windows located, and keys are given for cross-section details provided elsewhere in the plans.

5. FLOOR STRUCTURAL SUPPORTS

The floor framing plans provide detail for these crucial elements of your home. Each includes floor joist, ceiling joist, spacing, direction, span, and specifications. Beam and window headers, along with necessary details for framing connections, stairways, or dormers are also included.

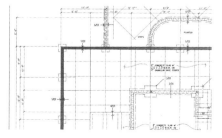

6. ELECTRICAL PLAN

The electrical plan offers suggested locations with notes for all lighting, outlets, switches, and circuits. A layout is provided for each level, as well as basements, garages, or other structures. This plan does not contain diagrams detailing how all wiring should be run, or how circuits should be engineered. These details should be designed by your electrician.

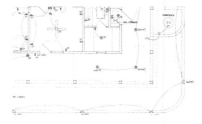

7. EXTERIOR ELEVATIONS

In addition to the front exterior, your blueprint set will include drawings of the rear and sides of your house as well. These drawings give notes on exterior materials and finishes. Particular attention is given to cornice detail, brick and stone accents, or other finish items that make your home unique.

ROOF FRAMING PLANS — PLEASE READ

Some plans contain roof framing plans; however because of the wide variation in local requirements, many plans do not. If you buy a plan without a roof framing plan, you will need an engineer familiar with local building codes to create a plan to build your roof. Even if your plan does contain a roof framing plan, we recommend that a local engineer review the plan to verify that it will meet local codes.

BEFORE YOU CALL

You are making a terrific decision to use a pre-drawn house plan it is one you can make with confidence, knowing that your blueprints are crafted by national-award-winning certified residential designers and architects, and trusted by builders.

Once you ve selected the plan you want or even if you have questions along the way our experienced customer service representatives are available 24 hours a day, seven days a week to help you navigate the home-building process. To help them provide you with even better service, please consider the following questions before you call:

■ Have you chosen or purchased your lot?
If so, please review the building setback requirements of your local building authority before you call. You don t need to have a lot before ordering plans, but if you own land already, please have the width and depth dimensions handy when you call.

■ Have you chosen a builder?
Involving your builder in the plan selection and evaluation process may be beneficial. Luckily, builders know they can have confidence with pre-drawn plans because they ve been designed for livability, functionality, and typically are builder-proven at successful home sites across the country.

■ Do you need a construction loan?
Construction loans are unique because they involve determining the value of something that is not yet constructed. Several lenders offer convenient contstruction-to-permanent loans. It is important to choose a good lending partner one who will help guide you through the application and appraisal process. Most will even help you evaluate your contractor to ensure reliability and credit worthiness. Our partnership with IndyMac Bank, a nationwide leader in construction loans, can help you save on your loan, if needed.

■ How many sets of plans do you need?
Building a home can typically require a number of sets of blueprints one for yourself, two or three for the builder and subcontractors, two for the local building department, and one or more for your lender. For this reason, we offer 5- and 8-set plan packages, but your best value is the Reproducible Plan Package. Reproducible plans are accompanied by a license to make modifications and typically up to 12 duplicates of the plan so you have enough copies of the plan for everyone involved in the financing and construction of your home.

■ Do you want to make any changes to the plan?
We understand that it is difficult to find blueprints for a home that will meet all of your needs. That is why Hanley Wood is glad to offer plan Customization Services. We will work with you to design the modifications you d like to see and to adjust your blueprint plans accordingly anything from changing the foundation; adding square footage, redesigning baths, kitchens, or bedrooms; or most other modifications. This simple, cost-effective service saves you from hiring an outside architect to make alterations. Modifications may only be made to Reproducible Plan Packages that include the license to modify.

■ Do you have to make any changes to meet local building codes?
While all of our plans are drawn to meet national building codes at the time they were created, many areas required that plans be stamped by a local engineer to certify that they meet local building codes. Building codes are updated frequently and can vary by state, county, city, or municipality. Contact your local building inspection department, office of planning and zoning, or department of permits to determine how your local codes will affect your construction project. The best way to assure that you can make changes to your plan, if necessary, is to purchase a Reproducible Plan Package.

■ Has everyone—from family members to contractors—been involved in selecting the plan?
Building a new home is an exciting process, and using pre-drawn plans is a great way to realize your dreams. Make sure that everyone involved has had an opportunity to review the plan you ve selected. While Hanley Wood is the only plans provider with an exchange policy, it s best to be sure all parties agree on your selection before you buy.

CALL TOLL-FREE 1-800-521-6797

Source Key
HPK25

CUSTOMIZE YOUR PLAN – HANLEY WOOD CUSTOMIZATION SERVICES

Creating custom home plans has never been easier and more directly accessible. Using state-of-the-art technology and top-performing architectural expertise, Hanley Wood delivers on a long-standing customer commitment to provide world-class home-plans and customization services. Our valued customers—professional home builders and individual home owners—appreciate the convenience and accessibility of this interactive, consultative service.

With the Hanley Wood Customization Service you can:

■ Save valuable time by avoiding drawn-out and frequently repetitive face-to-face design meetings

■ Communicate design and home-plan changes faster and more efficiently
■ Speed-up project turn-around time
■ Build on a budget without sacrificing quality
■ Transform master home plans to suit your design needs and unique personal style

All of our design options and prices are impressively affordable. A detailed quote is available for a $50 consultation fee. Plan modification is an interactive service. Our skilled team of designers will guide you through the customization process from start to finish making recommendations, offering ideas, and determining the feasibility of your changes. This level of service is offered to ensure the final modified plan meets your expectations. If you use our service the $50 fee will be applied to the cost of the modifications.

You may purchase the customization consultation before or after purchasing a plan. In either case, it is necessary to purchase the Reproducible Plan Package and complete the accompanying license to modify the plan before we can begin customization.

Customization Consultation $50

TOOLS TO WORK WITH YOUR BUILDER

Two Reverse Options For Your Convenience – Mirror and Right-Reading Reverse (as available)

Mirror reverse plans simply flip the design 180 degrees keep in mind, the text will also be flipped. For a minimal fee you can have one or all of your plans shipped mirror reverse, although we recommend having at least one regular set handy. Right-reading reverse plans show the design flipped 180 degrees but the text reads normally. When you choose this option, we ship each set of purchased blueprints in this format.

Mirror Reverse Fee (indicate the number of sets when ordering) $55
Right Reading Reverse Fee (all sets are reversed) $175

A Shopping List Exclusively for Your Home – Materials List

A customized Materials List helps you plan and estimate the cost of your new home, outlining the quantity, type, and size of materials needed to build your house (with the exception of mechanical system items). Included are framing lumber, windows and doors, kitchen and bath cabinetry, rough and finished hardware, and much more.

Materials List . . . .$85 each
Additional Materials Lists (at original time of purchase only) . . $20 each

Plan Your Home- Building Process – Specification Outline

Work with your builder on this step-by-step chronicle of 166 stages or items crucial to the building process. It provides a comprehensive review of the construction process and helps you choose materials.

Specification Outline . . . .$10 each

Learn the Basics of Building – Electrical, Plumbing, Mechanical, Construction Detail Sheets

If you want to know more about building techniques and deal more confidently with your subcontractors we offer four useful detail sheets. These sheets provide non-plan-specific general information, but are excellent tools that will add to your understanding of Plumbing Details, Electrical Details, Construction Details, and Mechanical Details.

Electrical Detail Sheet $14.95
Plumbing Detail Sheet $14.95
Mechanical Detail Sheet $14.95
Construction Detail Sheet $14.95

SUPER VALUE SETS:
Buy any 2: $26.95; Buy any 3: $34.95; Buy All 4: $39.95

Best Value

MAKE YOUR HOME TECH-READY — HOME AUTOMATION UPGRADE

Building a new home provides a unique opportunity to wire it with a plan for future needs. A Home Automation-Ready (HA-Ready) home contains the wiring substructure of tomorrow's connected home. It means that every room—from the front porch to the backyard, and from the attic to the basement—is wired for security, lighting, telecommunications, climate control, home computer networking, whole-house audio, home theater, shade control, video surveillance, entry access control, and yes, video gaming electronic solutions.

Along with the conveniences HA-Ready homes provide, they also have a higher resale value. The Consumer Electronics Association (CEA), in conjunction with the Custom Electronic Design and Installation Association (CEDIA), have developed a TechHome™ Rating system that quantifies the value of HA-Ready homes. The rating system is gaining widespread recognition in the real estate industry.

Developed by CEDIA-certified installers, our Home Automation Upgrade package includes everything you need to work with an installer during the construction of your home. It provides a short explanation of the various subsystems, a wiring floor plan for each level of your home, a detailed materials list with estimated costs, and a list of CEDIA-certified installers in your local area.

Home Automation Upgrade $250

GET YOUR HOME PLANS PAID FOR!

IndyMac Bank, in partnership with Hanley Wood, will reimburse you up to $750 toward the cost of your home plans simply by financing the construction of your new home with IndyMac Bank Home Construction Lending.

IndyMac's construction and permanent loan is a one-time close loan, meaning that one application—and one set of closing fees—provides all the financing you need.

Apply today at www.indymacbank.com, call toll free at 1-800-847-6138, or ask a Hanley Wood customer service representative for details.

DESIGN YOUR HOME — INTERIOR AND EXTERIOR FINISHING TOUCHES

Be Your Own Interior Designer! — Home Furniture Planner

Effectively plan the space in your home using our Hands-On Home Furniture Planner. It s fun and easy no more moving heavy pieces of furniture to see how the room will go together. The kit includes reusable peel-and-stick furniture templates that fit on a 12"x18" laminated layout board enough space to lay out every room in your house.

Home Furniture Planning Kit **$15.95**

Enjoy the Outdoors! — Deck Plans

Many of our homes have a corresponding deck plan, sold separately, which includes a Deck Plan Frontal Sheet, Deck Framing and Floor Plans, Deck Elevations, and a Deck Materials List. A Standard Deck Details Package, also available, provides all the how-to information necessary for building any deck. Get both the Deck Plan and the Standard Deck Details Package for one low price in our Complete Deck Building Package. See the price tier chart below and call for deck plan availability.

Create a Professionally Designed Landscape — Landscape Plans

Many of our homes have a front-yard Landscape Plan that is complementary in design to the house plan. These comprehensive Landscape Blueprint Packages include a Frontal Sheet, Plan View, Regionalized Plant & Materials List, a sheet on Planting and Maintaining Your Landscape, Zone Maps,

and a Plant Size and Description Guide. Each set of blueprints is a full 18" x 24" with clear, complete instructions in easy-to-read type. Our Landscape Plans are available with a Plant & Materials List adapted by horticultural experts to eight regions of the country. Please specify your region when ordering your plan see region map below. Call for more information about landscape plan availability and applicable regions.

LANDSCAPE & DECK PRICE SCHEDULE

PRICE TIERS	1-SET STUDY PACKAGE	5-SET BUILDING PACKAGE	1-SET REPRODUCIBLE*	1-SET CAD*
P1	$25	$55	$145	$245
P2	$45	$75	$165	$280
P3	$75	$105	$195	$330
P4	$105	$135	$225	$385
P5	$175	$205	$405	$690
P6	$215	$245	$445	$750
D1	$45	$75**	$90	$90
D2	$75	$105**	$150	$150

PRICES SUBJECT TO CHANGE   * REQUIRES AN E-MAIL ADDRESS OR FAX NUMBER

** 3-SET PACKAGE

TERMS & CONDITIONS

OUR 90-DAY EXCHANGE POLICY

BUY WITH CONFIDENCE!

Hanley Wood is committed to ensuring your satisfaction with your blueprint order, which is why a we offer a 90-day exchange policy. With the exception of Reproducible Plan Package orders, we will exchange your entire first order for an equal or greater number of blueprints from our plan collection within 90 days of the original order. The entire content of your original order must be returned before an exchange will be processed. Please call our customer service department at 1-888-690-1116 for your return authorization number and shipping instructions. If the returned blueprints look used, redlined, or copied, we will not honor your exchange. Fees for exchanging your blueprints are as follows: 20% of the amount of the original order, plus the difference in cost if exchanging for a design in a higher price bracket or less the difference in cost if exchanging for a design in a lower price bracket. (Because they can be copied, Reproducible blueprints are not exchangeable or refundable.) Please call for current postage and handling prices. Shipping and handling charges are not refundable.

ARCHITECTURAL AND ENGINEERING SEALS

Some cities and states now require that a licensed architect or engineer review and "seal" a blueprint, or officially approve it, prior to construction. Prior to application for a building permit or the start of actual construction, we strongly advise that you consult your local building official who can tell you if such a review is required.

LOCAL BUILDING CODES AND ZONING REQUIREMENTS

Each plan was designed to meet or exceed the requirements of a nationally recognized model building code in effect at the time and place the plan was drawn. Typically plans designed after the year 2000 conform to the International Residential Building Code (IRC 2000 or 2003). The IRC is comprised of portions of the three major codes below. Plans drawn before 2000 conform to one of the three recognized building codes in effect at the time: Building Officials and Code Administrators (BOCA) International, Inc.;

the Southern Building Code Congress International, (SBCCI) Inc.; the International Conference of Building Officials (ICBO); or the Council of American Building Officials (CABO).

Because of the great differences in geography and climate throughout the United States and Canada, each state, county, and municipality has its own building codes, zone requirements, ordinances, and building regulations. Your plan may need to be modified to comply with local requirements. In addition, you may need to obtain permits or inspections from local governments before and in the course of construction. We authorize the use of the blueprints on the express condition that you consult a local licensed architect or engineer of your choice prior to beginning construction and strictly comply with all local building codes, zoning requirements, and other applicable laws, regulations, ordinances, and requirements. Notice: Plans for homes to be built in Nevada must be redrawn by a Nevada-registered professional. Consult your local building official for more information on this subject.

TERMS AND CONDITIONS

These designs are protected under the terms of United States Copyright Law and may not be copied or reproduced in any way, by any means, unless you have purchased a Reproducible Plan Package and signed the accompanying license to modify and copy the plan, which clearly indicates your right to modify, copy, or reproduce. We authorize the use of your chosen design as an aid in the construction of ONE (1) single- or multifamily home only. You may not use this design to build a second dwelling or multiple dwellings without purchasing another blueprint or blueprints or paying additional design fees. Multi-use fees vary by designer—please call one of experienced sales representatives for a quote.

DISCLAIMER

The designers we work with have put substantial care and effort into the creation of their blueprints. However, because we cannot provide on-site consultation, supervision, and control over actual construction, and because of the great variance in local building requirements, building practices, and soil, seismic, weather, and other conditions, WE MAKE NO WARRANTY OF ANY KIND, EXPRESS OR IMPLIED, WITH RESPECT TO THE CONTENT OR USE OF THE BLUEPRINTS, INCLUDING BUT NOT LIMITED TO ANY WARRANTY OF MERCHANTABILITY OR OF FITNESS FOR A PARTICULAR PURPOSE. ITEMS, PRICES, TERMS, AND CONDITIONS ARE SUBJECT TO CHANGE WITHOUT NOTICE.

IMPORTANT COPYRIGHT NOTICE

From the Council of Publishing Home Designers

Blueprints for residential construction (or working drawings, as they are often called in the industry) are copyrighted intellectual property, protected under the terms of the United States Copyright Law and, therefore, cannot be copied legally for use in building. The following are some guidelines to help you get what you need to build your home, without violating copyright law:

I. HOME PLANS ARE COPYRIGHTED

Just like books, movies, and songs, home plans receive protection under the federal copyright laws. The copyright laws prevent anyone, other than the copyright owner, from reproducing, modifying, or reusing the plans or design without permission of the copyright owner.

2. DO NOT COPY DESIGNS OR FLOOR PLANS FROM ANY PUBLICATION, ELECTRONIC MEDIA, OR EXISTING HOME

It is illegal to copy, change, or redraw home designs found in a plan book, CDROM or on the Internet. The right to modify plans is one of the exclusive rights of copyright. It is also illegal to copy or redraw a constructed home that is protected by copyright, even if you have never seen the plans for the home. If you find a plan or home that you like, you must purchase a set of plans from an authorized source. The plans may not be lent, given away, or sold by the purchaser.

3. DO NOT USE PLANS TO BUILD MORE THAN ONE HOUSE

The original purchaser of house plans is typically licensed to build a single home from the plans. Building more than one home from the plans without permission is an infringement of the home designer's copyright. The purchase of a multiple-set package of plans is for the construction of a single home only. The purchase of additional sets of plans does not grant the right to construct more than one home.

4. HOUSE PLANS IN THE FORM OF BLUEPRINTS OR BLACKLINES CANNOT BE COPIED OR REPRODUCED

Plans, blueprints, or blacklines, unless they are reproducibles, cannot be copied or reproduced without prior written consent of the copyright owner. Copy shops and blueprinters are prohibited from making copies of these plans without the copyright release letter you receive with reproducible plans.

5. HOUSE PLANS IN THE FORM OF BLUEPRINTS OR BLACKLINES CANNOT BE REDRAWN

Plans cannot be modified or redrawn without first obtaining the copyright owner's permission. With your purchase of plans, you are licensed to make non-structural changes by red-lining the purchased plans. If you need to make structural changes or need to redraw the plans for any reason, you must purchase a reproducible set of plans (see topic 6) which includes a license to modify the plans. Blueprints do not come with a license to make structural changes or to redraw the plans. You may not reuse or sell the modified design.

6. REPRODUCIBILE HOME PLANS

Reproducible plans (for example sepias, mylars, CAD files, electronic files, and vellums) come with a license to make modifications to the plans. Once modified, the plans can be taken to a local copy shop or blueprinter to make up to 10 or 12 copies of the plans to use in the construction of a single home. Only one home can be constructed from any single purchased set of reproducible plans either in original form or as modified. The license to modify and copy must be completed and returned before the plan will be shipped.

7. MODIFIED DESIGNS CANNOT BE REUSED

Even if you are licensed to make modifica-tions to a copyrighted design, the modified design is not free from the original designer's copyright. The sale or reuse of the modified design is prohibited. Also, be aware that any modification to plans relieves the original designer from liability for design defects and voids all warranties expressed or implied.

8. WHO IS RESPONSIBLE FOR COPYRIGHT INFRINGEMENT?

Any party who participates in a copyright violation may be responsible including the purchaser, designers, architects, engineers, drafters, homeowners, builders, contractors, sub-contractors, copy shops, blueprinters, developers, and real estate agencies. It does not matter whether or not the individual knows that a violation is being committed. Ignorance of the law is not a valid defense.

9. PLEASE RESPECT HOME DESIGN COPYRIGHTS

In the event of any suspected violation of a copyright, or if there is any uncertainty about the plans purchased, the publisher, architect, designer, or the Council of Publishing Home Designers (www.cphd.org) should be contacted before proceeding. Awards are sometimes offered for information about home design copyright infringement.

10. PENALTIES FOR INFRINGEMENT

Penalties for violating a copyright may be severe. The responsible parties are required to pay actual damages caused by the infringement (which may be substantial), plus any profits made by the infringer commissions to include all profits from the sale of any home built from an infringing design. The copyright law also allows for the recovery of statutory damages, which may be as high as $150,000 for each infringement. Finally, the infringer may be required to pay legal fees which often exceed the damages.

BLUEPRINT PRICE SCHEDULE

PRICE TIERS	1-SET STUDY PACKAGE	5-SET BUILDING PACKAGE	8-SET BUILDING PACKAGE	1-SET REPRODUCIBLE*	1-SET CAD*
A1	$470	$520	$575	$700	$1,055
A2	$510	$565	$620	$765	$1,230
A3	$575	$630	$690	$870	$1,400
A4	$620	$685	$750	$935	$1,570
C1	$665	$740	$810	$1,000	$1,735
C2	$715	$795	$855	$1,065	$1,815
C3	$785	$845	$910	$1,145	$1,915
C4	$840	$915	$970	$1,225	$2,085
L1	$930	$1,030	$1,115	$1,390	$2,500
L2	$1,010	$1,105	$1,195	$1,515	$2,575
L3	$1,115	$1,220	$1,325	$1,665	$2,835
L4	$1,230	$1,350	$1,440	$1,850	$3,140
SQ1				$0.40/SQ. FT.	$0.68/SQ. FT.
SQ3				$0.55/SQ. FT.	$0.94/SQ. FT.
SQ5				$0.80/SQ. FT	$1.36/SQ. FT.
SQ7				$1.00/SQ. FT.	$1.70/SQ. FT.
SQ9				$1.25/SQ. FT.	$2.13/SQ. FT.
SQ11				$1.50/SQ. FT.	$2.55/SQ. FT.

PRICES SUBJECT TO CHANGE   * REQUIRES AN E-MAIL ADDRESS OR FAX NUMBER

PLAN #	PRICE TIER	PAGE	MATERIALS LIST	DECK	DECK PRICE	LANDSCAPE	LANDSCAPE PRICE	REGIONS
HPK2500011	C1	4	Y					
HPK2500012	L2	8	Y					
HPK2500013	SQ5	16						
HPK2500014	SQ5	17						
HPK2500015	SQ5	18						
HPK2500016	A3	19						
HPK2500017	A3	20						
HPK2500018	A3	20						
HPK2500413	A4	21						
HPK2500019	SQ5	22						
HPK2500020	SQ5	23						
HPK2500021	A3	24						
HPK2500022	A4	25						
HPK2500023	A3	25						
HPK2500024	A2	26						
HPK2500025	A4	27						
HPK2500026	C1	28						
HPK2500027	C1	28	Y					
HPK2500028	C1	29	Y					
HPK2500029	C1	30			OLA024	P4	123568	
HPK2500030	C3	31	Y		OLA004	P3	123568	
HPK2500031	C2	32	Y					
HPK2500032	C4	33						
HPK2500033	C2	34	Y					
HPK2500034	C2	35	Y					
HPK2500035	C2	36						
HPK2500036	C3	37	Y					
HPK2500037	L1	38						
HPK2500038	C4	39	Y					
HPK2500039	C1	40	Y					
HPK2500040	C2	41						
HPK2500041	C1	42						
HPK2500042	C3	43	Y					
HPK2500001	C1	44	Y					
HPK2500043	C3	45	Y					
HPK2500044	C2	46						
HPK2500045	C2	47	Y					
HPK2500046	C3	48	Y					
HPK2500047	C3	49	Y					
HPK2500048	C2	50	Y					
HPK2500049	SQ1	51	Y					
HPK2500051	L2	52						
HPK2500050	C3	53	Y					
HPK2500052	L1	54	Y					
HPK2500053	L2	55	Y		OLA024	P4	123568	

PLAN #	PRICE TIER	PAGE	MATERIALS LIST	DECK	DECK PRICE	LANDSCAPE	LANDSCAPE PRICE	REGIONS
HPK2500054	C2	56						
HPK2500055	C2	57	Y					
HPK2500056	C2	58						
HPK2500057	C2	59						
HPK2500058	A4	60	Y					
HPK2500059	C1	61	Y					
HPK2500002	C1	62	Y					
HPK2500060	C1	63	Y					
HPK2500061	A4	64	Y					
HPK2500062	A3	64						
HPK2500063	A2	65						
HPK2500064	A1	66						
HPK2500374	A3	67	Y					
HPK2500375	A2	67	Y					
HPK2500066	C2	68	Y					
HPK2500067	A4	68	Y					
HPK2500376	A4	69	Y					
HPK2500065	C1	69	Y					
HPK2500068	C3	70	Y					
HPK2500377	C1	70	Y					
HPK2500069	C3	71	Y					
HPK2500378	SQ1	71						
HPK2500070	C2	74	Y					
HPK2500071	C4	75	Y					
HPK2500072	C1	76						
HPK2500073	A4	77	Y					
HPK2500074	A3	78	Y		OLA004	P3	123568	
HPK2500075	A3	79	Y					
HPK2500076	SQ1	80	Y					
HPK2500077	A3	81	Y					
HPK2500078	L2	82	Y					
HPK2500079	C2	83	Y					
HPK2500080	C2	84	Y					
HPK2500081	C3	85	Y					
HPK2500082	C2	86	Y					
HPK2500083	C3	86	Y					
HPK2500084	C3	87						
HPK2500085	C2	87						
HPK2500086	C4	88						
HPK2500087	L1	89						
HPK2500088	A3	90	Y					
HPK2500089	A2	91	Y					
HPK2500090	C1	92	Y					
HPK2500091	A1	92	Y					
HPK2500092	A2	93	Y					

PLAN #	PRICE TIER	PAGE	MATERIALS LIST	DECK	DECK PRICE	LANDSCAPE	LANDSCAPE PRICE	REGIONS
HPK2500093	A3	94	Y					
HPK2500094	A2	95	Y					
HPK2500095	A2	95	Y					
HPK2500096	A3	96	Y					
HPK2500097	A3	97	Y					
HPK2500098	A3	98	Y					
HPK2500099	A4	99	Y					
HPK2500100	C1	99	Y					
HPK2500101	A4	100	Y					
HPK2500102	A2	101	Y					
HPK2500103	A3	102	Y					
HPK2500104	C3	103	Y					
HPK2500105	C1	104	Y					
HPK2500106	A2	105	Y					
HPK2500107	A3	106	Y					
HPK2500108	A3	106	Y					
HPK2500109	A3	107	Y					
HPK2500110	C1	107	Y					
HPK2500111	C2	108	Y					
HPK2500112	C2	109	Y					
HPK2500113	C3	110						
HPK2500114	C2	110						
HPK2500115	L1	111						
HPK2500116	L1	111						
HPK2500117	C2	112						
HPK2500118	C2	112						
HPK2500119	C4	113						
HPK2500120	C1	114						
HPK2500121	C2	115						
HPK2500122	C1	116						
HPK2500123	C2	117						
HPK2500124	A4	118						
HPK2500125	SQ1	119						
HPK2500126	SQ3	120						
HPK2500127	C4	121						
HPK2500128	C4	122						
HPK2500129	C3	123						
HPK2500130	C1	124						
HPK2500131	C1	125						
HPK2500132	C1	126						
HPK2500133	C1	126						
HPK2500134	C1	127						
HPK2500135	C3	128						
HPK2500136	C3	128						
HPK2500003	C3	129						
HPK2500137	C3	130						
HPK2500138	C3	131						
HPK2500139	C3	132						
HPK2500140	C3	133						
HPK2500141	C1	134						
HPK2500142	C1	135	Y					
HPK2500143	C2	136						
HPK2500144	C3	137						
HPK2500145	C3	138						
HPK2500146	C4	139	Y					
HPK2500147	L1	140						
HPK2500148	L2	141						
HPK2500149	A4	144						
HPK2500150	A3	145						
HPK2500151	A2	145						
HPK2500152	C4	146	Y					
HPK2500153	C4	147	Y					
HPK2500154	C4	148						
HPK2500155	C4	149	Y					
HPK2500156	SQ1	150	Y					
HPK2500157	C3	151	Y					
HPK2500158	SQ1	152	Y					
HPK2500159	A4	153						
HPK2500160	C1	154	Y					
HPK2500161	A4	155	Y					
HPK2500162	A1	156	Y					
HPK2500163	C1	157	Y	ODA012	D2	OLA010	P3	1234568
HPK2500164	A4	157	Y	ODA012	D2	OLA083	P3	12345678
HPK2500165	C2	158	Y	ODA012	D2	OLA024	P4	123568
HPK2500166	A4	159	Y					
HPK2500167	C2	160	Y			OLA001	P3	123568
HPK2500168	C1	161	Y	ODA011	D1	OLA018	P3	12345678
HPK2500169	A3	162	Y			OLA001	P3	123568
HPK2500170	A3	163	Y					

PLAN #	PRICE TIER	PAGE	MATERIALS LIST	DECK	DECK PRICE	LANDSCAPE	LANDSCAPE PRICE	REGIONS
HPK2500171	A2	163	Y					
HPK2500172	C1	164	Y					
HPK2500173	A3	165	Y					
HPK2500174	A3	166	Y					
HPK2500175	A2	166	Y					
HPK2500176	C3	167						
HPK2500177	L1	168						
HPK2500178	C1	169						
HPK2500179	C2	169						
HPK2500180	C2	170						
HPK2500181	C1	170						
HPK2500182	C1	171						
HPK2500183	C1	171						
HPK2500184	C1	172	Y					
HPK2500185	A4	173	Y					
HPK2500186	A4	174	Y					
HPK2500187	C1	175	Y					
HPK2500188	C1	176	Y					
HPK2500189	A3	177	Y					
HPK2500190	C3	178						
HPK2500191	C1	179						
HPK2500192	C2	180						
HPK2500193	C2	181	Y					
HPK2500194	C4	182	Y					
HPK2500195	C2	183	Y					
HPK2500196	C2	184	Y					
HPK2500197	C2	184	Y					
HPK2500198	C2	185						
HPK2500199	C2	186						
HPK2500200	C2	187						
HPK2500201	C4	188	Y					
HPK2500202	C2	189						
HPK2500203	C2	190						
HPK2500204	C2	191	Y					
HPK2500205	C4	192						
HPK2500206	C4	193						
HPK2500207	C4	194						
HPK2500208	C2	195						
HPK2500209	C2	196						
HPK2500210	L4	197						
HPK2500211	A4	198	Y					
HPK2500212	A4	198	Y					
HPK2500213	C4	199	Y					
HPK2500214	C1	200	Y					
HPK2500215	C1	201	Y					
HPK2500216	C1	202	Y					
HPK2500217	A3	203	Y					
HPK2500218	A3	203	Y					
HPK2500219	A3	204	Y					
HPK2500220	A3	205	Y					
HPK2500221	A4	206	Y					
HPK2500222	A4	206	Y					
HPK2500223	A4	207	Y					
HPK2500224	A3	208	Y					
HPK2500225	A4	208	Y					
HPK2500226	A4	209	Y					
HPK2500227	C1	210	Y					
HPK2500228	A4	211	Y					
HPK2500229	A4	211	Y					
HPK2500230	A4	212	Y					
HPK2500231	C1	213	Y					
HPK2500232	C1	213	Y					
HPK2500233	C3	214	Y					
HPK2500234	C1	215	Y					
HPK2500235	A4	216						
HPK2500236	A4	217						
HPK2500237	C2	218						
HPK2500238	C2	219						
HPK2500239	A4	220						
HPK2500240	C1	221						
HPK2500241	A2	222						
HPK2500242	A2	223	Y					
HPK2500243	SQ1	224	Y					
HPK2500244	A4	225	Y					
HPK2500245	C1	226						
HPK2500246	C1	227						
HPK2500247	A3	228	Y					
HPK2500248	A3	229						
HPK2500249	C1	229						

PLAN #	PRICE TIER	PAGE	MATERIALS LIST	DECK	DECK PRICE	LANDSCAPE	LANDSCAPE PRICE	REGIONS
HPK2500250	A4	230						
HPK2500251	A3	231	Y					
HPK2500252	A3	232	Y					
HPK2500253	A3	233	Y					
HPK2500254	A2	234	Y					
HPK2500255	A2	235	Y					
HPK2500256	A4	236						
HPK2500257	A3	237						
HPK2500258	C3	237						
HPK2500259	A4	238	Y					
HPK2500260	C1	238						
HPK2500261	A3	239						
HPK2500262	C1	239						
HPK2500263	C1	240						
HPK2500264	A3	240	Y					
HPK2500265	C1	241						
HPK2500266	SQ5	244						
HPK2500267	SQ1	245						
HPK2500268	SQ1	246						
HPK2500269	C1	247						
HPK2500270	C4	248						
HPK2500271	C3	249						
HPK2500272	C4	250						
HPK2500273	C4	250						
HPK2500274	C4	251						
HPK2500275	L1	251						
HPK2500276	L2	252						
HPK2500277	SQ1	253	Y					
HPK2500278	A4	254						
HPK2500279	C1	255	Y					
HPK2500280	C3	256	Y					
HPK2500281	C4	257	Y					
HPK2500282	C1	258						
HPK2500283	L4	259	Y					
HPK2500284	C1	260	Y			OLA040	P4	123467
HPK2500285	C1	261	Y			OLA089	P4	12345678
HPK2500286	A4	262	Y	ODA025	D2	OLA037	P4	347
HPK2500287	L1	263	Y			OLA037	P4	347
HPK2500288	C2	264						
HPK2500289	C3	265	Y			OLA004	P3	123568
HPK2500290	SQ7	266						
HPK2500291	SQ7	267	Y					
HPK2500292	SQ1	268	Y			OLA008	P4	1234568
HPK2500293	SQ7	269						
HPK2500294	SQ7	270						
HPK2500295	SQ7	271	Y					
HPK2500296	SQ7	272	Y					
HPK2500297	SQ7	273	Y					
HPK2500298	C2	274	Y					
HPK2500299	C4	275	Y					
HPK2500300	C3	276	Y					
HPK2500301	C3	277	Y					
HPK2500302	C4	278						
HPK2500303	L2	279						
HPK2500304	C2	280	Y					
HPK2500305	C2	281						
HPK2500306	L1	282	Y					
HPK2500307	L2	283	Y					
HPK2500308	SQ1	284	Y					
HPK2500309	SQ1	285						
HPK2500310	L1	286				OLA008	P4	1234568
HPK2500311	C1	287						
HPK2500312	C2	288						
HPK2500313	SQ1	289	Y					
HPK2500314	A4	290						
HPK2500315	C2	291	Y					
HPK2500316	C1	292						
HPK2500317	C3	293	Y					
HPK2500318	C1	294	Y					
HPK2500319	SQ1	295						
HPK2500320	SQ1	296						
HPK2500321	C1	297	Y					
HPK2500322	SQ1	298	Y					
HPK2500323	SQ1	299						
HPK2500324	SQ1	300						
HPK2500325	SQ1	301						
HPK2500326	A4	302						
HPK2500327	C2	302						
HPK2500328	A4	303						

PLAN #	PRICE TIER	PAGE	MATERIALS LIST	DECK	DECK PRICE	LANDSCAPE	LANDSCAPE PRICE	REGIONS
HPK2500329	C1	304						
HPK2500330	A3	305						
HPK2500331	C1	306						
HPK2500332	C2	307						
HPK2500333	C3	308						
HPK2500334	C4	309						
HPK2500335	C3	310						
HPK2500336	C2	311						
HPK2500337	C4	312						
HPK2500338	L1	313						
HPK2500339	C3	314						
HPK2500340	C4	315						
HPK2500341	L3	316						
HPK2500342	L2	317						
HPK2500343	C3	318						
HPK2500344	C4	319						
HPK2500345	C4	320						
HPK2500346	C4	321						
HPK2500347	L3	322						
HPK2500348	L4	323						
HPK2500349	L1	324						
HPK2500350	L1	325						
HPK2500351	C2	326						
HPK2500352	L1	326						
HPK2500353	L4	327						
HPK2500380	P5	330	Y					
HPK2500381	P5	330	Y					
HPK2500382	P4	330	Y					
HPK2500383	P4	330	Y					
HPK2500384	P4	330	Y					
HPK2500385	P4	330	Y					
HPK2500386	P5	330	Y					
HPK2500387	P4	330	Y					
HPK2500388	P5	330	Y					
HPK2500389	P5	331	Y					
HPK2500390	P5	331	Y					
HPK2500391	P4	331	Y					
HPK2500392	P4	331	Y					
HPK2500393	P5	331						
HPK2500394	P6	331	Y					
HPK2500395	P6	331	Y					
HPK2500396	P5	331	Y					
HPK2500397	P2	332						
HPK2500398	P4	332						
HPK2500399	P2	332						
HPK2500400	P2	332						
HPK2500401	P2	332						
HPK2500402	P4	332						
HPK2500403	P4	332						
HPK2500404	P1	332						
HPK2500405	P1	332						
HPK2500406	P2	333						
HPK2500407	P1	333						
HPK2500408	P1	333						
HPK2500409	P2	333						
HPK2500410	P1	333						
HPK2500411	P1	333						
HPK2500412	P1	333						
HPK2500354	P3	334						
HPK2500355	P4	336						
HPK2500356	P4	338						
HPK2500357	P4	340						
HPK2500004	P4	342						
HPK2500358	P3	344						
HPK2500359	P3	346						
HPK2500360	P4	348						
HPK2500361	P4	350						
HPK2500362	P3	352						
HPK2500363	P4	354						
HPK2500364	P4	356						
HPK2500365	P3	358						
HPK2500366	P3	360						
HPK2500367	P2	362						
HPK2500368	P3	364						
HPK2500369	P2	366						
HPK2500370	P3	368						
HPK2500371	P3	370						
HPK2500372	P3	372						
HPK2500373	P3	374						